AMERICAN
CULTURAL
PATTERNS

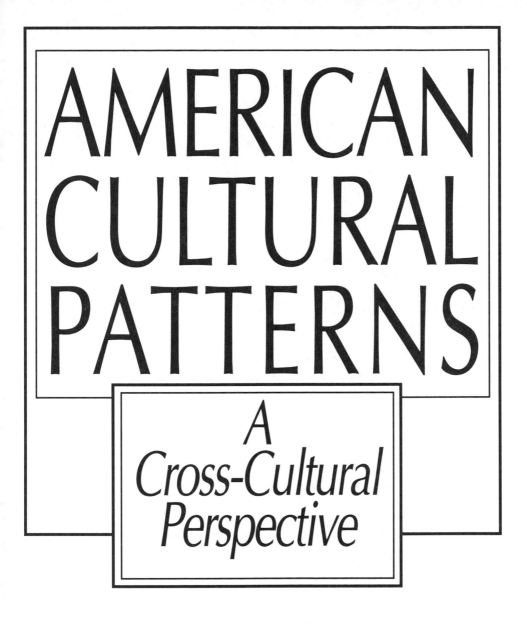

AMERICAN CULTURAL PATTERNS

A Cross-Cultural Perspective

EDWARD C. STEWART
AND
MILTON J. BENNETT

REVISED EDITION

Intercultural Press, Inc.

For information contact:
Intercultural Press, Inc.
PO Box 700
Yarmouth, Maine 04096 USA
207-846-5168
www.interculturalpress.com

Book design by Lurelle Cheverie
Cover design by Letterspace

Printed in the United States of America

03   02   01   00   10   11   12   13

Library of Congress Cataloging-in-Publication Data

Stewart, Edward C.
   American cultural patterns / by Edward C. Stewart and Milton J. Bennett.—Rev. ed.
      p.   cm.
   Includes bibliographical references and index.
   ISBN 1-877864-01-3
   1. United States—Civilization—Cross-cultural studies.   2. National characteristics, American—Cross-cultural studies.   I. Bennett, Milton J.   II. Title.
   E169.1.S836   1991
   973—dc20   91-4256
                                                       CIP

CONTENTS

INTRODUCTION

The need to improve cultural understanding led to the writing of the first edition of this volume some twenty years ago. Since then, research in cross-cultural psychology and intercultural communication has advanced our knowledge and skills in the field which has enabled more people to become more effective in intercultural relationships. Their numbers, however, remain relatively few, even as the need for understanding other cultures and for developing intercultural competence grows, fueled by the realities of living in an interdependent world.

Intercultural communicators are discovering how deeply critical events facing the world today are rooted in culture. Each morning the newspaper reminds its readers of the American trade deficit with Japan. American and European economists alike speak of the Japanese culture that blocks access to its market. The evening news reports the latest move in world power politics that threatens the peace, but the essential agreement on the deterrences needed to maintain international stability reposes uneasily on conflicting cultural patterns of negotiation and decision making. The cauldron of violence in the Middle East continues to reflect cultural conflict between social and political groups, as does the rioting that erupts periodically in urban centers around the world. Advances in intercultural communication have at times stripped away layers of misunderstanding only to confront the cultural roots of economic, political, and sociological events. Many of the national and international tensions, including threats to peace, cannot be addressed at present levels of knowledge and skill.

Another reason for cultivating cultural understanding stems from the changed position of the United States in the world. The decline of American political and economic influence has affected the role of individual Americans abroad and changed foreigners' attitudes toward them. Americans no longer occupy the privileged position they enjoyed only twenty years ago. This altered role has made nearly obsolete the word *advisor*, used in the first edition to refer to Americans working abroad. The new role Americans play as partners, hosts, visitors, and competitors demands the reformulation of a number of central issues in the realm of cross-cultural understanding.

In this book, cross-cultural problems are seen as arising from differences in behavior, thinking, assumptions, and values between Americans and people from other countries and cultures with whom they associate. These cultural differences often produce misunderstandings and lead to ineffectiveness in face-to-face communication. A deeper understanding of the nature of cultural differences would increase the effectiveness of Americans in cross-cultural situations. But to reach this goal, Americans must first become more conscious and knowledgeable about how their own culture has conditioned their ways of thinking and planted within them the values and assumptions that govern their behavior.

Cultural self-awareness is not always easy since culture is internalized as patterns of thinking and behaving that are believed to be "natural"—simply the way things are. Awareness of their subjective culture is particularly difficult for Americans since they often interpret cultural factors as characteristics of individual personality. This view of internalized cultural patterns, disregarding their social origins, is a characteristic of American culture. It is not a universal point of view.

Since this book is written from the perspective of Americans, their culture serves as the frame of reference while other cultures enter the discussion as contrasts. Like world maps that place the map's originating country in the center, there is a degree of ethnocentrism in this focus on American culture, but it also serves an important purpose for cross-cultural analysis. We would like to stress, therefore, that this convention does not imply that American culture is perceived to be at the center of the mosaic of world cultures.

While our analysis of cross-cultural problems in communication naturally identifies obstacles to intercultural communication between Americans and members of other cultures and suggests ways in which communication could be improved, it is not our objective to prescribe behavior. Instead, we shall offer schematic descriptions of some important aspects of American culture and show their practical consequences for intercultural communication. Geared to operational needs of practitioners, the treatment deliberately skirts numerous issues concerning the meaning of culture, values, and other matters of primarily theoretical interest.

The objective of this second edition, as of the first, is to supply a perspective on some of the cross-cultural problems encountered by Americans visiting, working, or living with foreign associates. Whether the association occurs within the United States or abroad, this book presumes that those from other cultures direct their lives from different points of view and that Americans will gain a deeper understanding of their own culture by looking at it from contrasting cultural perspectives. We expect applications of this understanding will be made by practitioners working as trainers, technicians, students, academicians, businesspeople, or others who are visiting extensively or living in other cultural environments. It should also appeal to those concerned with American studies, who may wish to use cross-cultural analysis as a means of bringing American culture into sharper focus.

Finally, we hope this book will be valuable to people of other cultures who wish to gain a deeper understanding of American behavior. We have sought to avoid the ethnocentric distortions which limit the usefulness of most cultural self-studies to foreign readers.

In the first chapter, the cross-cultural problem is represented in a basic contrast between Western and non-Western societies with examples of specific cultural barriers met by Americans abroad. In chapter 2, American patterns of thinking and cultural contrasts are traced from their concrete inception in perception to their abstract conclusion in conceptualization. Chapter 3 explores the implications and limitations of the Whorf hypothesis and other factors in language use, including the role of nonverbal behavior in American and contrasting communication patterns. Chapters 4 through 7 present the core American assumptions and values organized into four areas: form of activity, form of social relations, perception of the world, and perception of self and the individual. Assumptions and values discussed in these chapters are the dominant values commonly associated with the American middle class. Clearly, these do not include all the significant values shared by large numbers of Americans. The relativity of assumptions and values is stressed throughout this description by contrasting dominant American cultural characteristics with those of other domestic and foreign cultures. The final chapter examines the implications of the analyses appearing in the previous chapters for the actual practice of intercultural communication by Americans.

Throughout the book we have tried as much as possible to employ only common concepts and to avoid using the language and concepts of social science that lack familiar connotations. We have, however, adopted certain conventions of expression from the field of intercultural communication. Since the words *cross-cultural* and *intercultural* have similar definitions, we sometimes use them interchangeably, but we also apply them with more precise and separate meanings. *Cross-cultural* normally refers to any *comparison* of cultural differences (e.g., a cross-cultural study of values in the U.S. and Japan) or to situations in which such differences exist (e.g., a cross-cultural teaching situation). The word *intercultural* is usually added to *communication* or *relations* and refers to the actual *interaction* between people of different cultures. For example, in a cross-cultural work environment, Americans and foreigners necessarily engage in intercultural communication. We avoid using *international* since the word refers to a wide range of political and economic affairs that may be neither culturally comparative nor interactive. Despite avoidance of the word, we hope that the book's cross-cultural perspective will be recognized as a necessary complement to international studies.

The term *American* is used here as a short form of "citizen of the United States of America." While many people prefer *North American,* the authors believe that to include sovereign Canadians in the same grouping as Americans is misleading, despite many similarities between the populations of the two countries. It is even more misleading when you consider the fact that Mexico is also part of North America. The use of the word *American* to refer to the people of the United States has a long historical precedent, and we have chosen to accept it for our purposes here.

American culture refers to the dominant patterns of thinking and behaving of mainstream Americans, composed primarily, but not exclusively, of members of the white, male middle class. When discussing other cultures represented in American society, we will use the term *ethnic subcultures.* This distinction is artificial since American mainstream and ethnic subcultures constantly intermingle, reciprocally influencing each other. When discussing the interaction of ethnic minorities, we shall substitute *multicultural* for *cross-cultural* and *interethnic* for *intercultural.*

Additional terms we shall use in specific ways include the following: *sojourner* is anyone (in this case, an American) who travels abroad for a specific purpose or resides temporarily in a foreign country. The term *abroad* is used generically to mean "outside the U.S.A." Foreigners with whom Americans interact are called *associates* or *coworkers* unless a more specific label like *host* or *student* is appropriate. Since the meaning of *foreigners* can sometimes be ambiguous, *host country nationals* will occasionally be used to refer to people whom Americans encounter abroad.

The original edition of this book incorporated the work of Florence R. Kluckhohn without adopting her complete system of theoretical concepts. This edition still strongly reflects the influence of Dr. Kluckhohn's work. While care has been taken to represent Dr. Kluckhohn's ideas accurately, the authors assume responsibility for any differences in interpretation which may appear. The work of George M. Foster and Robin M. Williams, Jr. is also integrated into this analysis of American culture.

In addition to the published material referenced throughout the text, some unpublished sources have been used. These include interviews with military advisors in Laos, Thailand, and Latin America, United States Agency for International Development technicians, Peace Corps volunteers, medical missionaries, and hundreds of foreign and American students in international study programs. These sources have been augmented by the writers' own observations. The senior author, Edward Stewart, has for years served as a consultant to and conducted research for businesses in the United States, Japan, and Europe and has worked with government agencies in the U.S. and abroad that regulate technology. The other author, Milton Bennett, is an intercultural trainer, educator, and researcher whose work includes the preparation and debriefing of Americans working, traveling, and studying worldwide.

Florence Kluckhohn, George Foster, and Robin Williams, Jr. provided substantive critiques of an original draft of the first edition, setting the form persisting through this revision. The writers are indebted to them for their incisive, kind, and patient reviews. We remain grateful to David Hoopes, who has provided constant encouragement in his insightful editing of both editions of this book.

CONCEPTUALIZATION OF THE CROSS-CULTURAL PROBLEM

Lasting success in working or living with people from another culture ultimately rests on good human relations. Sometimes the relationship is specialized, as with an engineer doing business with other engineers. Their technical background and purposes may create a professional bond that allows them to establish successful temporary and restricted business relationships during a brief visit. Other guests in a foreign environment may depend on the tolerance of their hosts, simply "being themselves" and making no effort to accommodate to cultural differences. The short-term success of these kinds of professional or host-guest relationships sometimes leads people to discount the importance of cultural differences in cross-cultural interaction. But this sort of "success" cannot be sustained over time. Even technicians must eventually discard the role of expert and develop empathy for coworkers in the cross-cultural setting.

Until recently, little attention has been given to the effect of cultural differences or sociocultural factors on interpersonal relations. Even today the view that these factors constitute the critical ingredient of cross-cultural interaction is not widely held among people involved in international affairs. And outside the field of intercultural communication, the subject is still largely neglected by scholars. The most ambitious attempt to correct this deficiency is Richard Brislin's *Cross-cultural Encounters* (1981). In this book Brislin summarizes the existing research on cross-cultural interpersonal relations and demonstrates the complexity of the subject, helping to explain why practitioners have avoided it and why researchers have sought simple solutions based on a unified view of culture.

In practice, confusion is created by two basic aspects of culture. One aspect is *subjective culture*—the psychological features of culture, including assumptions, values, and patterns of thinking. The other is *objective culture*—the institutions and artifacts of a culture, such as its economic system, social customs, political structures and processes, arts, crafts, and literature. Objective culture can be treated as an externalization of subjective culture which usually becomes reified; that is, those institutions which are properly seen as extensions of human activity attain an independent status as external entities. They seem to exist "out there," and their ongoing human origins are forgotten.

In traditional universities the study of objective culture is well established in departments of social sciences and humanities. Perhaps this is because institutions and other external artifacts of behavior are more accessible to examination. Subjective culture is usually treated as an unconscious process influencing perception, thinking, and memory or as personal knowledge which is inaccessible to trainers or educators. In universities this aspect of culture is a newcomer and a minor thread in sociology, social psychology, and communication. Subjective culture becomes a major subject only in cultural anthropology. Although anthropologists typically make cross-cultural comparisons, they much more rarely investigate the practical aspects of intercultural communication. Instead, their major interest is in collecting information about the institutions of objective culture. While this kind of information provides useful background, it does not effectively prepare sojourners for the intercultural experience. Yet, it is precisely this information about objective culture which constitutes most of the cultural components of the majority of orientation programs for persons going abroad. The problem, as we see it, is to conceptualize subjective culture in such a way that it can be more effectively incorporated into preparing sojourners for living and working abroad. To that end, we will analyze the basic elements of culture as interpersonal dimensions relevant to cross-cultural cooperation.

Aspects of Cross-Cultural Interactions

For most people, including Americans, the distinguishing mark of cross-cultural interaction is the disappearance of the familiar guideposts that allow them to act without thinking in their own culture. Routine matters become problems that require planning or conscious decisions. They may not know when to shake hands, nod their heads, ask a question, express an opinion, or maintain silence. They may have to question the effectiveness of their techniques for giving advice and may need to search for proper channels of communication.

Faced with these cross-cultural uncertainties, people tend to impose their own perspectives in an effort to dispel the ambiguity created by the unusual behavior of host country nationals. They are unlikely to suspend judgment about differences in behavior because they assume unconsciously that their own ways are normal, natural, and right. Those of the other culture, therefore, must be abnormal, unnatural, and wrong. This presumption of superiority of one's own culture is, of course, characteristic not only of Americans but of most peoples of the world.

Cross-cultural ambiguity and reactions to it often become most prominent for the American in the world of work. In the foreign setting

> he sees what looks like familiar bureaucratic structures and technological systems, but the way they actually function is confusing. He meets people with professional training similar to his own but who do not always act in their work role as expected— yet he depends on them for getting the job done. Frustration becomes part of his everyday language if he finds no way to achieve fuller understandings of why things which look alike do not perform as they are supposed to (Useem, Useem, and Donoghue 1963, 179).

This problem may become especially acute when individuals work with foreigners in the context of a familiar organization since the environment provides them with little if any incentive to recognize the cultural biases of their behavior or to question the objectivity of their actions. An understanding of the biases and underlying predispositions of their particular culture should aid Americans in ridding themselves of the belief that their own assumptions and values should be the norm for all peoples. This change in attitude does not mean that Americans should discard their own culture (even if it were possible for them to do so) or even that they should value it less highly, but it should prepare them to perceive both their own behavior and that of coworkers more objectively.

Americans frequently go abroad in the role of consultant and may, therefore, be less directly involved in actual work than when they were at home. Thus, their goals abroad are usually less tangible than those they have at home. If work and social position are not clearly structured, individuals are thrown back upon their own resources in making decisions, evaluating situations, and pursuing courses of action. Performance on the job may be adversely affected when routine matters become major problems and cultural differences are intensified. Consultants may also be deprived of the social support available when working within a familiar organization, and they may be either isolated or else absorbed into a foreign social structure. Customary services and the advice or moral support provided by colleagues will also normally be missing.

Many Americans find when they arrive abroad that their work assumes a character quite different from what they were led to expect. A training problem takes on a new dimension when the sojourner discovers that the trainees, in addition to speaking only their native language, are illiterate. Sometimes a health program does not get off the ground because people do not have the concept of germs and are therefore unable to understand preventive health measures. Most upsetting of all, their culture provides an explanation of disease and health incompatible with Western scientific discoveries. In short, what is aptly labeled "training," "education," or "health" in the United States may acquire entirely different characteristics abroad.

A particularly disturbing problem faced by consultants may be the intransigence of local officials and government which makes the Americans' job one of persuading and influencing. They may be compelled to accept, perhaps bitterly, the frustration of their objectives, and when deprived of concrete achievements, Americans may experience feelings of failure. These feelings are often compounded by the realization that their services are not wanted. (This has been particularly true of the military advisors and, to a lesser degree, of Peace Corps volunteers.) They are accepted as a necessary evil or, at best, a neutral presence. They bring with them material resources and prestige, but their advice is not always welcomed.

American students, educators, and researchers face problems in some ways similar to those encountered by consultants, business executives, and other professionals living abroad. Ambitious educational goals that were set in the home environment may be out of reach in a foreign country. Researchers may find data that "should" be readily available concealed by layers of bureaucracy, and they may discover that their methods of inquiry, such as interviews or questionnaires, are inappropriate or ineffective. Students who expected that their host families would simply be providing sleeping quarters may be surprised at the intensity of cross-cultural adjustment that is demanded of them. Teachers are likely to encounter radically different attitudes toward learning and classroom behavior. The disappearance of familiar guideposts acts on academics as it does on others, provoking frustration and perhaps the assumption that American approaches to education are superior in all ways. In addition students and others engaged in educational exchange may feel that the unexpected problems have spoiled the pleasures anticipated in going abroad.

Teachers and visiting scholars abroad are in a position similar to that of other workers in seemingly familiar organizations. They may resist the recognition of cultural differences in favor of maintaining a semblance of their familiar roles—roles that encourage equality and an emphasis on the give-and-take that prevails in the American classroom. Yet, teachers will probably find, especially outside of Europe, that their students behave quite formally, are very deferential to the teacher and reluctant to participate in classroom discussion, and are inclined to rote learning. American educators may judge this behavior as indicative of a personal failing on their own or their students' part, rather than seeing it as a culturally different pattern.

Many, if not most, of the problems faced by Americans abroad are encountered in reverse by foreign students and scholars coming to the United States. American instructors are likely to demand "appropriate" behavior from these students and to judge aberrations as a failure to adapt. Ironically, in an attempt to adapt to American classroom patterns, foreign students sometimes overreact to the participatory atmosphere, monopolizing too much time and speaking dogmatically. This may appear as arrogant and domineering to the instructor, fueling further negative evaluation. Foreign students in the U.S., like American students abroad, certainly must learn to communicate effectively with the host country nationals and to cope with the local educational system. However, Americans with a knowledge of their own culture and an appreciation for cultural diversity can help foreign students immensely by openly recognizing their differing cultures and by explaining American patterns in culturally comparative terms.

Americans abroad readily observe and describe cross-cultural differences of language, customs and preferences. The fact that these kinds of differences may be easily perceived often obscures the deeply imbedded but more profound disparities in concepts of the world and human experience and in patterns of thought and modes of action, all of which affect the person-to-person interaction of Americans and their hosts. Subtle differences in the behavior, thoughts, and emotions of associates may not always be perceived by Americans, but as they cumulate they require interpretation, and the explanation most likely to occur to Americans is that their associates have a bias against them. In other words, the Americans may feel they are being stereotyped.

Contributing to this reaction and sometimes giving it substance is the fact that others do indeed have stereotypes of Americans, perhaps originating from Americans known previously or from hearsay, but more probably emerging from exposure to American films and television. Aspects of the stereotype may run counter to the American's emotional and cultural frames of reference. For instance, the stereotype of "rich American" may be perceived by an individual American as neither an accurate nor desirable label. Americans may be regarded as representatives of the U.S. government, whether they are on government business or not. The heightened meaning of nationalism abroad may lead hosts to assume that these Americans will speak the official line or pursue particular policies, regardless of their personal convictions. Sometimes this stereotype takes the form of "American CIA agent."

Americans, like foreigners, develop stereotypes of others. Media attention to the traditional aspects of other cultures may lead sojourners to expect their coworkers to be evasive, superstitious, ritualistic, or unsophisticated. Foreigners in the United States are constantly surprised by Americans asking them if they ride camels or if they have ever eaten ice cream. Ironically, Americans couple these misconceptions with a tendency to generalize to all foreigners certain American characteristics of human relations which they consider universal. When added to the stereotypes foreigners have of Americans, this tendency compounds communication problems and masks the deep cultural patterns that need scrutiny.

The core difficulty in cross-cultural interaction is—simply stated—a failure to recognize relevant cultural differences. Because of superficial stereotyping and the belief that one's own values and behaviors are natural and universal, Americans (and others) at home or abroad often fail to grasp the social dynamic that separates them from their associates. Unless sojourners recognize the unconscious assumptions that they make about human relations, they may never be able to establish effective intercultural relations. This failure to create a viable intercultural social context may compel sojourners to retreat into an enclave of compatriots, to "go native," or to return home. Any of these alternatives may preclude their accomplishing the objectives which took them abroad.

The Basis for Cultural Contrast

The objective of establishing an awareness of cultural contrasts leads us to begin with an observation reported by Americans who have worked and lived in many parts of the world. They often say that non-Western countries, mostly in Africa, Asia, and Latin America, differ from one another in some respects, but all share common characteristics often referred to as non-Western. Although the frequency of this observation does not necessarily verify it, westernization is often associated with other perceptions of differences that provide useful concepts for cultural analysis. For instance, non-Western countries frequently share a status as former colonies, or as territories within the spheres of influence of European countries. This historical burden, even today, endows them with a common fate. Formerly, these non-Western countries, with a few major exceptions, supplied cheap labor, raw materials, and markets to the industrial countries. Now, they make up the group of developing nations striving to break into the ranks of the industrialized states, with Japan having been the first to succeed.

Including the historical dimension of colonialism in a cultural analysis increases the scope of understanding, but social scientists are more at home with political, economic, and military events than with subjective culture. Therefore, most do not give systematic treatment to the ways of thinking of a people. Tönnies (1957), a German sociologist, is an exception. He analyzed the social changes that take place as nations develop from traditional, gemeinschaft societies into modern, gesellschaft states.

The social order of the gemeinschaft society is largely based on the customs and traditions of communities sharing the same language, race, religion, and ethnicity, and wielding economic power over their geographical region. Social belonging tends to be total, and community members seek satisfaction of all goals within their communities. Social sanctions and political control are based on informal and traditional ascriptions to elitist groups. Workers are defenders and supporters of the social order and are conscripted to their tasks. Opinions and beliefs are private in the sense that they are associated with the customs of the community rather than determined in open, public discussions. Identity of the individual is bound up with belonging to the community. The social fiber of gemeinschaft communities creates for its members an *interpersonal reality,* a concept which Diaz-Guerrero (1976) uses to distinguish Mexican culture from American culture which he refers to as having an objective reality. These concepts are applied more generally to gemeinschaft and gesellschaft societies.

As a country develops into a modern nation, the social intensity of gemeinschaft communities, their social ties based on emotion and sentiment, loosen to become a web of impersonal social relations supported by the formal and even contractual ties characteristic of gesellschaft societies such as the United States. Social ties are based on rational agreement and self-interest and are regulated by law. Groups are formed for specific purposes and accept members based on special interest or on technical, educational, or professional attainments. Identity is separate from belonging; the status of the individual citizen and member of the state takes precedence over membership in groups. The status enjoyed by the individual is a product of achievement rather than a birthright as political and professional ties replace traditional social links. The changes induced in objective culture at the level of political, social and economic institutions trickle down to the subjective culture of interpersonal interaction. Thought is rational and standards are utilitarian, creating an objective reality for members of gesellschaft societies (Mouer and Sugimoto 1986, 61).

The Tönnies dichotomy parallels in a historical frame the contrasts of Western versus non-Western and colonizer versus colonized, and it provides insights into subjective culture in gemeinschaft and gesellschaft societies. Though general and ideal, the analysis of interpersonal and objective reality of gemeinschaft and gesellschaft societies helps to explain the development of Western and American cultures.

The true relationship between gemeinschaft and gesellschaft is revealed by a historical glance at the role of technology in society, particularly the technologies for industry and war. Two technical innovations in particular were critical—gunpowder for firearms and coke-fired production of steel and iron for industry and war. Neither innovation was Western. Both technologies had appeared in China by A.D. 1000 (McNeill 1982, 24-39). Iron and steel production evolved in China under the aegis of a dramatic social innovation—market-regulated behavior, which replaced obedience to command. But in the centuries between A.D. 1000 and 1600, the gemeinschaft interpersonal reality of Chinese mandarins successfully held in balance the gesellschaft drive of successful entrepreneurs. Market-regulated behavior never entirely replaced obedience to command or gained full sway over production. In medieval China

> private riches acquired by personal shrewdness in buying and selling violated the Confucian sense of propriety. Such persons could be tolerated, even encouraged, when their activity served official ends. But to allow merchants or manufacturers to acquire too much power, or accumulate too much capital, was as unwise as to allow a military commander or a barbarian chieftain to control too many armed men (McNeill, 36).

Government policy was critical in controlling market-regulated behavior. Officials took over private production by creating state monopolies and levied taxes or imposed official prices to reduce levels of operation. The Chinese control of market-regulated behavior appears to qualify as a gemeinschaft curb on gesellschaft dynamism. China displayed political and social union, opposed the self-serving individualism of entrepreneurs, and placed the bureaucrat at the summit of prestige. In the eyes of Chinese imperial officialdom, the empire formed a single household (McNeill, 31). On occasion the official response to market-regulated behavior was to abort technology. For example, in 1436 the imperial court issued a decree forbidding the construction of new ocean-going vessels. The Chinese ships that vanished from the oceans were technically superior and several times the size of the Western vessels that arrived in the Indian Ocean some decades later (McNeill, 40-50). By the end of the fifteenth century, China had lost its technical edge to the West, which retained a clear advantage until the Japanese breakthrough of the last twenty years.

The Chinese cybernetic society of the fifteenth century found no equivalent in the West. Although Christian values were as hostile to the spirit of the marketplace as Confucianism, efforts of popes to establish hegemony over Christendom ended in failure. Earlier efforts made by monarchs had come to the same dismal end (McNeill, 68-69). Europe remained divided into locally divergent political structures, perpetually at odds with one another. By the thirteenth century, military and market expansions in Europe were rapidly depleting primary social bonds, replacing them with gesellschaft market behavior. The primary relations of the gemeinschaft bond within communities effectively ceased to regulate everyday conduct.

> This political situation permitted a remarkable merger of market and military behavior to take root and flourish in the most active economic centers of western Europe. Commercialization of organized violence came vigorously to the fore in the fourteenth century when mercenary armies became standard in Italy. Thereafter, market forces and attitudes began to affect military action as seldom before. The art of war began to evolve among Europeans with a rapidity that soon raised it to unexampled heights (McNeill, 69-70).

The shift from gemeinschaft social organization of interpersonal reality to gesellschaft forms of objective reality appeared as one of the conditions for the shotgun wedding of war and commerce. Gunpowder was the active agent. The earliest evidence for the existence of guns in Europe is 1326. Thereafter, the technology of guns and firearms developed rapidly, unrestrained by political or social controls. In Italy by the fifteenth century, a connection was made between science and warfare. Italians, trembling with fear, mobilized their best brains to help resist the superior cannons of the French armies invading Italian city-states. The sculptor, Michelangelo, and the scientists, Leonardo da Vinci and later Galileo, among others, were pressed into service, forging the link between science and military technology that has persisted to the present. The manufacture of improved firearms revolutionized warfare, leveled city walls, and wrought major changes in Western societies. Unlike the Chinese, Europeans appeared fascinated by the union of war, science, and commerce.

One of the ironies of the gemeinschaft dynamic is found in the history of Japan. In 1504 the Portuguese disembarked on Japanese shores carrying firearms. The Japanese quickly adopted them and improved them; within a generation their quality excelled that of the Portuguese weapons.

Armed with these refined Japanese firearms, lowly peasants killed lordly samurai with impunity, inflicting severe damage upon the gemeinschaft structure of the society. In 1642 Japan closed its shores to foreigners, banned firearms, destroyed existing ones, and obliterated all mention of them in records and manuscripts. For a period of two hundred years, Japan successfully reversed the development of military technology, destroying all traces of its prior existence to preserve the integrity of its social relations. In its isolation, Japan avoided Western colonization. When its shores were opened once more to the outside world in 1868, the Japanese embraced foreign technology, quickly modernized the nation, and by the 1980s, assumed the position of the second major economic power in the free world. This achievement, built on a gemeinschaft society, demonstrates that modernization does not require the acquisition of a gesellschaft dynamic, as occurred in the West.

Events of the 1970s have cast new light on the relation between gemeinschaft and gesellschaft. The economic and technical supremacy of the West (and particularly of the United States), usually associated only with gesellschaft, has been challenged by Japan. Japan is an industrial and modern state based on gemeinschaft organization in which social, political, and economic institutions blend one into the other, virtually inseparable. In the essentially one-party political system of Japan, political issues are settled within the same party by means of the gemeinschaft social dynamic of interpersonal reality. Both at the level of gemeinschaft institutions and of social interactions, Japan reveals a cultural base for its technology and industry which is different from the one supporting American and European development. The Japanese case of unexpected success in modernization, when compared with lessons from the West, convincingly demonstrates that the relationship between gemeinschaft and gesellschaft is more complex than suggested by a simple historical evolution from an agrarian to a modernized society.

The original formulation of Tönnies, describing societies in the broad strokes of gemeinschaft and gesellschaft , is too simple. The primordial attachments of gemeinschaft based on blood, region, race, custom, and even language and religion persist in gemeinschaft societies. The social dynamic of personalism is exploited in social movements and revolutions. In times of danger, patriotism may strengthen, but as the studies of the military in World War II demonstrate, civil bonds (the appeal of ideology and patriotism) do not drive the fighting spirit in combat as much as loyalty to fellow soldiers (Shils 1957, 138).

An example of this dynamic within American society is the heightened awareness of ethnicity since the 1950s. Ethnic group identity and a sense of gemeinschaft belonging became a partial replacement for what was perceived as second-class citizenship in the larger society. The new sense of group identity provided political clout for these previously impotent minorities. The development of communes, human relations institutes, encounter groups, evangelical religion, black power, radical student movements, and other social phenomena similarly indicate gemeinschaft tendencies in American society.

The simple dichotomy of gemeinschaft and gesellschaft is further complicated by variation from society to society. For example, the people of Thailand are members of a gemeinschaft society, rural and traditional. But Thais think of themselves primarily as autonomous individuals rather than as part of a family or extended group. Their self-concept resembles that of a middle-class member of a gesellschaft society. On the other hand, the Japanese, who, like Americans, live in a highly industrialized nation, define themselves predominantly in relationship to others. The implications of these various definitions of the self are twofold: a given aspect of a non-Western culture may sometimes be more similar to a corresponding feature of Western culture than to that of other non-Western cultures; and secondly, industrialization does not necessarily assume the emphasis on the individual found in the United States.

Treating Tönnies' gemeinschaft/gesellschaft dichotomy as separate categories clearly does not work. While providing some basic contrasts, it does not accommodate variations among and within cultures. If, however, we discard the notion of categorization and treat gemeinschaft and gesellschaft as opposite ends of a spectrum instead of exclusive categories, the two social dynamics succeed in providing an important entry into cultural analysis. It is a bias of American thought to perceive similarities in others and to downgrade differences and variations, particularly when describing non-Western societies. Americans do not typically appreciate that each society incorporates a full range of cultural variations, and differences between two societies are found when patterns of the same cultural components are compared.

In this book, many dimensions have been employed in addition to the set established by gemeinschaft and gesellschaft. The approach we have used to select cultural components as well as to stress cultural variation, has much in common with the value orientations used by Florence Kluckhohn. Her model of cultural variations is based on the proposition that all human beings, irrespective of background or conditions of life, face a limited number of common human problems. One such problem is how to relate to one's cultural compatriots, the critical question singled out by Tönnies. Kluckhohn identifies four additional problems: relationship to time, relationship to nature, form of activity, and the nature of man (F. Kluckhohn 1963, 221-22). The full range of possible solutions to these universal human problems is found in each society although a dominant solution is usually present. Different dominant solutions represent generalizable cultural positions, and deviance from them in any given culture represents intracultural variation.

The dimensions of analysis used in this book exceed by far the five of Kluckhohn, but the basic idea is the same. Both American and foreign societies will be described primarily according to their dominant cultural positions within the full spectrum of solutions available to members of a given society. Differences in dominant positions will be used to provide contrasting examples to American culture.

A worldwide review of dominant cultural patterns shows that American culture usually lies at one end of the spectrum for each problem while the cultures of non-Western societies tend to occupy positions at or near the opposite end. For example, Iranians, Ecuadorians, and Taiwanese Chinese differ in the qualities they value in a person. But in comparison with middle-class Americans, the members of each of these societies place more stress on gemeinschaft features of family and position in society. In the United States, individual achievement is usually valued above family. In this and most other cultural assumptions and values, the American middle class differs from the majority of non-Western culture groups. It is legitimate, therefore, to compare peoples of non-Western countries as a group with Americans even though the non-Western countries themselves differ markedly.

Assumptions and Values

People typically have a strong sense of what the world is really like, so it is with surprise that they discover that "reality" is built up out of certain assumptions commonly shared among members of the same culture. *Cultural assumptions* may be defined as abstract, organized, general concepts which pervade a person's outlook and behavior. They are existential in that they define what is "real" and the nature of that reality for members of a culture. Assumptions are not themselves behavior, which is concrete, discrete, and specific. Additionally, cultural assumptions exist by definition outside of awareness. That is, we cannot readily imagine alternatives to them. In this sense, assumptions are like primitive or zero-order beliefs, defined by Daryl Bem as

> so taken for granted that we are apt not to notice that we hold them
> at all; we remain unaware of them until they are called to our
> attention or are brought into question by some bizarre circumstance
> in which they appear to be violated (1970, 5).

Members of different cultures possess various ideas of reality since their assumptions about both the world and experience differ. Most

Americans, for instance, implicitly assume an objective reality in which the world external to themselves is physical and material and does not have a soul or spirit. The truth of these assumptions may appear to be self-evident, but, as we have seen, they are not shared by people in many parts of the non-Western world. Large groups of people throughout South- and Southeast Asia endow nature with an essence similar to the one reserved by Westerners for humans alone. Westerners, and Americans in particular, are predisposed by their assumptions to exploit the physical environment to their own purposes. Conversely, Indians or Southeast Asians find themselves attempting to synthesize or integrate with nature because they assume that this is the natural relationship. In this animistic view, human beings are just another form of life and do not possess unique attributes which set them apart from other forms of life or from topographical features of the environment such as mountains or valleys.

Basic assumptions such as the perception of the self and the perception of the world can be inferred from actions of an individual; however, several assumptions are usually required to fully explain any particular behavior. Furthermore, these basic perceptions do not inevitably fix the direction in which an individual acts. For example, middle-class Americans usually think of themselves as individuals, the world as inanimate, other people as competitive but capable of cooperation, and action as necessary for survival. Do these assumptions mean that a particular individual should become a businessperson or a social worker, a voter or a nonvoter, a deductive or an inductive reasoner? While individuals' decisions in these areas will reflect the basic cultural assumptions, they are likely to be based on personal preferences that are less abstract, less generalized, and less organized. For instance, Americans buy automobiles, houses, and other physical possessions not so much because they assume that nature is exploitable but because they desire the material comfort and social status represented by these objects. They buy particular automobiles and houses largely based on personal preference.

The justification for inferring cultural assumptions becomes clear in a cross-cultural context. While Americans may differ in the reasons they give for their behavior and in the personal preferences they exhibit, the fact remains that they do not often start their mornings by placing small packets of rice (or potatoes) on the ground and in the bushes around their houses. In the United States, such behavior would be seen as eccentric at best while among Balinese Hindus the same behavior is considered normal. The Balinese and Indian assumption of an animated spirit world that needs feeding stands in contrast to the American assumption of an inanimate material world as an explanation of these differing behavior patterns. Other stark contrasts like this one and many more subtle differences among cultures indicate that generally accepted behavior in cultures is consistent with specifiable basic assumptions.

While cultural assumptions refer to basic beliefs about the nature of reality, *cultural values* refer to the goodness or desirability of certain actions or attitudes among members of the culture. As such, values prescribe which actions and ways of being are better than others. In their comprehensive review of all the different ways in which the term *value* has been used, Clyde Kluckhohn et al. (1951) conclude that the one idea common to all usages is that of "oughtness." Like assumptions, values are not in themselves behavior. Rather, they are processes that govern what people in a particular culture agree they ought to do.

Material comfort is an example of an American cultural value. Americans are therefore likely to decide that they should install central heating or air-conditioning in their homes to neutralize the extremes of cold and heat. The Japanese, who generally value remaining close to nature over material comfort, might decide under similar circumstances to use space heaters for winter and fans for the summer. Besides acting as criteria for guiding behavior, the values of both Americans and Japanese have cognitive and emotional content. Americans have the concept of furnaces, radiators, and heat controls. They can also see their furnaces and remember the smell of the heat coming on early in the fall; as for the air-conditioning, they sense the coldness, hear the noise, and feel the draft. The combination of concept and emotion makes climate control a part of the American reality. So, in general, values provide the criteria for guiding behavior because they possess content and emotion and they contribute to social reality (see Robin Williams 1970, 440).

Explicitly avoided in the usage of value are particular preferences of individuals, such as choices in air conditioners, foods, cars, magazines, etc. To include this meaning under value would make the concept too broad to have utility since cultural generalizations would become lost in the myriad of individual variation to be found in any culture. This variation reflects personality differences and remains in the province of individual psychology. But beyond personal preferences, there are important subcultural variations as noted by Kluckhohn and Strodtbeck.

> In most of the analyses of the common value element in culture patterning, the dominant values of peoples have been overstressed and *variant* values largely ignored.... Our most basic assumption is that there is a *systematic variation* in the realm of cultural phenomena which is both as definite and as essential as the demonstrated systematic variation in physical and biological phenomena (1961, 3).

While acknowledging the importance of subcultural variation in values, the cross-cultural analysis in this book requires a deliberate focus upon the dominant value pattern of middle-class Americans. Variant patterns will be introduced only for the purpose of avoiding too great a distortion of American society. In finding contrasting examples from other societies, we shall again turn to the dominant regularities, rather than to intracultural variations. We are aware, however, that we shall not be able to do full justice to the rich diversities found in either American middle-class society or in non-Western cultures.

Yet another case of deviation from the dominant value orientation occurs when behavior is geared to fulfill an expectation rather than driven by the value. For example, Americans may attempt to behave in ways that seem to fulfill the social expectations of self-reliance. To see themselves as self-reliant, they might take some action that does not really reflect the value of self-reliance, for example, taking out a loan from a bank rather than borrowing from relatives. In other words, people will sometimes attempt to fulfill social stereotypes of what they should be. We shall use the term *social norm* to refer to this kind of surface conformity with social expectations.

Behavioral Prescriptions

In concluding this conceptualization of the cross-cultural problem, it is appropriate to consider the possibility of providing Americans going abroad, or foreigners in the United States, with a list of dos and don'ts. Why not tell Americans never to point their feet at a person when in Thailand, not to pat a child on the head in Laos, always to use polite and flowery expressions in Saudi Arabia, and not to expect punctuality in Guatemala. In short, it should be possible to draw up a list of behaviors ranging from those that are desirable to those that are taboo. This approach is misleading for two major reasons.

The evaluation of behavior as desirable or taboo pursues the elusive goal of objectivity. Behavior is concrete but ambiguous: the same action may have different meanings in different situations, so it is necessary to identify the context of behavior and the contingencies of action before sojourners can be armed with prescriptions for specific acts. Fulfillment of this strategy is impossible since the enumeration of possible events lies beyond the state of the knowledge of human behavior. In addition, knowledge of the individuals with whom sojourners will be working would be required. This information is seldom available and where found is inadequate. The illusion of mastering desirable and taboo actions places blinders on Americans and foreigners alike, invites inflexibility, and falls short of equipping them for effective interaction.

When simplistic behavioral prescriptions are discarded, sojourners need some other method for diagnosing problems and predicting successful courses of action. It can be argued that Americans abroad—particularly in innovator roles—should act neither as Americans nor as host nationals. In particular, "going native" is neither possible nor desirable. Ideally, sojourners should adopt a third culture (Useem, Useem, and Donoghue 1963) based on expanded cross-cultural understanding. The first step in doing this is to know the assumptions and values upon which one's own behavior rests. Equipped with this crucial foundation, sojourners must be able to systematically contrast these assumptions and values with those of the host culture and discover the areas of cultural difference that are relevant to their particular situations. This knowledge can be used initially to empathize with the different feelings and expectations of host country nationals. Finally, relationships with foreign associates and mutual knowledge of relevant cultural differences can be used to create the unique common ground required for successful intercultural communication.

CULTURAL PATTERNS
OF PERCEPTION
AND THINKING

In everyday small talk among Americans, the subject of perception repeatedly crops up. American conversation is sprinkled with words such as "see," "hear," and "perceive." People will say "I hear that...," or someone may ask, "What do you see happening now?" A common statement is "I saw what was coming next."

The number and variety of references to perception and its synonyms suggest that the concept is diffuse and ambiguous. Americans speaking in English use the concept with two distinct meanings. For instance, if a hiker out on a trek says, "From the mountain, I saw the village in the valley," perception is an observation in which physical features of the world register in the brain. But when the same hiker then says, "I saw that it was time to turn back and descend to the village," perception is like a judgment, referring to an appraisal of a situation.

Based on these observations, we can see that human perception resembles a Janus-like figure consisting of two faces, one looking inward and one looking outward (Platt 1968, 63-64). The inward-looking face is associated with subjective processes of perceiving and thinking such as perspective, intuition, opinions, and beliefs. The outward-looking face monitors features of the physical world and registers sensory impressions of objects which in the case of "vision," for instance, are attributes such as shape, color, texture, and size. The outward face of perception is objective; only imperceptibly does it shade off into the subjective and inward face. Table 1 is a visual rendition of the perception/thinking process.

We have adopted an old convention to analyze the three principal mental processes depicted in the table: sensing, perceiving, and thinking. Within this tradition, sensing and perceiving are at the surface and relate to apprehension of the external world while thinking takes on depth as in the expression "deep thoughts." Actually, perception lies between sensation and thought and links them, and it is in this linking that the human mental process manifests its Janus-like nature—with one face glancing outward toward the surface while the second face looks inward, "buried in thought."

The fourth and deepest process, encoding or the creation of symbol systems, merges with thinking but also suggests a special thought-driven use of percepts for communication—as in the sounds of a Beethoven symphony, the visual imagery of the Statue of Liberty, and the signs of written English. With mathematics, the last traces of surface or sensory stimuli have vanished.

The four processes, listed in the right-hand column in Table 1, have counterparts in structure listed in the left-hand column. Beginning with sensation at the surface, proceeding to perception, cognition, and ending with symbol systems, each structure closely parallels the four processes in column three. Our focus will be on how the structure and processes are manifest in the product, column two.

Table 1.   Representation of Human Experience

STRUCTURE	PRODUCT	PROCESS
Sensation	Sensory Stimuli	Sensing
S • U • R • F • A • C • E		
Perception	Percept Perceptual Objects Images Concepts	Perceiving
Thought/ Cognition	Patterns of Thinking	Thinking
Complex Symbol Systems	Pictorial Style Musical Form Language Mathematics	Encoding/ Symbolizing

Deep Mind

This asks deep thought: an eye within the mind,
Keen as a diver salving sunken freight,
To sink into the depth, yet searching there,
Not lose itself in roving phantasies;
That all end well and mischief follow not
First for the State, which is our chief concern,
Then for ourselves; . . .

AESCHYLUS: "THE SUPPLIANT MAIDENS" (LINES 411-417)
TRANSLATED INTO ENGLISH VERSE BY G. M. COOKSON.

Sensation

Human beings live in a world of overwhelming sensations. The human eye is capable of identifying some 7,500,000 distinguishable colors (Geldard 1953, 53). The human ear has been estimated to respond to 340,000 discriminable sounds (Geldard, 24). Smell, taste, touch, pain, and the other senses signal information about physical conditions that are immediately important for survival (see Gregory 1970, 12). Pain, touch, and especially kinesthesis (movement) make us aware of our bodies and of interaction with objects in the environment. But human beings live with only a vague awareness of the waves of stimulation that envelop the sensory organs, are encoded, and eventually reach consciousness. Perception transforms the infinite ambiguity of sensory signals—colors, sounds, tactile sensations—into meaningful objects that we live with—tools, shelter, food, caresses.

> We are so used to objects, to seeing them wherever we look, that it is quite difficult to realize that they present any problem. But objects have their existence largely unknown to the senses. We sense them as fleeting visual shades, occasional knocks against the hand, sniffs of smell—sometimes stabs of pain leaving a bruise-record of a too-close encounter. The extraordinary thing is how much we rely on properties of objects which we seldom or never test by sensory experience (Gregory, 11).

The above quotation highlights the paradox of perception: from signals received by the physiological sensory organs our mind constructs a realistic world composed of images, thoughts, and feelings, which, in turn, affects how we organize those same signals. The paradox begins with the uncertainty of fleeting sensory stimuli and ends with the objects with which we live and with the expectations that go beyond them. Apparently, the goal of the human visual system is to construct a "rigid-image description" of the observed objective world, transforming transient events of sensory stimuli into a world of perceptual objects stable in time and space (Marr 1982, 267, 340, 350). Other sensory operations can be assumed to follow this pattern.

Perception

The stable world we perceive is built in a succession of perceptual stages through which objective features of the sensory stimuli are encoded in increasingly complex structures of the brain. This encoding occurs first in the perceptual process (see the center column of Table 1) as percepts, perceptual objects, images, and concepts.

Percepts. Objective perception, or simply perception, is unconscious in the sense that the individual is usually unaware that the process is taking place, responding only to its products appearing in the mind as percepts and then objects. The red splash of color becomes a rising sun, and the sharp cry, an animal enraged. The sensations are transformed into percepts by being organized into *figure* and *ground.* We see the sun (figure) against the sky (ground) and hear the animal raging in the forest of the night. (We will return in a moment to discuss the significance of figure/ground.) A percept is what the mind makes of the raw data of sensation.

Perceptual Objects. From percepts the mind constructs perceptual objects which are characterized by permanence and represent an adaptation of the organism to its environment. During the brief moments of perceiving, percepts are coupled to perceptual stimuli derived from the senses; but once they are uncoupled, they are lodged in the mind and transformed into a world of perceptual objects stable in generalized time and space. Objects, to a degree, lose associations with specific contexts and specific perspectives of the perceivers. Ambiguity and uncertainty diminish as perceptual objects acquire a reality apart from the conditions of perceiving.

Images. Images are internal or cognitive representations of external objects or events, "pictures within the mind" (McConnell 1986, 245). These occur in different forms. "An eye within the mind" or "diver salving sunken freight," both from Aeschylus (see Table 1), serve to illustrate *imagination imagery.* Our minds manipulate such images detached from "eyes" or "divers." A second kind of image, *memory,* serves to validate and to generalize percepts. We sense an affinity for a stranger in the crowd. We reconstruct and search memory and soon find an image of an old friend who has features resembling those of the stranger. Memory and imagination imagery may serve as vehicles for abstractions of thought (see Richardson 1969). Images enter into all patterns of thinking but with considerable variation from person to person.

Concepts. A concept is a mental abstraction, usually generalized from specific examples (McConnell, 241), that may serve as a unit of thinking. Concepts (underlying appearance) are deeper than percepts or images. Their distinguishing quality is lack of perceptual content, although they may be defined by imagined percepts as in using the metaphor "deep" for "mind," and "I see" for "understand" or "know." Concepts are used to identify relationships which go beyond mere description. It is at this point that the sensation-driven process of perception shifts to the thought- or concept-driven process of thinking. Although the change of one into the other is imperceptible and continuous, at the extreme ranges, perceiving and thinking are radically different processes.

Patterns of Thinking. At the cognitive level of deep structure, the products of both sensation-driven and thought-driven processes—percepts, perceptual objects, images, concepts—are selected, categorized, and organized so that the mind extends its mastery of objective reality by creating a cognitive, or subjective, reality where meaning is assigned and relationships elaborated. This involves bringing to bear the stored knowledge (memory), emotional predispositions (feelings/intuition), and subjective thought processes (mindsets) on the continuous influx of new sensory/perceptual data. At the core, thinking is the mental ability to govern adaptation and to search for meaning below the sensation-driven surface and beyond the reach of facts.

Since the plunge below the surface to the depths of thought takes only about half a second, object perception is quickly overwhelmed by the subjective processes of thinking. As we probe the depths of the mind, the influence of sensory stimuli diminishes while that of thinking increases. Thus while the sensation-perception-thinking process presents itself as an unbroken strand, a clear distinction can be made between sensation at its surface and the mental activity taking place at the deepest levels.

Symbol Systems. The next stage in the mental process is the creation of complex symbol systems which can be encoded and represented in notations, signs, and symbols and shared with others. Pictorial and musical forms (which may also be considered "languages") can be shared universally. Language (communicative) and mathematics (or the "language" of mathematics) can be shared among those who understand them.

Pictorial styles appear to integrate visual dimensions of perception into complex symbols which can be compared with the grammar and vocabulary of language and which appear in painting, sculpture, and other visual arts. Musical forms, in a similar fashion, integrate auditory percepts and emotions into harmony, rhythms, and melody which make up a language of music.

Language retains links to perception in the form of sounds of speech, but meaning in language is mostly determined by deep, thought-driven processes. These meanings are generally shared within and generate from the community that uses the language. Mathematics involves a genuinely abstract language that exists beyond sensation. Our principal concern here, however, is more with perception and thinking than with symbol systems. Because so many of these processes occur out of our awareness and because they are so heavily influenced by the assumptions and values we learn from our cultural environments, perception and thinking play a central and critical role in shaping the attitudes and determining the behaviors which are special to each culture. It is these attitudes and behaviors, including the assumptions and values on which they are based, that we are examining here and to which we refer as subjective culture.

The American Model of Perception and Thinking

Before we can arrive at an objective appraisal of American patterns of perception and thinking, it is necessary to understand that the distinction between objective sensation at the surface and more deeply embedded subjective thinking is a culture-based idea. It is not a universal model for the human mental process. The use of "deep" to describe thought was a startling breach of traditional forms of thinking when it first appeared during the fifth century b.c. in ancient Greece, and it has influenced Western, including American, thinking ever since. It is in striking contrast to early Buddhist thinking and to thinking patterns which prevail among, for instance, the Chinese and Japanese today.

The idea that thought is deep emerges clearly in the works of Heraclitus and of Aeschylus. Heraclitus apparently was the first to use the metaphor of depth to describe thought (Snell 1953, 17-22). It was rapidly adopted by other Greek thinkers and resulted in a significant shift in the Greek paradigm for thinking. Prior to that time Greeks lacked a hinge between the sensory organs and the internal world. The Greek understanding of the external world, as reflected, for instance, in the works of Homer, was confined to concrete instances such as the glint in the eagle's eye, the gleam of sunlight on a helmet, the glistening sweat on the backs of oarsmen, a glimpse of Helen's face, or the glow of embers. Human relations were also seen as surface in the form of obligations, duties, and relations among people. The metaphors of Homer were more horizontal than vertical, referring to size, extent, or number, including ranking. Homer lacked the lexical means for direct expression of qualities such as friendship and thinking which are not readily represented in surface metaphors. Achilles and Ulysses did not weigh alternatives and reach decisions, since there was no personal agency to make choices. Instead, victory or defeat, life or death, were determined by the balance of Zeus and by the intervention of fate in the form of gods and goddesses (see Snell, 1-18).

The change in paradigm, which connected the external world to the processes of deep thought, was captured by Aeschylus in his earliest surviving play, *The Suppliant Maidens*. When King Pelasgus is compelled to decide the fate of the suppliants, he says:

> Surely there is a need of deep and salutary counsel; need for a keen-sighted eye, not o'ermuch confused, to descend like some diver, into the depths, that to the State above all things this matter may work no mischief, and may come to a fair issue for ourselves...(Smyth 1956, 45).

Thus was the new paradigm given timeless expression. A translation of the passage into English verse is given in Table 1.

The ancient Greek notion of mind that we now call deep structure and the affirmation of its individual locus of judgment and decision making are firmly in place in American culture. It is the material stability of the physical world yielded by thought-driven patterns of perception and thinking that stands out in American cultural thought. An examination of Buddhist ideas of perception—which still affect thinking in areas of Asia where Buddhism has been strong—will help bring into sharper focus the distinctive features of American ways of thinking.

In India, it is the fugitive uncertainty of perception which has been singled out as the core of experience. The early Buddhists in India took perception as central to knowledge (Jayatilleke 1963, 428). They seized upon fugitive sensations as the keystone of their thought, describing the sensible world as made up of momentary flashes of energy (Stcherbatsky 1962, 79). Sensation was but the reflex response to those flashes. These Buddhists believed that only the first moment could be known directly before it was annihilated. The present moment alone was captured by sensation, not the preceding nor the following one. The reality of that single moment was unutterable; it existed outside conceptual determination and beyond words (Stcherbatsky, 186). The stability of the objective world was an illusion born of words that were inherently separated from reality. The use of sensory evidence to support concepts about reality was of no value (Nakamura 1964, 140) since the sensation, the ultimate reality, was instantaneous and could not generate the permanence of the physical world. Stability in time and space, the Buddhists reasoned, was a construction of the imagination (Stcherbatsky, 80-83).

This view of perception influenced the way Buddhists ordered their knowledge about the world and life. Their perceptual theory minimized the distinction between direct sensory information and knowledge obtained through fantasy or inference, inducing them to treat perceptual objects and mental products similarly. Concrete objects and abstract concepts were situated side by side on a single dimension, and abstract ideas could be represented as concrete objects. The objective world was exhaustively described but without the rank ordering which Westerners impose on reality by classifying objects and events according to their importance (Nakamura, 130-33).

These contrasts in conception are evident when the contemporary thought patterns of Americans are compared with those of the Chinese or Japanese. The American proverb, "still waters run deep," (as a way of describing a quiet, thoughtful person) would be rendered differently by the Chinese. In Mandarin, a profound thinker would be described as "great" or "valuable" rather than deep. Also, in Japanese, horizontal allusions to size, rank, or multiplicity more often render the quality of thought than vertical allusions to depth. Both for the Chinese and Japanese, the thinking process is seen as much less deep than it is by Americans and other Westerners. External social roles and relationships, for instance, receive much more emphasis than the nature of one's thought processes. Put differently, the Chinese and Japanese tend to have a highly developed sociological sense but make relatively little use of psychological analyses.

The difference between Buddhist and Western approaches to perception appear in the distinction between operations of the brain. The process of sensation may be roughly equated to an analog device such as a clock which to a degree can represent functions and objects directly (Gregory 1970, 162-66). Such sensations as those of color, for instance, are continuous and, within the scope of the eyes, practically infinite. Sensations are representative of the physical stimuli, the wave lengths which produce sensations. But sensations are transformed into percepts and eventually into objects and images—the constructed symbols; and a system such as language comes to resemble digital devices. In the words of Gregory,

> So we are forced to the conclusion that the brain is biologically an analog system. With the development—or invention—of language man's biologically analog brain can work in a digital mode. This is so remarkable that we can hardly begin to understand it (163).

It seems clear that the Buddhist view of perception and thought stresses the analog functions of the brain—the fugitive sensations that flow from bursts of energy which constitute the elusive remains of a brief reality. The Western view of perception emphasizes the digital symbolization of percepts that form the basis for the permanence we attribute to the world. The idea that the world is continuous, stable, and material derives from the interaction between sensory perception of objective stimuli and abstract contributions from the brain itself. Human beings resolve the paradox of a stable world composed of fleeting percepts by integrating these two modes in everyday experience. But if this is a universal process, what is the source of cultural differences in patterns of thinking? One answer lies in the way people in different cultures order the world of sensations they receive by creating category boundaries, that is, classifying, categorizing, sorting, and storing the sensations. Central to this process is the principle of figure and ground.

Figure and ground can be explained with a simple demonstration. When we draw a closed ring on a blank piece of paper and then look at it, we see a circle, that is, the space inside the ring and not simply the ring described by the line itself. This space inside the ring, which may now be seen as the figure, seems to be raised above and to have more texture than the space outside the ring, which is now the ground. The same figure/ground relation appears if we draw three straight lines and connect them at their end points. We see a triangle. Figure/ground organization is a general principle which applies to all percepts and in part defines what is meant by transformation from sensation to perception. Second, the transformation of sensation flux into figure/ground is also an example of a digital symbolization of fleeting visual shapes of analog perception.

Although the interpretation of figure and ground is a biological function of creating percepts, at a practical level the perception may display the influence of experience. For instance, it is difficult for the tourist walking on the beaches in Guam to identify a stone used as a tool by the early inhabitants of the island. At first, all stones look alike. It takes some experience before the novice learns to identify by appearance those stones that may be old tools. Although the organization of sensory signals into perceptions of figure and ground is natural for everyone, identifying the specific object perceived will usually be affected by learning from one's environment.

Cultural differences are found almost exclusively in the subjective processes of interpretation, in the way something is thought about rather than in objective perception. Thinking at this level can be seen as the construction of category boundaries that define figure/ground objects, transforming them into perceptual objects. An almost literal example of this process occurs in the training of an airplane pilot, who must learn to distinguish the figure of an airstrip from the ground surrounding it. (It may distress the reader to know that this is often a difficult task.) In addition, category boundaries define the extent to which a figure is subcategorized. For instance, when skiers inspect snow before the day's run, they will subcategorize it into various types: light powder, medium-packed, corn, etc. The distinction among these types will probably escape nonskiers, who simply perceive snow.

Most particular boundary constructions are learned, and culture is an important factor in this learning. Culture guides us in what to consider "figure." Micronesians, for example, are far more likely than Americans to see wave patterns—interactions of tide and current on the ocean surface that are used for navigation. To a typical American, the ocean is just "ground," and only boats or other objects are "figure." But this same American may single out an automobile sound as indicating imminent mechanical failure, while to the Micronesian it is simply part of the background noise. In general, culture engenders in us the tendency to perceive phenomena that are relevant to both physical and social survival. In terms of cultural differences, the critical point to grasp, of course, is that what is "figure" or important to one culture may be "ground" to another.

Perceptual boundaries are mutable. For instance, children who speak Trukese, a Micronesian language, do not make a distinction between blue and green. One word, *araw*, refers to both colors, and is the response to both "What color is the sea?" and "What color is the grass?" Yet these children routinely learn to perceive the difference in color as part of their training in English as a second language. The mutability of perceptual boundaries supports the idea that organizing stimuli into categories is a psycho-cultural activity rather than an automatic physiological process.

The boundaries used to categorize stimuli, such as those indicated by the words *green* and *blue,* are not arbitrary and free-floating interpretations. Boundary markers belong to a system of representation possessing its own structure. In English, for instance, blue and green are abstract adjectives which can be used as metaphors for emotional experiences as in a "blue mood" or "green with envy." The power of blue and green to express emotion derives from both the symbolism associated with the colors they represent and from their privileged position in the English language as abstract qualifiers. A word used to represent an object affects the perception of similar objects. The representation of perceptual features is in subtle ways affected by language rather than by the object itself. Perception is distorted to accommodate to the structure—vocabulary, grammar, style—of the language. But the reverse also happens. There is an accommodation in which the language may be stretched to fit perception. An example occurs with the analog perception of the natural world in continuous gradations and variations. Blue gradually merges into green since no boundary exists that clearly separates them. But language itself establishes discrete categories. There is no ambiguity between the words *green* and *blue* but when these two labels are applied to represent the hues of sea, sky, or palms, ambiguous areas of the continuum—blue-green, green-blue—make accurate description more difficult. These ambiguous areas usually receive longer names (aquamarine vs. blue; emerald vs. green); observers react more slowly to them and disagree in identifying them (Roger Brown 1958, 241).

Variations in how the perception of the continuum of the environment is differentiated may contribute to difficulties in intercultural communication since the areas of the continuum that are ambiguous are suppressed and become a source of anxiety. The words used to represent the suppressed areas may be charged with meaning unperceived by a stranger to the culture and its language. In the words of Leach, "Language gives us the names to distinguish the things; taboo inhibits the recognition of those parts of the continuum which separate the things..." (1964, 35). Evidence for this theory is apparent in the classification of animals in English.

Animals fit into four classes according to their social distance from humans: pets, tame farm animals, field animals or game, and remote wild animals. Leach points out that those animals that don't neatly fit the classification receive special attention. The dog, for instance, is not only pet but also tame farm animal (the shepherd dog, for instance), and wild animal. As a pet, the dog belongs to the class of "not food" for English speakers although in other parts of the world the dog is raised for food. Dogs also serve as the source of verbal abuse in phrases such as "son of a bitch." Leach writes:

> In seventeenth century English witchcraft trials it was very commonly asserted that the Devil appeared in the form of a Dog; i.e., God, backwards. In England, we still employ this same metathesis when we refer to a clergyman's collar as a "dog collar" instead of a "God collar" (27).

Other animals sharing the ambiguity of the dog are the cat, horse, ass, goat, pig, rabbit, and fox. These animals "appear to be specially loaded with taboo values, as indicated by their use in obscenity and abuse by metaphysical associations or by the intrusion of euphemism (Leach, 41).

The observation that perceptual category boundaries are learned and are arrived at by subjective processes of interpretation which lead to different experiences of reality contradicts the natural view of Americans that one lives according to a specific, objective reality. In fact, the perceiver responds to culturally influenced categorizations of stimuli.

> To categorize is to render discriminably different things equivalent, to group the objects and events and people around us into classes, and to respond to them in terms of their class membership rather than their uniqueness (Bruner, Goodnow, and Austin 1956, 1).

The construction of boundaries produces images and concepts which classify the content of our experience and provide a means of coping with the complexity of perception. Although cultural differences are found in the natural categories which represent physical perception and images, their overall significance is slight when compared with the abstract artificial categories of thought-driven processes.

Differences in Style of Thinking

The continuum between sensory perception and abstract symbolism (as provided in Table 1) provides a rigorous framework for examining differences in thinking and in values across cultures. For example, Americans tend to focus on functional, pragmatic applications of thinking; in contrast, the Japanese are more inclined to concrete description, while Europeans stress abstract theory. As a result, Japanese thinking would seem to be much closer to the perception end of the continuum than American thought, and European thinking would lie further toward the symbolic end. This is as expected since description (Japanese) is linked to the sensory aspects of perception while function (American) is tied to central processing of perceptual data, and theory (European) is linked to symbol systems and is most distant from immediate perception.

It is likely that a way of thinking close to the perception end of the continuum would be particularly adept at attaching meaning to the immediately perceived events, and such seems to be the case with the Japanese. Japanese thought is as close to analog perception as any other defined pattern of thinking. As might therefore be expected, the Japanese are typically more sensitive than Americans to nonverbal behavior, an analog form of communication. They have a searching perception that notices the appearance of people, what they do, and how they do it. Americans, on the other hand, are not noted for their perceptual skills. They rely much more than do the Japanese on digital, verbal messages, and they usually display more interest in how to get things done than in who is doing it. Americans, while drawing inductively on a perceptual world of objective things and events, construct a moderately abstract functional reality rather than a concrete perceptual one.

Americans going abroad are inclined to respond to the similarities they meet rather than the differences. Searching for the familiar and failing to recognize cultural differences, they may interpret clashing styles of thinking as social conflict. In the incident reported below, a conflict in styles of thinking between a group of Americans and a British engineer creates an impasse which is misinterpreted and projected to the social level of human interaction.

Twenty executives were brought together to participate in a training program. The executives were members of a large American corporation; they had been drawn from the northeastern part of the United States. One or two had been hired from other companies, and one was an Englishman recently arrived from abroad. The training program was designed so they could become acquainted with each other before beginning the process of setting policy for a new plant built by the corporation in the southern part of the United States. As preparation for one of their training sessions, they had read a recent book on management techniques. During the session they discussed its content so as to clarify their own policies on management. The group quickly became polarized.

The majority of the American managers occupied one position (a few remained silent) while the British engineer—highly trained and experienced—took an opposite position in the discussion. As the managers talked, their language became more heated and the comments more personal. The Americans used words and phrases such as "cost-benefit," "productivity," "making a profit," "making the best use of your time," and "change." The British engineer frequently insisted that he did not understand what the Americans were talking about. He repeatedly emphasized the necessity of knowing the specific context in which a given working situation or problem had arisen. He emphasized his own experience as a trained engineer and how, out of his training and experiences, he had been able to develop concepts and rules-of-thumb that he could apply to new situations as they arose. He felt it was relatively futile to attempt to predict the highly general and vague possibilities that the managers might encounter in their new plant; these were meaningless issues to him.

The Americans in this example were exhibiting a characteristic pattern of thinking which is inductive and operational. Heavy emphasis is placed on efficiency but little attention is paid to the overall framework in which one's actions take place. Future projections are made and criteria for measuring success considered, but they are generally embodied in operational principles involving benefit ratios, profit margins, and the like. In this case, they were agreeing on policies based on a rational response to objective facts which they interpreted according to a set of predetermined operating principles.

In contrast, the British engineer was specific in his search for guidance from his own ideas and past experience. He wanted to consider concrete instances to which to apply his theories and to avoid adopting the general principles of the Americans which he considered vague anticipations of the future. He judged that the Americans were concerned with uncertain generalities which might not come about, that their thinking was unclear, and that their use of language was confusing. For their part, the Americans judged the Englishman to be obnoxious, antagonistic, and disruptive to the harmonious working of the group. Neither the Englishman nor his American colleagues recognized the source of their difficulty. The cultural differences in patterns of thinking were readily projected to personal and unfavorable characteristics of individuals, who were then assigned disruptive social motives.

The American View of Facts

From the case study, we conclude that American thinking is more closely oriented to action and getting things done than to the "direct perception of impermanent forms." Americans focus on operational procedures rather than perceptions of the situation. This way of thinking is rational, Americans believe, and efficient. The connection to perception, as defined earlier, is that Americans assume that rational thinking is based on an objective reality where measurable results can be attained. This cultural orientation provides one of the principal keys to understanding the American pattern of thinking. It is the American view of "fact." The significance of this key can be illustrated by a personal experience of one of the authors in South Korea.

The writer visited the demilitarized zone north of Seoul which separates South Korea from North Korea and entered the tunnels which the North Koreans had dug through the mountains. When the military command in South Korea discovered the underground passageways, they reasoned that if the tunnels had not been discovered in time to prevent the North Koreans from launching a surprise attack, Seoul would have been under severe military threat. After the visit, the writer spoke with an American army colonel in military intelligence who was stationed in Korea. In response to a question, the colonel said that eighteen months before the discovery of the tunnels, the intelligence officers had enough information in hand to conclude that the North Koreans were digging through the mountains. When asked to explain the eighteen-month delay, the colonel answered that most of the intelligence information was collected by South Korean foot soldiers patrolling the mountains and consisted of reports that there were sounds coming from the earth and that the ground was shaking. The colonel said that those reports were considered "imagery" and "gossip" of a kind often obtained from South Koreans and were not given any weight.

When the Koreans asked the Americans what they should do to be taken seriously, the American consensus was that "imagery" should be transformed into "facts." First, the source of the information needed to be objectively identified; the patrols should be assigned numbers. Next, the sounds should be measured on some scale—from one to ten, for instance. Sound could range on this scale from a murmur to a clap of thunder overhead. The shaking could run from a slight shudder to an earthquake. When reporting these facts, the information should include the time and the position of the patrol when the observation was made. If these conditions had been met, the Korean gossip or imagery could not have been ignored by American intelligence.

From the episode of the tunnels, we can derive several qualities of American patterns of thinking in contrast to Korean. Americans separate perceptual content which is "objective" and hence measurable from that which is only "imagery." Also, Americans appear to employ a specialized category for information that excludes information by word of mouth or gossip, while the Koreans do not. These observations illustrate some particular aspects of the American concept of fact.

First, facts possess perceptual content; they are empirical, observable, and measurable. Second, facts are reliable so that different observers will agree about them. Third, facts are objective and therefore valid. They are impersonal and exist separately from perceptual processes and from observers. In American thinking, facts exist in the external world and not inside the mind. Fourth, both the reliability and validity of facts are associated with measurements using coordinates of time and space, leading Americans to speak of "historical" but not "future" facts. Americans also say "as a matter of fact," and refer to local or particular facts but not general facts, which would strip the concept of its meaning.

Despite these assumptions about facts, Americans are also quite comfortable engaging in counterfactual speculations where a false identity, action, or event is used to gain insight or information of some sort. In interviews, Americans will often use a hypothetical question such as "If you were the president, what would you do about the threat of a nuclear power plant explosion?"

American facts, their quantification, and the counterfactual mode of thought are avoided in other cultures. The Chinese apparently use counterfactual thinking sparingly if at all. The French and the Indians stoutly resist counterfactual speculation in interviewing, apparently sensing a manipulation of their own personal identities. We can only conclude that the American conception of facts and the use of counterfactual thinking are not universal.

American Pragmatism

American thinking distinguishes between the internal world of thought and the external world of action but emphasizes operations such as decision making that straddle the two. American mental formations favor what is called *procedural knowledge*, which focuses on how to get things done. In contrast, Germans favor *declarative knowledge*, which consists of descriptions of the world (Ryle 1949). The American approach is functional and emphasizes solving problems and accomplishing tasks. The measure of success lies in the consequences of concept-driven action. This distinctive functional style is embodied in American *pragmatism*. Pragmatism lacks the theoretical commitment that Edmund Glenn identifies with the Russians (1981, 80) and the perceptual commitment of the Japanese, lying somewhere in between. The American drive to attain impact has led to the cultivation of a variety of approaches to problem solving, decision making, and conflict resolution intended to avoid the deficiencies of intuition and common sense. Pragmatism employs psychology, game theory, and mathematics to channel human thinking and judgment into applications. This technical approach to human behavior, sometimes called *technicism* (Stanley 1978, 200), is deeply embedded in the consciousness of most Americans, many of whom mistakenly consider it universal. It clearly is not, as indicated by the fact that the Japanese and other cultures lack this prototype of conceptual decision making. The concepts of *alternatives, probability* and *criterion,* to mention three that we shall discuss, mean something very different to the Japanese than they do to Americans.

When selecting a course of action, the Japanese seldom consider alternatives systematically. Instead, they are more likely to arrive intuitively at one course of action. The difference between the Japanese and American approaches is illustrated in the following episode which illustrates the different attitudes of the American and the Japanese toward planning in general.

> A Japanese and an American administrator were planning a program for a group of visitors who were arriving in Tokyo from overseas. The American collected cost information on four different places where the visitors could be lodged during their one-week visit. These were a business hotel, a guest house, a dormitory (or similar lodgings), and an apartment complex. He weighed the advantages of each according to convenience, accessibility of transportation, food, etc. against the different prices involved. He then showed the results to his Japanese colleague. The Japanese looked at the figures and asked how they were going to stay at four different places at the same time. The American answered that of course they were not going to stay at four different places. The figures were simply a feasibility study. His colleague replied, "We also do feasibility studies, but most often we just pick the best one, and we do that very well."

The use of probability has seeped through American culture to a degree unknown to the Japanese and others. When Westerners cooperate with Japanese in technical areas, a number of conceptual gaps can arise to produce misunderstandings and tensions. Two examples given below illustrate some of these difficulties. Both episodes occurred in Japan in the course of conducting research with Japanese and Western technical companies.

> An American manager, situated in Tokyo, received an order for his company's products produced at a plant three hours away by train. He knew that the plant was running near full capacity, but he decided to call his plant manager, an excellent Japanese engineer trained in a leading Japanese university, and ask him for his estimate of how long it would take to fill the order. The Japanese declined to give an answer. The American pressed for an estimate but failed to persuade the Japanese to respond. The

stand-off led to tension between the two men, which came out
weeks later when they accidentally met face-to-face in a training
session and discussed the situation with assistance from the
trainer.

The Japanese explained his response or lack of response by saying that,
for him, numbers represented countdowns, commitments to deliver.
The American understood his position but said that he had only been
asking for a "guesstimate," not a commitment. The American was
comfortable using data to estimate probable but indeterminate out-
comes. The Japanese was not.

This episode conveys a fundamental difference in how Americans
and Japanese work with measurements, probability, and plans. It is
particularly important because it demonstrates again how these kinds
of differences are often interpreted as interpersonal conflict. American
technicism includes a readiness to speculate freely with numbers. American production figures, for example, are often reported as a percentage
of the full capacity of the plant, and they invariably include small errors.
Japanese production figures are strictly counts of actual units produced.
The same difference holds in the area of quality control. In the American
system, product samples are inspected and the results used to generalize
about the quality of the total production. This is also an example of
technicism—the use of statistics and probability to increase efficiency.
The Japanese adopt the attitude of craftsmen and insist on quality
inspection for each item produced, making an inspection of samples
irrelevant. Responsibility for Japanese quality control naturally falls to
the production line and to each individual worker.

The Japanese manager in the above episode acted in the best
Japanese style. First, he did not share with the American uncertainties
of planning for the order; Japanese typically do not discuss their plans
until after the countdown. Second, he would not commit himself to
deliveries based on probability rather than countdowns. Therefore, he
was caught in a difficult cultural predicament.

A second episode presents a technical view of speculation, probability, and risk analysis. The incident was reported by a Scandinavian
assigned to survey and approve the construction of a ship contracted to
a Japanese ship-building company.

The surveyor, who was working with the Japanese, identified a
structural problem in the design of the ship. He insisted that a
horizontal component of the structure be changed from a
rectangular to a triangular shape to improve the distribution of
forces on the vertical components of the structure. The Japanese
responded by accumulating an enormous amount of data
supporting their design, which they brought to the surveyor a few

days later. Overwhelmed by the data, he approved the design presented by the Japanese. Nevertheless, the surveyor remained uneasy, believing that the metal in the ship's structure would develop fissures after some years of service because of metal fatigue. Later, the surveyor recognized that the Japanese calculations had taken into account normal functioning but had not included risk analysis and had specifically omitted speculations about long-term metal fatigue. The Japanese considered it superfluous to conduct experiments to test the design. If the design was as good as its representation in the drawings, they expected the ship to be good. Their approach to safety consisted of a refined and detailed examination, but their testing ordinarily omitted speculations about improbable conditions that would test the limits of the technology. The Scandinavian surveyor, with experiences in the tempestuous North Sea, was more willing to speculate about unusually severe conditions.

This Scandinavian surveyor's experience would probably be very similar to that of an American technician placed in the same position. On the surface there appears to be miscommunication or perhaps an effort to cut corners, but the deep message is another story. The American (and in this case Scandinavian) approach to probability and the analyses of risk differ from that of the Japanese. If we consider the differences in the context of patterns of thinking, we can see that the Japanese attitude is compatible with perceptual thinking, while the Western attitude is functional and based more on abstract considerations. The use of speculations and probability in risk analysis requires a strong commitment to find out what will happen if certain conditions are fulfilled, which by assumption are possible but improbable. This attitude is unduly abstract for a mental disposition inclined toward rigid and measurable perceptions.

We have introduced these lengthy episodes and their analyses as evidence that the American pattern of thinking directs American actions along very different channels from those of the Japanese (and others), even when it involves technical personnel working with abstractions such as probability. The Japanese, relying on perceptual thinking, choose to work with the certainty of precedents and rules—even those of bureaucracies—rather than with probability.

The operational cast of American (and European) thought apparent in the preceding discussion places it closer to the symbolic end of the perception/symbolism continuum. For instance, Americans are oriented toward the future, an abstract state of mind lying outside perception. Reliance on a vision of the future may raise doubts about the practicality of American thinking. These doubts, though, can be laid to rest by noting that the temporal aim is toward the near future, making the orientation more functional than that in other societies where people orient themselves to a future measured by decades and generations. Second, the future appears in American thinking in the form of anticipated consequences of actions. The projection into the future is conveyed by human intentions and actions rather than by abstract time. Anticipated consequences of actions is a functional concept used in models of decision making and provides a link between thinking and action. We shall return to this subject when we discuss the value of activity. Here it is sufficient to note that the American time orientation represents a midpoint on the continuum—a position that combines some aspects of concrete action with the symbolism of abstract probability.

The primary content of perceptual thinking has been described here as images that are classified according to such perceptual dimensions as color, shape, size, and position. In American thinking, perceptual dominance yields to functional attributes of what a person can do with things in the form of concepts instead of images (a computer is not just a high tech instrument used for games; it is a high-speed tool used for calculating data). Further along the continuum, operations for classifying objects increase in abstraction and scope until classifications can be based on a single common feature, a *criterial attribute* (Cole and Scribner 1974, 101-02). Any one system of thought has access to each level of abstraction, but Japanese thinking tends to dwell on complex perceptual attributes and avoids all-encompassing general principles while American thinking reaches for that single dimension, the criterial attribute.

Negative Reasoning and Null Logic in American Thought

A typical American analysis of a practical issue tends to focus on obstacles that may block courses of action and to consider ways of neutralizing those blockages in advance. These improbable, negative events enter into their thinking as practical forms of arguments known as *negative reasoning*. In the American cultural context, we shall refer to this way of thinking as *null logic*. It is this dynamic that explains the American concern with avoiding failure in the future by taking action in the present. Null logic is easily recognized in its applications. It directs preventive programs in technology; for instance, parts of aircraft are automatically replaced after a predetermined number of flying hours and before they malfunction. In the area of health, people take a polio vaccine before they succumb to the illness. In education, children may take reading readiness training before they start to learn to read and meet impediments. Safety in industry is based on the analysis of a chain of cause and effect leading to potential accidents. Safety programs are designed to avoid the critical act that causes the accident. From an early age, the typical American child learns to avoid acts that bring about undesirable situations and to select those that get around barriers. Much of the content of American functional thinking concerns circumventing barriers to action. Thus, children often learn to avoid failures or poor grades rather than to attain excellence. Analysis consists primarily of what can go wrong and how to avoid it to attain success.

American null logic seems to be a variation of a more general pattern of Western negative reasoning. Such reasoning involves the assumption that a claim is **not** valid until it is proven to be so. The American variation is distinguished by (1) an emphasis on anticipation of consequences in decision making, (2) an intimate association with action, (3) the implicit presence of the problem solver, and (4) the balancing of negativism by optimism based on the belief that hard effort succeeds. These are cherished American prototypes which occupy less room in European negative reasoning where theory and logic enjoy higher status and don't generate the push to "get things done" that is characteristic of Americans. As a consequence, Americans working with the Flemish or the French, for instance, may see their counterparts as cynical, while the Europeans view the Americans as romantic and naive about the ways of the world.

Nakamura describes another contrast to American null logic in Indian ways of thinking. Indians display a fondness for negative expressions, preferring to define objects by what they are not. "Non-one" is said for "many or none," and yoga disciples revere five moral precepts: nonviolence, sincerity, nontheft, chastity, and nonacquisition. Three of the five in Sanskrit, flagged with *non* in English, are expressed in negative form (Nakamura 1964, 52-59). Europeans and Americans prefer positive expressions for defining objects and virtues. The negative perspective at the foundation of this Indian way of classifying objects and concepts appears, we would suggest, in Western science, technology, and behavior in the form of negative reasoning. The American contribution is to render negative reasoning operational in the form of null logic. Thus, at the practical level, Americans cannot always expect warm compliance with their procedures in industry, education, or even health. In many non-Western cultures null logic is not a motivating force. Instead, the approach to a course of action proceeds through intuition and painstaking description of actual conditions.

The Implied Agent in American Thinking

As we have seen, Americans tend to conceive of human activity as problems requiring human agents to find solutions. American problem solving exposes what appears to be the backbone of American culture: a mental orientation toward practical actions which incorporates a subjective point of view. We will call this orientation the *implied agent* and explain it as the psychological disposition to collect, process, and display information as if an actor or observer were present. In the following example, the implied agent becomes a motorist trying to find his or her way to the airport.

> Traffic signs in the American city assume that drivers need directions on how to get to certain destinations. For instance, in Washington, D.C., drivers can pick up directional signs miles distant from the destination. Directions are given by signs placed where drivers must make a choice between two or more alternative routes and again where they will inform the drivers that they have made the correct choice. The principle of giving directions to reach the airport seems clear enough, but consider the situation in a Japanese city where signs are posted according to a different principle. In Tokyo, drivers on their way to the international airport find that the road is marked for the airport only after the last point of choice is behind and the only possible destination up front is the airport.

In this example, American signs help direct drivers to the airport; Japanese signs assure them they have made the correct choice. American signs guide while Japanese signs label. A similar conclusion can be reached with temporary road signs such as those announcing road construction. American signs in principle are placed well ahead of the place where drivers must select an alternative route when a detour is required while signs in Ecuador, Japan, and elsewhere are placed in principle at the site of the construction, where they actually describe the conditions of the road. When drivers read the sign, they have passed the last choice point and have to proceed with caution or stop, turn around, and retrace their path.

Although there are many exceptions to these principles of "direction" and "description," the two seem to serve as prototypes in the United States and in Japan. The American pattern of collecting and conveying information in a way that guides behavior is at the core of the concept of the implied agent. The information conveyed is particular, action-oriented, causal, and practical. It assumes an agent outside the self and the immediate situation that is capable of observing information and acting upon it. This contrasts with the perceptual thinking of the Japanese and others, which maintains a concept of self which is centered in the immediate act of perception.

The concept of implied agent provides us with a convenient way of describing the American preoccupation with causation. The idea of a "natural happening" or "occurrence" is not familiar or acceptable for Americans as it is for the Chinese and many other non-Westerners. Events do not just occur or happen naturally; they require a cause or an agent that can be held responsible. Americans are not satisfied with statements of occurrence until they have determined who is responsible—who did it or who caused it to be done. "Where there's smoke, there's fire" means that each effect or event has a causative agent. The English language reflects this quality of American (and English) thinking. For example, in English one cannot grammatically refer to a natural occurrence of rain without an agent. Unlike other Romance languages that allow the statement, "Is raining," the English speaker must invent a dummy subject to say, "It is raining." The *it* in this English statement is the agent.

The implied-agent concept extends into most practical areas of American life. For instance, the American strategy of management appears to revolve around answering "why" questions: Why did an individual act as he or she did? Why is a particular objective appropriate? Why did a plan not work (and who is responsible)? An informal study was conducted with an international company in Tokyo, in which Western managers were asked to list the difficulties they had with their Japanese colleagues. Every list contained the complaint that the Japanese do not answer "why" questions. Two examples illustrate the problem.

1. The materials shipped to Japan from the states ordinarily arrived at the port of Osaka, where they were quickly passed through customs in about a day or so. But on one occasion the shipment came through Yokohama. The passage through customs took more than three days. The American manager asked his Japanese assistant to go to the port and find out why it had taken so long. The Japanese manager traveled to Yokohama and returned with information about how the shipment had been processed through customs. The American manager was dissatisfied with the information and asked the Japanese assistant to return to Yokohama. While the delay was all right this one time, headquarters had to know the reason for it, and the manager cautioned his assistant that it should not happen again. The Japanese manager once more traveled to the port. When he returned, the American manager received a great deal of information about the passage of the shipment through customs, including details about the forms filled out, names of

customs agents, and time schedules for the shipment going through each part of the customs procedure— but still no explanation as to why it had taken so long. Finally the American began to realize that he had run up against something he did not clearly understand. He relented from pressing his Japanese assistant, whose willingness and ability were beyond dispute. In the end, the American decided that there was no real reason for the delay other than the fact that the customs officials in Yokohama were not familiar with the shipments for the company and therefore had conducted customs inspection with punctilious formality. Customs agents in Osaka, on the other hand, were familiar with the periodic shipments, knew the company officers, and therefore passed their shipments through customs rapidly.

2. An American manager arrived at a hotel some twenty minutes before the expected arrival time of his vice president, who was flying in from the States. He checked at the desk and was alarmed to discover that the reservation for his superior had been switched to another hotel. He was angered at the change made without his approval, but he did not immediately attempt to find out why. He dashed to the second hotel, where he met his vice president. Although the second hotel was equal to the first one, the change seemed capricious. He wanted to find out why the switch had been made. Later, he asked his Japanese assistant to inquire. The inquiry soon became bogged down with explanations of procedures on how the reservations were made. The American arrived at the conclusion that his question was not going to be answered, and it was not.

These two episodes document the American predilection for "why" answers and the Japanese preference for "what" answers. From the Japanese point of view, the individual should already know "why," and it is a mark of immaturity for one to have to ask. Americans make exactly the opposite judgment, feeling that the "what" is obvious and mature people should inquire into the underlying "why"—they should discover the agent. At a more fundamental level, Americans like information put together in lineal cause-and-effect chains, ideally strung out along a single dimension. In contrast, Japanese prefer increasingly refined details without insisting upon logical or lineal links. These detailed expositions probably indicate circular movement in thought, compared to the more straight-line, operational thought of Americans.

American Analytical Thinking

As we have seen, Americans anticipate future problems by searching for a single factor with which to explain events. This effort demands abstract thought, null logic, and an implied agent of causality. It also demands *analysis*. Analysis dissects events and concepts into the pieces which can be linked in causal chains and categorized into universal criteria. This kind of thinking stands in contrast to a more integrated approach, sometimes called "holistic" or "synthetic" (from "synthesis"). In comparison to American thought, many other cultures such as Japanese, Chinese, and Brazilian are more synthetic than analytical in thinking style.

The analytical cast to American thought appears cold and impersonal to many. One of the actions of youth in the 1960s was to turn away from analysis and restore synthesis in their thinking, which seemed more humanistic. But the coldness of analytical thought is mitigated somewhat when we recognize that its mode of operation is through problem solving and the implied agent. Both of these principles introduce subjectivism and human purpose into an otherwise austere reality created by operational analysis. In American culture, emotions have no overt role in thinking. But human subjectivity is nevertheless present, disguised in practical forms such as the implied agent.

The style of thinking that derives principles from analysis of data is called *inductive*. In Western science, the inductive style is represented by the generation of models and hypotheses based on empirical observation. Somewhat aside from traditional science, everyday American inductive thinking is operational, leading to a stress on consequences and results and a disregard for the empirical world as such. What is important is the ability of the individual to affect the empirical world. In contrast to the American operational style of thinking, Europeans tend to attach primacy and reality to ideas and theories. Their *deductive* and more abstract style of thinking gives priority to the conceptual world and symbolic thinking. Deductive thinkers are likely to have more confidence in their theories than in the raw data of empirical observation, so it suffices for their purposes to show one or two connections between their concepts and the empirical world. They do not feel compelled in the American way to amass facts and statistics. They prefer to generalize from one concept to another, or from concept to facts, by means of logic. They have faith and trust in the powers of thought; Americans place faith and trust in methods of empirical observation and measurement.

The American way of thinking produces disciplines in the social sciences that are more likely to be empirical and to stress empirical methods in other disciplines than in European countries. Scientific work is often seen as confirming and elaborating the organic theories of other scientists and philosophers rather than being new. There is a tendency for deductive thinkers to consider ideas as organic and living parts of reality. They may consider a new idea to be a "revelation" or a "discovery," while the more inductive American thinker will consider a concept more in the nature of a "construct" or an "invention" to be defined mainly by examples. This difference in styles of thinking may be illustrated by the comment of Don Martindale, an American sociologist, on the observation by Ferdinand Tönnies, a European, that "in the organic world the concept itself is a living reality." Martindale (1960, 91) observes that "presumably the concept of a man, like an actual man, gets up in the morning, puts on its pants, shaves, and in other ways prepares for a busy day."

These observations of American and European styles of thinking indicate some cultural differences in emphasis that may be associated with intercultural misunderstandings. The crude comparisons suggest that there is a single style characteristic of Americans and another of Europeans. In fact, a third contrasting style—*relational thinking*—involves a high degree of sensitivity to context, relationships, and status and exists in cultures where the social order approaches a gemeinschaft pattern. Analytical thinking, by contrast, tends to prevail in societies that, by comparison, resemble a gesellschaft pattern. Relational thinking is found in many countries as well as in certain subcultures in the United States.

In an important study of conceptual styles, Rosalie Cohen (1969) found in children from low-income American homes a relational pattern of thinking encountered more often in non-Western societies. Cohen defined conceptual styles as "integrated rule-sets for the selection and organization of sense data" and noted that the styles can be defined "without reference to specific substantive content and they are not related to native ability" (841-42). Within each conceptual style, certain assumptions and relationships are logically possible and others are not. She found two major styles in the United States: analytical, which we have discussed and which is the dominant pattern of thinking, and relational, a style which is less abstract and more sensitive to the total social context.

Perhaps Cohen's most important contribution is the notion that these conceptual styles are associated with different family and friendship structures. People with relational patterns of thinking come from backgrounds in which neither equality among persons nor differentiation of roles are as accentuated as they are in the background of those with analytical patterns of thinking. Culture groups where the analytical type appears are more formally organized; privileges, responsibilities, and status in the groups are distributed in orderly fashion. The individual in these groups has a greater freedom to leave the group and to "refuse to act in any capacity not defined by his job" (Cohen, 853). This conceptual style is identified with the American middle class.

On the other hand, relational types are more deeply embedded in their membership groups. They are expected to identify with the group as a whole rather than with formal functions associated with their roles in the group; they have to be ready to act in any capacity at any time. Functions in the group, including leadership, are shared more widely among members than is found with groups composed of analytical persons.

These distinctions parallel findings revealed in the study of cross-cultural differences, where the demonstration of an association between conceptual style and social organization is significant. Particularly important is Cohen's conclusion that the educational and social institutions which Americans create are particularly suited to the analytical conceptual style. The social organizations, curricula, pedagogy, and discipline in the schools provide unfavorable environments for the relational conceptual style. This condition may cause difficulties for many foreign and American students in higher education. American instructors who complain that some students lack the ability to think analytically may be encountering the same relational conceptual style found by Cohen among children in low-income families.

One of the major differences between analytical and relational styles is how subjectivity is treated. The analytical style separates subjective experience from the inductive process that leads to an objective reality. The relational style of thinking rests heavily on experience and fails to separate the experiencing person from objective facts, figures, or concepts. Thus students with relational inclinations are said by their instructors to confuse concepts with impressions gained through observation or experience. In their writing and thinking, these students tend to give equal value to personal experience, empirical fact, and concepts derived from persons in authority. They fail to make the distinction between the objective and the subjective, which is required in the analytical academic world.

In contrast to the American analytical style, Chinese thinking is strongly relational and for this reason lacks clarity from a Western point of view. The Chinese do not analyze a topic by breaking it into parts. Their thinking is based upon concrete conceptions weighted with judgment (Granet 1950, 8-30). It lacks the power of precise analysis and abstract classification, but it excels in identification by evoking concreteness, emotion, and commitment to action. Chinese thought strives for unity between events or objects and their given signs or symbols, so that references to the conceptions in the spoken word itself tend to be taken for the act (Granet, 40). An event may be explained by pointing to another event that occurred at the same time, even though by Western logic the two are not connected. This movement from event to event provides the displacement characteristic of Chinese thought which has been called *correlational logic* (Chang 1952, 215). In contrast, Western thought tends to relate things with abstract concepts or principles.

Social influences in relational thinking are particularly important in gemeinschaft societies. The critical role of social influences is partly explained by the procedures used in learning. Even knowledge which is based primarily on sensory impressions is social in kind. Knowledge as well as identity are embedded in social processes. The question that arises is how learning can take place while these social assumptions are supported. The answer for both analytical and relational thinking is that learning requires a model for imitation. Learners match the model with their own production or performance. Learning by use of this model requires a strong and well-defined relationship between the learner and the teacher, who assumes the role of "master." This is the typical pattern of apprenticeship learning in which the learner assumes a deferential and subservient role. Not only are skills and knowledge transferred, but the learner also acquires attitudes of deference to the master, perpetuating the social forms of authority in the society. Imitation is found throughout the world, and it is a dominant form of learning in many societies. It is particularly noticeable in traditional activities such as the martial arts in China and the tea ceremony in Japan.

Based on the evidence available, it is clear that styles of thinking vary from culture to culture, sometimes dramatically. The abstract, analytical, pragmatic approach of Americans is very different from the European style emphasizing theory and organic concepts. And as a group, the Western styles vary substantially from the relational style of the Japanese and the Chinese who are more likely to think by means of analogy, metaphor, and simile. Much of the difference between East and West in our example can be grasped in language. As we have seen, language is an encoding in symbols of the images, concepts, and patterns of thinking that are all part of the cognitive process. In the next chapter, we shall examine the relation between language and patterns of thinking and behavior in American culture.

CHAPTER THREE

LANGUAGE
AND
NONVERBAL BEHAVIOR

If we view languages only as communication tools—sets of words that can be exchanged for other sets and yield the same meaning—we court the role of "fluent fools" as we translate words without their original cultural context. Language serves as a tool for communication, but in addition it is a system of representation for perception and thinking. The functions of tool and representation intersect, but for the analysis of cultural differences we shall separate them and concentrate on the representation of experience. This function provides us with verbal categories that guide the formation of boundaries between concepts and objects and defines the role of language in separate cultures.

American Attitude toward Language

Americans, like everyone else, recognize that differences in language must be dealt with in cross-cultural situations. But since most Americans speak only one language, they are usually dependent on finding English speakers or translators. Once they succeed in their search, Americans are likely to believe that the problem of language is solved. They assume that words alone are conduits for conveying meaning and tend to ignore the more subtle role of language in communication. According to this assumption, the message reaches the receiver, and the words unload their content and deliver their meaning intact (Reddy 1979). If the message is misunderstood, either the receiver is faulted for not listening, or the sender is blamed for selecting the wrong words. (According to American norms, both senders and receivers share responsibility for miscommunication.)

The assumption of a closed association between words and their meaning has a long history in Western thought, tracing back at least to Aristotle.

> In this conception, words were merely mechanisms, or something of a dealer's choice in expressing an essence of being and reasoning which all men, or at least all educated men, share. Hence, reality and reasoning about reality are considered universal in nature and in application, and unaffected by language. The same truth should be apparent to all men. This assumption has survived for a long time (Fisher 1972, 97).

Most American speakers of English operate with this assumption. Language is seen as a mechanism, and little if any thought is given to how language affects reasoning.

Language and Thinking

A memorable statement of language representing experience appears in Benjamin Whorf's often quoted statement:

> We dissect nature along lines laid down by our native languages. The categories and types that we isolate from the world of phenomena we do not find there because they stare every observer in the face; on the contrary, the world is presented in a kaleidoscopic flux of impressions which has to be organized by our minds—and this means largely by the linguistic systems in our minds (Whorf 1956, 213).

In this statement, Whorf advances what is often called the Whorf hypothesis: language largely determines the way in which we understand our reality. This is known as the "strong hypothesis," but Whorf is inconsistent in his treatment of the influence of language on thought. In other writings, he takes the position that language, thought, and perception are interrelated, a position called the "weak hypothesis."

The practical question raised for intercultural communicators by the Whorf hypothesis is whether a message delivered in one language (e.g., English) maintains its intended meaning when conveyed to a person (e.g., an Indonesian) for whom English is a foreign language. The hypothesis is particularly critical in the case of a message being translated into a second language before it is transmitted. According to the strong hypothesis, the second language would both constrain and channel the internal process of perception and of thinking. Therefore, the translated version should convey a different meaning. But the weak hypothesis predicts the possibility that the second language could be shaped to render the same meaning in the translated version as in the original. The issue raised by the Whorf hypothesis is of considerable importance in negotiations, diplomacy, and even everyday exchanges. A satisfactory explanation of it requires a close examination of the context of communication and the communicator's psychology of awareness.

Everyone who has been involved in cross-cultural interaction has a stock of anecdotes about how something said was misunderstood. In analyzing these miscommunications, the reader should bear in mind that no one commands the full capacity of even his or her own native language, much less that of any other language. When communicating, the demands of the situation often require immediate responses, compelling the communicator to rely on verbal habits and familiar thoughts rather than to search for messages the receiver will plainly understand. Furthermore, most communicators lack the insight to construct a message that neutralizes the influence of language. Both speaker and receiver are much more likely to resort to familiar forms. Whether the linguistic resources for perfect translation of one language into the other exist or not, the competence of the people involved and the demands for immediate responses constrain deploying the full resources of a language in intercultural communication. Much of the meaning of language is extracted by the receiver from the context in which messages are transmitted rather than from the dictionary meaning of the words.

An example of language creating context is found by returning to color experiments, again with blue and green. A recent study used this familiar color contrast to determine the influence of color vocabularies on perception (Kay and Kempton 1984). The participants in the experiments were English speakers accustomed to using words *green* and *blue* and native speakers of Tarahumara—a Uto-Aztecan language of northern Mexico—who, like the Trukese mentioned earlier, have one term for both English words. The experiments required the subjects to discriminate among color chips in the blue to green range. When the English speakers were allowed to use the names of the colors (or "name strategy," as the researchers called it) in making their judgments, their discrimination of colors was more precise than that of the Tarahumara speakers. When the experimenters deprived the English speakers of their vocabulary by using chips of a color intermediate between blue and green and by referring to them as both green and blue, the perceptual differentiation of the Tarahumara speakers was the same as that of the English speakers. The experimenters concluded that speakers increased their differentiation of color when the name strategy was available, that is, green and blue, but that language did not directly affect the initial sensory stimulus, only their recognition and reporting of it. The experimenters also concluded

> that the name strategy seems to operate at an utterly nonconscious level, since sophisticated subjects to whom the name strategy is described nevertheless report that the color in question "looks different" (Kay and Kempton, 75).

This finding about the psychology of awareness is important since it explains why Americans can rely so much on language while disregarding the Whorf effect. If we are unconscious of our reliance on language strategies to recognize and report sensory data, then we are likely to assume falsely that the same objective reality exists for all people. From the evidence available, we can conclude instead that language creates a master framework for perception (Fisher 1972, 95).

Language and Objects of Perception

Some Americans are surprised to discover that the enumeration of objects and the classification of space receive different representations in various languages. American English has only one way to count things (one, two, three, etc.) while Japanese and Trukese each have many different counting systems. In part these systems classify the physical appearance of objects. For instance, one long thing is counted with different words from one flat thing or one round thing in Trukese. We could imagine that experience with objects in general is much richer in cultures where language gives meaning to subtle differences in shape. Indeed, the aesthetic appreciation the Japanese have for objects seems more developed than that of Americans, whose English language lacks linguistic structures to represent shapes and perceptual thinking in general. In addition both the Japanese and Trukese use a set of words to count people that is different from all those used for objects. We might speculate that research on human beings that quantifies behavior "objectively," so common in Western cultures, would not occur as easily in cultures with more refined counting systems.

In American English, things can be either "here" or "there" or, colloquially, "over there" when implying the distance is greater. In the Trukese language, references to objects and people must be accompanied by a *location marker* that specifies their position relative to both the speaker and listener. A pen, for instance, must be called *ei piin, ena piin* (that close to you but away from me), *enan piin* (that far away from both of us but in sight), or *ewe piin* (that out of sight of both of us). Again, we may assume that Trukese people experience space more richly than do Americans, whose language does not provide so many spatial boundary markers and for whom space is therefore more abstract.

Language in Social Relations

The experimental evidence available clearly supports a Whorf effect in social perception. People's perceptions of social events and situations, social relations, roles, and even their own behavior are distinctively in keeping with the different conceptual structures of their languages (Fisher 1972, 99).

Perhaps the simplest and best known examples are linguistic differences in *status markers*. Thai, Japanese, and some other Asian languages have elaborate systems of second-person singular (you) words that indicate the status of the speaker relative to the listener. In Thai there are also variable forms of the first-person singular to indicate relative status. Thus, I (relatively lower in status) may be speaking to you (somewhat higher in status) or to you (much higher in status), using a different form of *I* and *you* in each case. It seems apparent that cultures with languages which demand recognition of relative status in every direct address make one more keenly aware of status difference than does American culture, where English provides only one form of the second person. European cultures, most of whose languages have two forms of *you* indicating both status distinctions and familiarity, may represent the middle range of this dimension. Europeans are more overtly attentive to status than are Americans, but Europeans are no match for Asians in this regard.

Kinship terms are also used in some cultures to define social relationships and to indicate status, and they may be even more complex than status markers. Americans who have read nineteenth-century Russian novels—by Dostoyevski or Tolstoy, for instance—often find it difficult to keep track of the relations among the characters and to understand their motives. Part of the difficulty lies in the intricate web of extended kinship relations that existed in nineteenth-century Russia and that was marked by some three hundred kinship terms. In Russian families

> all members of the household were considered relatives, even though they might not have been so in terms of blood or marriage. They ate together, shared the work—and defined their relationships to one another by the use of very precise kinship terms (Farb 1974, as quoted in Christian 1980, 248).

Translations of Russian novels into English do not make these relationships clear since English lacks the kinship terms. Also, the society inhabited by contemporary English speakers differs radically from that of the Russians of the last century. The failure to represent in English the critical social terms of Russian society and Russian language compels the American reader to interpret the social dynamics of Russian culture in terms of American social and cultural dynamics. This deficiency makes it difficult for Americans to understand the actions and motivations of characters and sometimes even the plot of a novel (Christian, 248).

Language Structure As a Model for Thinking

Thus far we have used semantic examples to examine the influence of language on thought. To complete the case for the Whorf effect, we should briefly consider the impact of the structure or syntax of language on thinking. Two aspects of linguistics, forms of verb tense and subject/predicate structure, yield evidence of cultural representation in thought.

The Trukese language lacks an elaborate future tense, and Trukese people appear to be more concerned with living in the present than in planning for the future. For instance, arrangements for future events such as meetings or boat trips are always tentative, when they are made at all. While it may be an overstatement to say that the lack of a future tense dictates present-orientation, Whorf (1956) made a similar observation about the Hopis, whose language also lacks a future tense. The Hopi people use statements of intention to refer to future events, and Hopi behavior, like Trukese, displays qualities of present-orientation. Americans, using the well-developed future tense in English, aim toward the near future, stress planning, and project the future in making decisions.

A tentative but useful analysis of the English language has been made by Fisher (1972), who identifies two structural qualities in English that suggest a linguistic compatibility, if not a base, for the kinds of objective descriptions and action orientations that are preferred by Americans. The first quality is the subject/predicate structure of the language, which predisposes the speaker to interpret as fixed the relationship between subjects or things and their qualities or attributes. The structure of English tends to suggest that the lake is blue, even though the waters are in fact grey under an overcast sky, reddish at sunset, and green from the reflection of grass growing on the banks. The structure of the language suggests to the user that experience should be represented as *is* or *is not*, a digital rather than an analog representation. This speculation is indirectly supported by Fisher when he writes,

> It takes much more to describe conditions which are not exactly one way or another—a problem which modern scientists face when they use English to discuss molecular motion or relativity (120).

Chinese, like English, provides for subject-verb-object sequence but avoids the "is-or-is-not" polarity. Chinese encourages complementary ordering of relations which would be opposites in English, such as black and white. Instead of the English polarity of man and woman, Chinese renders a reciprocal relation between the two. From the American point of view, the Chinese man at times appears feminine, and the woman, masculine. Chinese articulates the middle values, what would be a continuum in English stretching between polar extremes. Chinese thinking avoids using ends of the dimensions to grasp the nature of the universe. Instead, the Chinese fix attention on the quality of the continuum (Fisher, 120). For example, emotions which in English are polarized (e.g., love and hate) would likely be expressed in Chinese through the use of complementary pairs of moderate emotions such as deference and politeness, social obligations and privileges, and congeniality and despondency rather than the juxtaposition of extreme opposites.

Chinese seems to function as an analog system compared to the more digital character of English. Thus, English is weak in representing gradations of emotional feelings and moods but gains effectiveness in rendering discrete mechanical and technical descriptions. Because of the abstract quality of digital representation, English presents opinions as statements of fact, as in "Ted Williams was the best baseball player in the American League." English also obscures subjectivity by conveying it as part of a presumably objective process, as in "We found that more force was necessary to quell the disturbance." Affirming more than is known creates instability and imprecision, but it stimulates intellectual curiosity and originality, and ultimately it leads to research (Glenn 1981, 86).

Speakers of English are also forced by the subject/predicate form to constantly represent causality. When there is a predicate in the language but no subject, the structure of English requires that the speaker assume one. As noted in chapter 2, the word *it* often suffices for the missing subject, as in, "It happened one night." The implication is that happenings do not simply occur on their own (as they can in Italian, for instance); there is something (it) behind them. In the sentence, "It will rain," the *it* may become an implied agent, as evidenced by the common news show banter: "How's the weather going to treat us today?" Fisher comments,

> In its conception of action and events, English is an actor-action-result model, and tends to suggest that perception of this universe and what happens in it. The actor-action-result pattern is very useful for conceptualizing mechanics, business and much of science. It suggests the question "What caused that?" or "What effect will this have on the end result?"(120).

The action orientation of English and its causal concern were discussed earlier from the point of view of the implied agent. We can conclude that an imposing array of assumptions, values, and linguistic features of English predisposes Americans to interpret events in the world as lineal chains of causes and effects.

Dichotomies and Negative Construction

The existence in English of extreme dichotomies influences how Americans manage their relations with others. Specifically, English speakers are compelled by their language to use one of two opposites in questions. As a consequence, Americans commonly use evaluations in questions and descriptions, and they find it easier to be critical than positive or neutral. These qualities of American thought are revealed in the structure of qualifiers (adjectives) in English. The structure will be illustrated by contrasting it to Portuguese.

Many adjectives in English naturally combine in pairs, as demonstrated in the list below:

FAR—NEAR	WIDE—NARROW
HEAVY—LIGHT	OLD—YOUNG
HIGH—LOW	LONG—SHORT
GOOD—BAD	

To the native English speaker's ear, "far and near," "high and low," "long and short" and the remaining pairs of adjectives sound as if they belong together and complement each other. This pairing of adjectives displays the tendency of English to form dichotomies.

At first glance, it may appear that the pairs of English adjectives are opposite but equal in their power to describe positions on the continuum. In actual use, however, the two members of the pair are not equal. This can be seen when the adjectives are used to ask questions, as in, "How far is it to the window?" and "How far is it to Montreal?" The questions are not phrased, "How near is it to the window?" or "How near is it to Montreal?" English phrases all such questions with *far*, which refers to all positions between far and near. Thus, the one polar opposite, *far*, may be considered the subject of the distance dimension. It conveys the meaning of separation by distance, while *near* (or close) conveys more a meaning of specific relation in space. For instance, asking how close the chair is to the window implies that the chair is already close. This same effect can be seen in the question "How old is she?", which refers to the general continuum of age. The question "How young is she?" suggests that a specific assumption about the person's age is being made.

As we saw in the earlier contrast with Chinese, English demands that a continuum be represented by its extreme poles rather than by concepts drawn from the middle ground between opposites. In the case of English adjective pairs, we see that the continuum must be represented by only one pole. American thinking is thus forced into both dichotomizing and selecting one extreme as the subject of the question.

The equivalent Portuguese adjectives can also be presented in pairs, as indicated below:

DISTANTE—PERTO	LARGO—ESTREITO
PESADO—LEVE	VELHO—JOVEM
ALTO—BAIXO	COMPRIDO—CURTO
BOM—MAU	

To a native Portuguese speaker's ear, these pairings do not enjoy the same natural cadence of "far and near," "high and low," "long and short." In general the Portuguese qualifiers do not pair so naturally as those of English but are replaced by a substantive and logical relation between *distante e perto, alto e baixo*, and *comprido e curto*. The Portuguese word pairs enjoy symmetry but convey the feeling of separate prototypes rather than ends of the same dimension. In this sense, they are closer to the meaning structure of *near*, which connotes a specific relationship in space rather than to the structure of *far*, which denotes the quality of the space.

The weaker polarization of Portuguese pairs is reflected in the way questions are asked in that language. In Portuguese, "How far is it to...?" becomes "*Qual é a distancia a...?*" which is literally translated as "What is the distance to...?" The question sounds natural in Portuguese, but in English it sounds stiff, even though it is grammatically correct. The Portuguese question asks simply for a location in space, as opposed to the equivalent English question that conveys separation in space and stresses the polarity of far versus near. Portuguese emphasizes the subject common to the paired adjectives and, in this regard, it is like the Chinese stress on the middle ground between complementary ends of continua.

The separation of opposing adjectives in English conveys another implicit meaning, which appears with the usage of *bad* and *good* in asking questions. If we are dining out and approach the head waiter of the restaurant with the question, "How good is the food here?" we can expect a straightforward answer. It is good, or bad, depending on the quality of the food, the mood of the waiter, or his degree of loyalty to the restaurant. On the other hand, if we approach him with the question, "How bad is the food here?" we have made a statement by way of asking the question. We convey our low opinion of the food served.

The example of *good-bad* illustrates that *good* is general but *bad* is precise. The latter term refers only to judgments close to its pole. The meaning of the two adjectives is positive for *good* and negative for *bad*. Although not apparent at first, nearly all the other pairs of adjectives exhibit the same feature: the English words in the left column are positive and the ones in the right column are negative. This feature is displayed if we use these adjectives as descriptors. For instance, we may wish to praise the financial officer, who keeps a close watch on the figures reflecting the company's performance. If we describe the officer as shortsighted, we fail in the effort to praise. We are compelled to describe the person as being farsighted whether the description is correct or not. When we use the other pairs of adjectives as descriptors, we reach the same conclusion: high morals versus low morals, and wide (or broad) interest versus narrow interest. Sometimes the negative descriptions are quite colorful. Someone who loses in a financial transaction comes out on the "short" end of the deal, and superficial performances are those of "lightweights," although "lighthearted" is a more positive term than "heavyhearted." *Old-young* does not fit this formulation so neatly, since *old* tends to be the more negative descriptor in American culture.

The evaluative construction of questions involving adjectives in English does not transpose to Portuguese. Portuguese renders our example of "How good is the food?" as "*Como é a comida aqui?*" ("How is the food here?"). If prospective diners wish to inquire substantively, Portuguese introduces the notion of quality, "*Qual é a qualidade da comida aqui?*" (What is the quality of the food here?"). Speakers of Portuguese thus avoid the risk of implicitly appraising the quality of the food in the question.

By combining the features of dichotomization and negative construction, we can conclude that in English precise qualifiers are negative while ambiguous ones are positive. These linguistic features generalize to American behavior with ease. In English it is easy to criticize and to find fault. Since the vocabulary for negative evaluations is precise and concrete, only moderate intelligence is required to find fault. The pleasant task of praising is more difficult since it takes brilliance to overcome mushy language and not sound as if one is only gushing (E. Stewart, 1985, 27).

The negative precision of English qualifiers yields a linguistic base for the null logic of American thought. The structure of the language naturally accommodates a pattern of managing others by specifying what should **not** be done, and it allows precise calibration of penalties for infractions. American motivation and discipline operate on negative grounds (Stewart, 27). Positive action is open to personal choices since the individual should be creative and avoid conformity and imitation. Thus, the individual is not told what to do since positive rules of behavior court conformity and encourage imitation—both undesirable in American culture. Instead, authority and regulations in American society tend to be exercised from the negative side: the individual is told exactly what not to do, and typically, punishments for infractions are far more precise than rewards for appropriate behavior. In other cultures such as Chinese and Brazilian, the exercise of authority is much more likely to be made by rules prescribing and regulating desirable actions.

Clarity and Ambiguity in Language

For Americans, clarity in language usage is better than ambiguity since precision leads to practical action. If the message is understood, then language and communication are good. As we have seen, however, English has some structural qualities that are inherently ambiguous, such as the use of nonspecific adjectives in questions. The combination of vague vocabulary and the desire for language to serve as a precise tool sometimes draws Americans into using unusual linguistic devices.

A typical phenomenon among American speakers is the selection of a general noun which lacks precision and to which is added another noun or adjective as modifier. The modifier may be equally vague, but the combination registers precision to the American ear through the phenomenon of *verbal dynamics*. For instance, the word *students* sounds better as *student body*, and *value*, as *value orientation*. *Science* is often rendered as *scientific method*, and a book may become *reading material*. As can be seen from the examples, verbal dynamics includes preferred general nouns. Often used are *approach, behavior, development, facilities, growth, learning*, and *process*. Preferred nouns or adjectives used as modifiers include *dynamic, experimental, exploratory, personal, productive, operational*, and *self-*. Combinations from these two samples of words furnish formidable representations of social norms, such as *dynamic process, self-learning*, and *personal growth*.

The juxtaposition of two or more words that modify each other captures the American preoccupation with processes and illustrates the operational emphasis in American thinking. Such is the case in a reference by a Washington, D.C., newspaper to the "traffic-bearing facility" over the Potomac. A bridge is a structural concept; it is a thing. The verbal dynamic of "traffic-bearing facility" shifts the focus from the structure to the function of the structure. Structure is derived from the interaction between both components of the phrase, since either word alone is too vague to denote any particular object. An examination of verbal dynamics usually reveals a loss of precision. The compound term is understandable only to those accustomed to the shift in emphasis from definite objects to ambiguous processes.

Languages apparently pass through different stages of evolution. An early stage, characterized by inflections, yields to a second stage employing prepositions which, in turn, evolves into the use of adjectival nouns as represented by verbal dynamics. The Chinese language has evolved along this course and English seems to be pursuing the same path. Linguistic evolution does not explain, however, why Americans should be further along in their verbal dynamics than other English speakers. The disparity has to be explained according to unique features of the use of language in the United States.

The American people have experienced a strong impetus to discard the ways of the Old World and adopt those of the new. The immigrants usually encouraged their children to become Americanized. Young people eagerly accepted the language and the ways of the new country and turned their backs on the language and customs of the old. Until recent times, the United States has perhaps been the only country in which speaking two languages was a mark of low status. The impulse to adopt the language of the country, English, was facilitated by an emphasis on simple vocabulary, a disregard for style, and the use of slang as an expression of affiliation and social conformity. American use of English has generally resisted convergence with literary traditions. Even scientific language has been heavily infiltrated by jargon, which accomplishes for scientists the same function as slang in the social context. In either case, vocabulary tends to be limited, and usage is consequently rather loose and vague. For instance, where a British speaker of English might say "bestow a prize," the American says "give a prize." Quite a number of such general words as *give* and *get* are used by Americans with modifiers attached when necessary to make the meaning somewhat more explicit. The British, on the other hand, seem to employ vocabulary more precisely.

These examples draw attention to how the ambiguity of verbal dynamics introduces uncertainty into intercultural communication. As with the other areas of language discussed in this chapter, verbal dynamics is a phenomenon that is representative of culture. Consequently, any translation of language—literal or figurative—must take into account cultural context.

Nonverbal Behavior

As we have seen, languages differ in representing experience in fundamental ways. For instance, Chinese appears to be more of an analogic language than English (Condon and Yousef 1975, 132). The digital tendency of English leads it to the creation of discrete abstract categories, dividing the continuity of human feelings, perception, and thought. These categories are represented by words which are arbitrary symbols in the same way that on/off codes are arbitrary symbols for a computer. But verbal messages in face-to-face interpersonal communication are invariably accompanied by nonverbal behavior that provides an analogic background for the digital words (Watzlawick, Beavin, and Jackson 1967, 53). Voice, gestures, eye contact, and touching are all direct analogic expressions of emotion; that is, they represent emotion rather than referring to it with words. People in social situations who are attuned to the presence and the feelings of others will respond more substantively to the analogic meaning of nonverbal communication than those who are not. Only a small percentage of the meaning created in a social communication exchange is based on language (Rosenfeld and Civikly 1976, 5), so understanding the more important nonverbal aspects of communication is vital to an overall comprehension of intercultural events.

When language is used predominantly as a tool of communication, as is the case with English spoken by Americans, nonverbal behavior is unconsciously perceived more as a commentary on the verbal message than as a part of the message itself. This can be seen in the communication of sarcasm or kidding. Expressions such as "my, what a nice tie" can be modified by a tone of voice that indicates the listener shouldn't take the words seriously. In other words, the nonverbal cue (tone of voice in this case) establishes the sarcastic context in which the words should be interpreted.

Nonverbal behavior may also communicate directly. The person's face that moves from a casual speaking distance of three feet to a two-foot distance has a strong relational impact on the listener. It is the direct emotional experience of the meaning interpreted from perception that gives power to nonverbal communication. Tone of voice, gestures, facial expressions, interpersonal distance, touching, and other expressive emblems are more representative of the feelings and emotions of a relationship than are the words that might describe it. Perhaps for this reason, and because it is perceived as less controllable, nonverbal communication is more believable than verbal communication in interpersonal relations. For adults, discrepancies between verbal and nonverbal information (as in the former example of sarcasm) are usually resolved in favor of the nonverbal cue. And, because these relational cues are seldom the subject of formal study, they tend to operate out of conscious awareness. This combination makes nonverbal behavior a potent factor in intercultural misunderstanding. We may unconsciously assume that everyone is using our own culture's cues and respond unquestioningly with the wrong interpretation.

One particularly difficult area of nonverbal behavior is paralanguage— the tone, pitch, stress, volume, and speed with which language is spoken. For example, Americans rely heavily on voice pitch within sentences (but not within words) to establish the nature of a conversational relationship. A medium falling tone at the end of the question "What can I do for you?" indicates a normal interaction. Too sharp a drop in pitch changes the tone of the question to one of a demand or a brush-off. Extending the pitch drop makes the question more inviting or friendly. This convention does not hold for all languages. In Chinese, for example, pitch may change within words, but it does not change systematically at the end of sentences. When English is spoken with Chinese inflection, sentences lack the rise and fall in pitch that Americans expect in friendly conversation. To the American ear, this flat speech sounds brusque, imperious, or angry. Similarly, Americans may respond to British speakers of English as condescending, Germans as rude, and Latins as excitable. While there may on occasion be some justification for the American response, it is more likely that the speaker's normal paralanguage is simply being misinterpreted.

In the area of kinesics, or body language, Americans tend to be moderately expressive. In contrast to people in many Asian cultures, Americans use gestures freely, but compared to those in Mediterranean, Latin, or Arab cultures, Americans seem quite restrained. Americans may mistakenly interpret Asians as inscrutable or devious and Italians as theatrical, based only on unrecognized differences in gesturing norms. Americans interpret a smile as pleasant or happy, or at least as a vacuous attempt to please, as in the smile of some airline attendants. In Japanese society, on the other hand, the smile enjoys a much wider area of application. Smiles disguise embarrassment, mask bereavement, and barely conceal rage, while happiness hides behind a straight face.

Other nonverbal behavior such as eye contact, touching, and interpersonal spacing follows similar patterns. Americans rely significantly on eye contact as a measure of trust and honesty. The lighthouse sweep of Japanese eyes and the shifting or downcast eyes of those from cultures where direct gaze is considered rude, if not aggressive, disturb Americans. Standing close in conversation may signal fight or flight for Americans while representing the appropriate distance for conversational interaction prescribed by another person's culture. Both spacing and touching are rather precisely coded with social or sexual meaning for Americans. Thus, the norms of Arabs and, to a lesser degree, of Latins, may suggest to Americans that these peoples are socially aggressive and sexually promiscuous. (Differences in other nonverbal behavior, such as dress or prolonged eye contact between men and women in public, causes Arabs and Latins to reach the same conclusion about Americans.)

Interpretation of nonverbal behavior is also affected by the processes of perception discussed in chapter 2: a cue that may be a figure in one culture may be ground in another. It would thus be incorrect to assess the different meanings of a gesture or voice tone in several cultures without first knowing whether that stimulus was being recognized at all. For instance, American English speakers can imply criticism with a tone of voice that trails off as it rises in inflection. This intonation pattern, sometimes used by American supervisors to gently correct work performance, may pass unnoticed by Southeast Asians and others for whom English is a second language. Additionally, only part of a constellation of nonverbal behaviors may be discriminated by the listener or observer, leading to even more complex possibilities for misinterpretation. An example of this occurs in arguments between American blacks and whites. Whites commonly react to the raised voice and facial set of blacks, but they may fail to perceive the presence or absence of change in personal distance accompanying the vocal and facial cues. For blacks, change in distance is the crucial cue that indicates whether or not the confrontation is physically threatening (Kochman 1981). All cultures have their own nonverbal codes, and since a large number of meaningful signs and symbols exist in the code of one culture but either don't exist or exist only partially in other cultures, cross-cultural analysis of nonverbal cues is required for each separate culture.

Americans tend to see nonverbal behavior as ancillary to verbal communication, while elsewhere, as in Japan, the nonverbal code may be used to convey the major message. In either case, interpersonal nonverbal behavior, like language, is usually representative of deep cultural values. This can be seen in the following example from Mexico.

An American visitor to Mexico was describing his family to a Mexican. To describe his young children, the American tried to convey their ages by indicating their height. He held up his right hand, the palm open and facing down horizontally at the height of his child from the ground. At first the American did not notice the look of dismay on the face of the Mexican in response to the hand gesture. It was only later that the visitor found out what had gone wrong with the conversation. The gesture he had used is similar to the movement of the hand in petting a dog or some other animal on the head. Mexicans accept that hand gesture as a description of the height of a dog, pig, or some other animal, but human beings are measured with the palm open and held vertical to the ground at the appropriate height.

The Mexican and American attitudes toward the two kinds of hand gestures can be associated with the views of reality of members of the two societies. Americans accept an objective reality where people and animals are both biological elements in the world. The boundary separating man from the animals wavers in the Darwinian climate of the United States. But Mexicans are not ardent Darwinians, and they insist on an interpersonal reality restricted to human beings, which excludes privileged status for pets and other animals. Both verbal and nonverbal codes and the thinking patterns they represent act to construct meaning. Since American nonverbal communication is secondary to verbal, Americans are poorly prepared to cope with the strength of nonverbal communication in societies such as the Thai or Mexican. While systems of verbal and nonverbal representation of experience are powerful in themselves, they only compose the surface level of deep structures and dynamics of reality. Underlying these verbal and nonverbal patterns, influencing them and also driving the higher levels, are cultural values and assumptions.

FORM OF
ACTIVITY

The exploration of values is popular in the United States. The analysis of human behavior is everybody's pastime and, for teachers, "value clarification" is a classroom buzz word. Social scientists have put values into practical service with quantitative measurements, detaching them from their sometimes arcane, philosophical moorings. This practical and quantitative twist to an appreciation of values prompts the observation by some foreigners that Americans have no *real* values or culture at all. And indeed, for all the romanticizing of values that occurs in the culture, Americans seem largely oblivious to how their behavior is steered by these basic concepts of "oughtness."

To analyze American cultural patterns and values, four different components have been selected: *form of activity, form of relations to others, perception of the world,* and *perception of the self.* In this and each of the following three chapters, different aspects of the four components are considered, ranging from the most systematic and descriptive values and assumptions to those social norms which serve mainly as platitudes or rallying cries for Americans. While the orientations discussed are not in all cases manifest by specific behavior, they do indicate the unconscious bases for evaluation that are likely to be employed by Americans at home and abroad.

Contradictions among assumptions and values are probably universal throughout societies. Each component of a culture affects and, in turn, is limited by the others. In American culture, for instance, the stress on the value of equality among all people is sometimes incompatible with the value placed on achievement or on individual freedom (Robin Williams 1964, 27-28). Nevertheless, the structure of assumptions and values for any culture exists as a system; each component must be considered in light of the others.

Despite variations and contradictions, there exists an overall integration to the pattern of middle-class American culture. It is possible to simplify its description by isolating various components and considering them one at a time as prototype expressions. This process involves abstracting from behavior the assumptions and values that are probably never found in a pure and isolated form; several cultural assumptions and values are usually necessary to explain a given behavior. However, exploring prototypes provides a framework for comprehending the components of the culture and the complexity of their relationships with one another.

Orientation to Action

Action in the real world requires a source since, for Americans, it does not simply occur by itself. An agent or, in the more abstract sense, a cause is required. This assumption in American culture has been noted earlier with the term *implied agent*. The implied agent assumption is so pervasive in American culture that a contrast is required to silhouette its formidable role. In Japanese society, actions are conducted behind the scenes in such a way that events appear to unfold spontaneously and naturally. If there are prime movers, they remain concealed, acting through a medium. Those who search for Japanese decision makers or responsible authorities invariably return empty-handed. In contrast, the American assumption of an implied agent encourages identification of prime movers; decisions have their makers, problems their solvers, accidents their causes, and successes and failures their heroes and villains.

Furthermore, the implied agent exists for the purpose of getting things done. The orientation to action, or the phase preceding behavior, is frequently conceived of as *decision making*. This concept has two meanings in American culture. In everyday life, the idea of decision making is often a vaguely understood social norm used to justify a wide range of behavior. For instance, casual conversations about goals, summer jobs, and extended travel may all be justified as part of deciding on a career. In its more formal sense, decision making incorporates a loose constellation of assumptions and values in American culture that have been systematized as procedures for guiding activity. For example, an element usually included in the decision-making process is "defining the goal." That there should be a goal and that its clarification should serve as a guide to more effective action represents a sequencing of three American assumptions: human beings are responsible for setting their own directions in the world, clarity is preferable to ambiguity, and contemplation should lead to action. This kind of decision making has attained a formal status in psychology and management, representing a typical American application of technical knowledge, what we are calling *technicism*, to human affairs.

In face-to-face situations the locus of both the action and the decision to act lies with the individual. From an early age, American children are encouraged to believe that they themselves are the best judges of what they want and what they should do. Even in those instances where Americans cannot decide for themselves, they still prize the illusion that they can. Thus, when they need to consult a banker, teacher, counselor, or expert of any kind, they perceive it as seeking information and advice to help them make up their own minds. Experts are treated as resource persons and not as decision makers. Americans believe, ideally, that they should be their own source of information and opinions and that they should solve their own problems. For example, aesthetic judgments are frequently equated with personal preferences; Americans are therefore likely to resent external canons for judging the worth of art. If the individual likes it, it is good; the value derives from the self. The result is an intense self-centeredness—so striking and pervasive that a prominent American psychologist, Carl Rogers, has mistaken it as a universal value (1964, 166).

Although American culture provides examples of situations in which one person makes a decision for another, more striking instances of this kind of displacement of decision making usually occur in non-Western countries. In many parts of the world, parents choose spouses for their children. In this and in other situations, the decision maker is not the person most affected by the decision, but the occupant of a traditional role in the social group—in the example above, the parents.

Another variety of decision making prevalent both in the United States and, to a larger degree, in the non-Western world is that in which decisions are localized in a group. Many matters that require action by a family or community in the non-Western world will be settled by a private decision among Americans. Furthermore, the manner in which the individual participates in the group may differ considerably among societies. Americans usually expect to be able to express their opinions and to exert an influence on the final decision. To fulfill their expectations, Americans are quite concerned with matters of procedure, agendas, and voting. These concerns are not ritualistic or ceremonial as they may be in some cultures; they serve the purpose of ensuring fairness to all and of facilitating action. Even when bypassing formal procedures, Americans may be persuaded by a plea that everybody be given a chance to speak and to have an equal voice in the decision. When interacting with members of different cultures who do not hold the value of fairness and equality for all members of a group or who do not discriminate between procedures and substantive questions, Americans may be accused of subterfuge or evasiveness when they raise matters of procedure or agenda (see Glenn 1954, 176).

The American value of majority rule is not universal. The Japanese reject the majority voice in decision making. Rafael Steinberg writes:

> One Western concept that has never really functioned in Japan, although written into constitution and law, is the idea of majority rule. The Confucian ethic, which still governs Japan, demands unanimity, and in order to respect the "rights of the minority" the majority will compromise on almost every issue until a consensus of some kind is reached. This principle applies not only to government, but to business board rooms, union halls, association meetings and family councils. No one must ever be completely defeated, because if he is, he cannot "hold up his face" (*Washington Post* June 7, 1964).

Although consensus decision making is slow by American standards, implementation of a decision with a consensus in place is quite rapid compared to the American efforts to garner support for decisions "after the fact."

The role of group leader or chairperson in groups which make decisions by consensus is quite different from what it is in American groups, where the chair is expected to be primarily a facilitator—one who ensures that every individual is able to express opinions freely. In Japan the typical formal or semiformal group decision is reached by a system that provides for "feeling around"—groping for a voice, preferably that of the chairperson, who will express the group's consensus.

> The code calls for the group to reach decisions together—almost by a sort of empathy. The function of a chairman is, therefore, not to help people express themselves freely but to divine the will of the group, to express its will and state the decision reached— presumably on the basis of divined will. This ability of the chairman is called *haragei* (belly art) (Kerlinger 1951, 38).

Americans are likely to perceive this kind of behavior as lacking in leadership. In fact, the public acts of the chairperson are largely ceremonial, serving to seal breaches in the corporate body and to display a solid front to the outside world. Efforts to reach decisions are typically made behind the scenes, and consensus may in actuality conceal a position of "no contest" on the part of various factions, after concluding that they lack the necessary power to impose their own will. Under such circumstances, Japanese culture offers to power-deficit factions the refuge of an umbrella of consensus, unfurled in open meetings and supported by symbols of harmony, benevolence, and fate that encourages factions to buckle down and adjust to a course of action not their own. Unanimous decisions in Japan often reflect a resolution of power rather than a synthesis of opinions and interests based on egalitarian values—as Americans often believe.

In American society, patterns of decision making that approach non-Western patterns, such as the Japanese, can be found in selected areas. In the political sector, in cases of city or county commission hearings, a group meeting, ostensibly held to reach a decision, may represent only public confirmation of a decision previously made behind closed doors by critical members of the group. These cases of political decision making deviate from the cultural norm which holds that all members of the group who will be affected by a decision are capable of helping to make it and should take part in the process of reaching it. Americans generally assume that the participation of individuals in meetings can actually affect the outcome of decisions considered and that deliberations of the group will be both substantive and rational.

Since Americans assume that decision making is localized in individuals, even in groups the individual participates in reaching decisions as a person, as a vote, or as the occupant of a role. In this context, decisions are ideally reached on the basis of anticipated consequences for the individual. In contrast, however, American medical doctors reach decisions about patients' symptoms in a different manner. The patient's report and the doctor's observations are matched against categories of diseases. The doctor's diagnosis and prescription follow automatically from the particular category in which the constellation of symptoms falls. The process by which the doctor makes a diagnosis and prescription is pertinent because it conforms with the manner in which people in many non-Western societies habitually reach decisions. Individuals merely apply preestablished principles to classify an issue; their actions follow from the result of the classification.

Classification was the crux of the matter in the following example taken from an interview with a USAID technician in Cambodia responsible for training the police:

> When we first tried to get a program of first aid for accident victims going, we did have some trouble because people said if somebody was struck by a car, it was fate, and man had no business in interfering because the victim was being properly punished for

> past sins. We explained to them that auto accidents are different.
> They are not due to supernatural intervention, but rather to
> causes, to violations of the laws. Now we get policemen to give
> first aid.

It is noteworthy that the technician did not attempt to change the ways of
the Cambodians along American lines by emphasizing the personal
consequences of suffering or by appealing to the personal humanitarian-
ism and sense of duty of the Cambodian policeman. Instead, the technician modified the scheme of classification by which the Cambodians had
evaluated automobile accidents and been led to decide that the victims
were not their concern. Accidents were reclassified into the human
sphere, where their effects could be ameliorated by human effort.

In another case on a Pacific island, the reclassification of the
function of a hospital saved a woman's life.

> The daughter of an island family anticipated a difficult breech
> birth of her first child. All efforts by the visiting Americans to have
> her go to the American hospital nearby were rebuffed. The birth
> occurred on the wood floor of the family house and was attended
> by a midwife. With heroic effort, the midwife saved the woman's
> life, but the child died immediately. Thereafter, an infection set in,
> threatening the woman's life again. Further efforts to persuade the
> family that the daughter should go to the hospital were unsuccessful
> because, as the father explained, American hospitals could only
> treat Americans who were not susceptible to the island spirits.
> Since this was clearly a case of spirits who had not been properly
> placated, there was nothing to do. The Americans finally suggested
> that the skillful stitching of the midwife had "trapped" some bad
> spirits inside the woman, and only the hospital was capable of
> undoing this work to release them. The daughter went to the
> hospital and has since borne several healthy children.

Not only is the individual the locus of decision making for Americans,
but he or she is also held responsible for the decision and any resulting
action. The idea of individual responsibility is reflected in the typical
questions, "Who did this?" or "Who is responsible?" Generally, the
relationship between decision making and responsibility is symmetrical,
meaning that decisions and subsequent action go together. An exception
to this in American culture may occur in government circles, where it is
not unusual for an administrator to call in an individual who is asked to
make a decision on a given issue. Once the decision is reached, the
decision maker departs, leaving the issue and decision in the hands of the
administrator.

In non-Western cultures where the locus of decision making is not the
individual, the question of responsibility is relatively meaningless. Re-

sponsibility is likely to be diffused in cultures where people have strong ties to their immediate family or community and who reach decisions by consensus. Among Japanese, for instance, the relationship between participation in decisions and action is asymmetrical. The Japanese consider it brash for individuals to make definite decisions regarding themselves or others. It is offensive for individuals to urge the acceptance of their opinions as a course of action. They must use circumlocution and maintain a rather strict reserve (Kerlinger 1951). The individual Japanese is subjugated to the group and, when faced with a decision leading to action,

> shrinks and may go to what seem fantastic lengths to avoid making a decision. Even if he should commit himself verbally to a course of action he will frequently end by doing nothing. He lacks a sense of personal responsibility; he feels only a sense of group responsibility. If at all possible, he will try to throw the onus of decision responsibility on a group or, at least, on some other person (37-38).

This pattern of asymmetrical decision making is to some degree characteristic of all peoples whose self-reference is the group or for whom decisions should be unanimous (Goodenough 1963, 511-15).

Decision making focuses on the preliminary step to action, whereas conceptualizing the world in terms of problems shifts the focus to obstacles that block smooth action. The American emphasis on problem solving construes disagreement as a negative factor that must be solved. The sentence, "He (or she) is going to have a problem with this idea" means that the person is expected to disagree with the proposal, and some problem solving may be necessary. Conversely, the phrase "no problem" is synonymous with "I agree." If the barriers are stubborn and their solution requires preparation and planning, problem solving must be preceded by decision making. The impersonal and abstract American orientation avoids conceptualizing problems or decisions as issues of human relations, but occasionally social factors intrude deeply into decisions and problems. When this is the case, Americans turn to conflict resolution.

Since the idea of problems and problem solving is a popular and pervasive social norm, it includes anything that can be defined as negative. It is the job of the problem solver to establish what the barriers are—the specific obstacles that need to be overcome. The labeling of barriers has some predictable effects on foreigners. First, the focus on barriers may seem harsh and critical for members of cultures with an orientation toward group survival or integration; they may see this focus as unduly negative and critical of people who should be supported. Second, host country nationals are sometimes resentful when they recognize that their country, themselves, and their work may be barriers for their American associates—obstacles in the American's smooth path to successful action.

In contrast to the American orientation to problems, some foreigners may state that there are no problems at all, even when they are confronted with things obviously going wrong. For instance, when American foreign student advisors tell Arab students that there is a problem with their registrations or transcripts, the students often refuse to acknowledge that the situation represents a problem. Part of the reason for this may be that the students assume the advisor will simply take care of any difficulties. Another possibility is that what constitutes a problem in some cultures (including those of the Arab world) is so severe that only major calamities fit the category. In general, members of non-Western cultures are likely to accept that somehow things will work out, so they do not naturally organize information into the form of problems that demand action.

The idea of problem solving seems to be rooted in the American concept of a rational order in the world that explains events and determines particular occurrences. The rational order is based on the assumption that the world is mechanistic and that things worthy of effort are material. Such a world is saturated with facts, figures, and techniques—the stuff of a reality brimming with problems to be solved. Americans are not typically philosophers or logicians. They are impatient with theory, but neither do they see experience itself as the only source of effective performance. Rather, they see training and education as ways of acquiring the tools that will prepare them for effective problem solving. Americans abroad are prone to use these tools exclusively, believing that in dealing with non-Westerners it is sufficient to tell them what they should do and how to do it. The assumptions and values of the non-Westerner may be either ignored or treated as yet another problem to be solved.

Usually, Americans do not conceive of only one possible course of action for a given problem. Instead, they tend to conceive of alternative courses of action and choose one. This attitude is comparative; a particular course of action is best for a given purpose rather than being the only possible one. The notion of absolute rightness is repugnant to Americans in the world of action (see Glenn 1954), although it can be observed in the sciences, which are assumed to be free of cultural baggage, and in religion, particularly with fundamentalist sects.

The outcome of decision making and problem solving is a course of action and a plan for implementing it. Both course and plan reflect the ideas that action and the world itself are composed of a chain of events held together by lineal connections of causes and effects projecting into the future. In the ideal case, a single cause determines an effect. Since Americans focus on the future rather than on the present or the past, the isolation of the critical cause leads American decision makers to adopt one-dimensional criteria for measuring the results of their actions. The concept of a simple cause connected with effect in a lineal chain encourages an action orientation and strengthens the expectation of being able to control the world. In contrast, if events are understood to be determined by multiple causes and contingencies, as in the Chinese conception, the planning of actions and controlling of events are beyond human capabilities.

The final aspect of the American orientation toward action is an emphasis on choice. After anticipating the future and, specifically, the consequences or effects of their actions, Americans choose the course that will produce the preferred consequences. The conception of desirable consequences is reached through practical empiricism. The desired effects are preferably visible, measurable, and materialistic. While the material or empirical effects of an action are more or less objective, practicality is not. What is practical for one person (or culture) may not be for another. Practicality refers to the adjustment to immediate situations without much thought for long-term effects or principles. From the point of view of non-Westerners, this "means-orientation" or "operationalism" of Americans often appears to sacrifice the end for the means.

Variations of Form of Activity

Foreign visitors in the United States quickly gain an impression of life lived at a fast pace and of people incessantly on the move. This image indicates that *doing* is the dominant form of activity for Americans. The implicit assumption that "getting things done" is worthwhile is seldom questioned (F. Kluckhohn and Strodtbeck 1961, 17). The ramifications of the doing assumption impinge upon other values and assumptions of the culture and pervade the language of Americans, as in the colloquial exchanges of greeting: "How're you doing?" "I'm doing fine—how are you coming along?" All aspects of American life are affected by the predominance of doing.

> Its most distinctive feature is a demand for the kind of *activity* which results in accomplishments that are measurable by standards conceived to be external to the acting individual. That aspect of self-judgment or judgment of others, which relates to the nature of *activity*, is based mainly upon a measurable accomplishment achieved by acting upon persons, things or situations. What does the individual do? What can he or will he accomplish? These are

almost always the primary questions in the American's scale of
appraisal of persons (F. Kluckhohn 1963, 17).

Kluckhohn's definition of *doing* is compatible with other characteristics of Americans such as the importance of achievement, the emphasis on visible accomplishments, and the stress on measurement. *Doing*, however, should not be interpreted as one end of an active-passive dichotomy, since people from cultures which are not distinguished by a *doing* orientation can be very active (F. Kluckhohn and Strodtbeck, 161). The converse can also hold: some persons in cultures oriented toward doing can be relatively inactive. In American culture, however, along with the assumption of doing, there is a dominant value of keeping busy: "Idle hands are the devil's workshop." Approximate synonyms to "keeping busy" approach the status of accolades, as when someone is described as "active" or "energetic." Heroes in American culture are likely to be action-oriented people. (In 1985 Clint Eastwood, an adventure-film actor, was voted the "most admired man" by American young people.) Being active may also refer to career-related activity. When someone is characterized as no longer active, it frequently means the person has retired. Both the assumption of doing and the value of being active are dominant patterns in American life.

In the non-Western world, the two remaining forms of activity, *being* and *being in becoming*, are dominant (F. Kluckhohn and Strodtbeck, 15-17). Differences in values and assumptions regarding these qualities sometimes confuse Americans abroad, who expect the influential persons in a community to be distinguished by their deeds. It may turn out, however, that intellectual, contemplative, or meditative persons are the ones who are respected, honored, and listened to.

> In the *being* form of activity, there is a preference...for the kind of activity which is a spontaneous expression of what is conceived to be "given" in the human personality.... It might even be phrased as a spontaneous expression in activity of impulses and desires; yet care must be taken not to make this interpretation a too literal one (F. Kluckhohn and Strodtbeck, 16).

Since concrete behavior usually reflects several assumptions and values simultaneously, the kind of activity described above is restrained by the demands of other aspects of the culture (F. Kluckhohn and Strodtbeck, 16).

The value of being resembles that of self-actualization—"the motivational and cognitive life of fully evolved people" (Maslow 1968, 72). The description of self-actualizing people and their "peak experiences" seems to be a central expression of the being variation of activity. Several features are typical of the peak experience: during peak experiences objects tend to be seen as intrinsic wholes, without comparisons;

perception can be relatively ego-transcending, appearing unmotivated; the peak experience is intrinsically valued and does not need to be validated by the reaching of goals or the reduction of needs; during the peak experience the person is fused with the experience, which occurs outside the usual coordinates of time and space (Maslow, 74-76). These characteristics are common in descriptions of experience given by members of cultures governed by being as the predominant form of activity. The being value orientation lacks a psychological foundation in the concept of "needs" and in the development of an individual self. The negative implication found with needs, as suggested by "need-reduction," is replaced by an active investment in occupying and improving one's position in the social structure. Thus, the peak experience as a summit expression of being reflects the gemeinschaft dynamic of belonging and of participating in activities that amplify meaning through social expression of the person.

The third variation of form of activity, being in becoming, governs whole persons in their development. While doing emphasizes visible and measurable actions and being stresses a transcendent state of belonging, being in becoming emphasizes "...that kind of activity which has as its goal the development of all aspects of the self as an integrated whole" (F. Kluckhohn and Strodtbeck 1961). All areas of personality, intellect, emotions, and motives receive due attention. Although *becoming* is secondary among Americans, the orientation emerged as a cultural motif in the 1960s and assumes a dominant position in movements with sources in humanistic and transpersonal psychology and in growth theories in education.

With the possible exception of Japan, particularly in Zen Buddhism, being-in-becoming does not appear to be the dominant pattern in any major culture. As a secondary value orientation, becoming is understood to develop over the active range of the life-span among some Europeans. Among other groups, such as practitioners of Yoga in India and Sufiism in Islamic societies, being-in-becoming accepts the goal of integrating the self into a larger and sometimes transcendent reality of the spirit.

Work and Play

One of the most important distinctions in the form of activity in American life is the separation of work from play. Work is done for a living. It is what people must do, and even though they may enjoy it, it is not to be mixed or confused with play. Play, on the other hand, is relief from the drudgery and regularity of work. It is pursued separately to be enjoyed in its own right even though many Americans engage in recreation with the same seriousness of purpose they expend on work.

Americans abroad often find the distinction between work and play absent in their foreign associates. Counterparts may appear to take work very casually. Non-Westerners (outside of Asia) do not usually allow work to interfere with the amenities of living and are likely to expect Americans to create a similar integration of personal life and work. For example, the Latin American does not make the American distinction between work and play (or business and play). Latin American meetings may become social events, and no compulsion is felt to be brief and businesslike (Hall and Whyte 1960). Americans may be frustrated by the difficulty they experience in concluding an agenda. Even in Japan and other Asian countries, work has a broader definition than in the U.S. For instance, drinking beer or sake with fellow employees or supervisors at the end of the day may be an expected work activity.

The American workplace mirrors the major values of the society, particularly the work ethic. Although it has weakened since the 1960s, the Puritan ethic of hard work (and no play) still prevails. While the Japanese have their own tradition of hard work, there are contrasts between work in these two cultures that illuminate basic values in both. In comparison to the Japanese system, American work is channeled through job descriptions, with rules controlling conditions for work and management. The technicism of American culture goes hand in hand with specialization of both workers and managers in the workplace. Consistent with their orientation toward independent action, American workers are self-reliant and more aggressive than their Japanese counterparts in controlling and modifying the conditions of their work. They do not hesitate to take an adversary position against management, and when they strike, they aim to inflict damage on their employers. Americans see themselves and their lives as separate from the company. Managers and workers alike exhibit personal initiative in moving from company to company in pursuit of better pay and higher positions. These inclinations reveal self-centeredness and the essence of the American style of work—enlightened self-interest.

The rise of Japan as a major industrial nation has generated considerable interest in the U.S. as to how the Japanese became a serious competitor so quickly. Most studies of the Japanese workplace conclude that Japanese culture provides part of the explanation of how the Japanese industrial plant could rise so quickly from the ashes of defeat in World War II. Although many Western practices were acquired, particularly in industry and business, they were adapted to Japanese culture.

A significant difference in the Japanese workplace is in how the workers and managers conduct their activities. Whereas Americans exercise direct and primary control over tasks by means of skills and technology, the Japanese have developed a number of ways of mediating their activities according to situations and human relations. Neither the Japanese worker nor the manager ever considers that tasks should be performed directly by individuals on the basis of skills or with the assistance of technology. In all instances, the Japanese organize activity around human groups and the relationships of their members, assigning less importance to skills and technology in favor of exercising social control over their actions. Japanese managers employ secondary control in their activities, usually taking action through the media of groups and social situations. Unlike Americans, the Japanese do not develop an adversary relationship between workers and managers. The cultures of their organizations generate strong forces to avoid uncertainty and conflict. For example, strikes are often advertised and conducted during lunch hours or under conditions that do not inflict damage on the employer. Japanese workers argue that it is their company, too, so why harm it?

Both Japanese workers and managers in the large, privileged companies have much less mobility than Americans. The Japanese establish a close alignment with their companies from which they derive their sense of security, their power and status, and the material benefits of their work. The Japanese group displays its fusion during the process of *ringi*, the social relations mediated process of institutionalizing a course of action. We hesitate to call this process decision making, preferring to speak of it as the "guiding activity in the company," since it concentrates on the process of implementing rather than deciding. In any case, the commitment of Japanese workers and managers to company activities through the medium of social relations is the key to the strength of the Japanese industrial plant.

Time and Temporal Orientation

Contemporary American values of time can be traced back to colonial days in Virginia where an early change in attitude toward time and labor occurred. The discovery of the profitability of tobacco in colonial Jamestown impelled agents of the Virginia Company to manipulate land and labor to maximize production. By the 1620s, the concept of *time thrift* had begun to replace the original work discipline that placed no emphasis on hourly output and required only four hours of daily labor (Richard Brown 1976, 43-44). The time thrift idea received a strong boost early on from Benjamin Franklin in his admonition, "Remember that time is money." Support from technology arrived in the form of mass-produced timepieces. By 1840 cheap clocks were everywhere and soon became a necessity in American households.

What made clocks so appealing was their contribution to household efficiency. They permitted much more precise organization and use of the working day. Since most residences were also places where family members earned their livelihood, efficiency in the home and on the farm altered the pace of life and caused a major social change in the direction of modernity. Clocks also liberated people from the confines of their homes by facilitating participation in a wide range of meetings and events outside the home. Rural people could now plan their attendance at public gatherings more readily than ever before (Brown, 134-35).

These excerpts from American history illuminate the background of the contemporary use of time in the workplace. Time thrift is the basis for measuring productivity by output per unit of time rather than by the quality of the product. When time thrift is used for controlling production, it is called a "deadline." Deadlines compel Americans to lay aside their own opinions and preferences on the grounds that ironing out differences through discussion and coordination will take too long, and thus endanger compliance with the deadline. In exchange for their cooperation in meeting a deadline, members of a work group may be promised that "next time" they will have an opportunity to express their own views more fully. But usually, the next time is also a deadline.

Control of work by means of time does not suit all societies into which Americans have introduced the procedure. In an American company in Japan employing both American and Japanese managers, the chief complaint of the Japanese about the American managers was their use of deadlines to control work. What makes the finding important is that both Japanese and American managers agreed without exception that the Japanese met deadlines better than the Americans. Therefore, we cannot attribute the Japanese irritation to their disinclination to act in a timely fashion. It seems that the Japanese resented the impersonal control imposed and probably would have been more pleased with arbitrary but personal authority.

Orientation toward time is a stable cultural difference (F. Kluckhohn and Strodtbeck 1961). People orient themselves and direct their actions according to where their culture places emphasis along the continuum of time orientations. For example, orientation to the present is characteristic in Latin Americans. In other societies, people are oriented to the past and consequently turn to traditions for guidance. The most abstract temporal orientation is toward the future—the dominant American value. As we have seen, Americans tend to take an abstract and operational view of the present, collect information in causal links, and focus on intermediate steps required for change or progress toward the future. The time span is short. For Americans the future is not measured in decades or generations as it is for Brazilians, who are oriented to the present, or Indians, who are oriented to the past. The future Americans plan for must be within reach of the individual, so it is projections for the near future that are actively used to influence present actions.

The near future of six months, a year, or sometimes longer, has been operationalized in American management in the form of objectives. An employee is asked to write out his own work objectives for the next year or so, and these are then used as criteria to evaluate his performance. Projects to develop management by objectives in other societies have often failed, as might be expected, since the use of objectives depends on being oriented to the future as well as to other values. People with past or present orientations may assume a fatalistic outlook toward the future and may be upset by aggressive attempts to structure the unknowable.

In American culture, the orientation toward the discernible future and the high value placed on action yield the principle that one can improve upon the present. Action and hard work will bring about what the individual wants; hence, Americans are described as having the attribute of *effort-optimism* (C. Kluckhohn and F. Kluckhohn 1947). Through effort one will achieve one's ambitions. No goal is too remote, no obstacle too difficult for the individual who has the determination to expend the effort. Hard work is rewarded by success. The converse also holds—failure means the individual did not try hard enough, is lazy, or is worthless. These harsh evaluations may be moderated by assumptions of bad luck. Nevertheless, they remain vital American values and shed light on the frustrations of Americans abroad who try to initiate action and attain goals with people who are oriented to the past or present. As Rudyard Kipling put it: "A fool lies here who tried to hustle the East."

Effort-optimism, with its underlying orientation toward the future, gives rise to one of the most frequent and pervasive problems for Americans working with foreign clients from past- or present-oriented societies. American advisors, researchers, and others complain about the delays involved in trying to accomplish anything. Their morale is lowered and their optimism dampened by the frustrations that accompany giving advice or directing inquiries to people of different cultural backgrounds. As an example, foreign student advisors report dissatisfaction with students who fail to heed their advice. The advisors typically judge their own performance by how well advisees comply with their suggestions, and so noncompliance by students represents to the advisor a failure to achieve. In general, the failure to achieve (or at least maintain their optimism) strikes at the heart of the American's value system. From the point of view of foreign clients, the advisor may be judged more for the reliability of the relationship established with the client than for the quality or the practicality of the advice given. While the Americans stress doing, most foreign clients are likely to stress being.

To avoid the American consequences of failure, some advisors who work abroad interpret their experiences in terms of the long-range effects their work will have. Others point out that their mere presence and personal example are beneficial. Still others consider the mission abroad as a learning situation; the next mission will be more successful since the advisor or visitor has profited from the frustrations and experiences of the last one. This reaction reflects the value Americans place on training and education as well as the orientation toward the future— in this case, the next mission. Finally, there is the tactic used by some returned Peace Corps volunteers: they construe their experience abroad as an education in international understanding, mainly for themselves and others in their own culture.

Motivation

Doing could simply describe daily and weekly rounds in people's lives, but Americans identify an agent to drive routine lifekeeping activities. This agent, whom we have met before, is the dynamic part of the personality that appears in motives and imparts purpose to behavior. The concept of motive, and the process of motivation associated with it, provides the link between agent and sequential action. Motives are inferences about what arouses people to action, while motivation explains the direction and purposefulness that Americans identify with human conduct. Americans may characterize people who advance in their careers as ambitious, or they may see people who help others as altruistic. Both ambition and altruism serve as motives that drive people to act as they do. In general, the concept of motivation specifies how actions are connected and directed, and in everyday life it provides a convenient explanation for performance. It is appropriate to say people excel because they are well motivated or that they fail because they lack motivation. These observations are frequently based on circular reasoning, where the behavior proves the motivation (or lack of it) which caused the behavior. The redundancy of motivational theories does not detract from their attractiveness to Americans, who flock by the thousands to "motivational seminars," assumedly to acquire motives that will cause them to act even more successfully.

The importance of motivation in American society may be associated with the fact that the American image of the individual tends to be general and vague. Motivation helps to fill this void since it is a dynamic concept that associates the individual with action and leads to the belief that one **is** what one **does**. Individuals isolated in a mechanistic world attain fulfillment through achievement—the motivation that propels the American and gives the culture its quality of "drivenness" (Henry 1963, 25-26). Restless and uncertain, Americans have a recurrent need to prove themselves and thereby attain an identity through success and achievements. Hence, accomplishments must be personal, visible, and measurable since the culture does not provide a means of evaluating and knowing the person except through externals of performance and attainment. It is this kind of motive that has been called *achievement.*

The achievement motive has been intensively studied in the United States and in other societies. The results of the research reported by David McClelland (1961) portray individuals with a high achievement motive as people who enjoy taking the initiative in making decisions. They prefer to participate in activities that challenge their skills and abilities. They are usually confident of success, but they tend to be too optimistic when the conditions for a successful performance are unknown. When information is available that permits an objective appraisal of success, these people are inclined to use it for a rational assessment of the situation in terms of personal abilities and skills. Persons with high achievement needs, often identified with the entrepreneur, have been described as risk takers. This attribute emerges from the research studies as a complex quality, subject to many contingencies. McClelland concludes that those who have high achievement motivation appear to prefer situations involving risk "only when they have some chance of influencing the outcome through their own skills and abilities" (1961, 214). In this conclusion, the focus returns to the individual and to a social dynamic of gesellschaft.

Although achievement is the dominant motive for Americans, *ascription* exists as a variation. Ascription is marked by an emphasis on being, where identity is more a function of being in a role than of performing independent actions. An individual may be defined as a member of a family, for instance, as is occasionally still found in New England and the more traditional parts of the South, or the individual is defined according to status or profession, as in the military. It is this kind of motivation, rather than achievement, that is shared by many cultures throughout the world as the dominant value. Many people in non-Western cultures act to preserve and enhance their particular position within the social structure—behavior that is consistent with ascriptive motivation and typical of a gemeinschaft society. Considerations about tangible progress and improvement are secondary in importance in ascriptive societies, if they are present at all.

Individuals with an ascriptive motivation are usually enmeshed in reciprocal relations with members of their family, community, trade, or profession. These social links are much more binding than they are for Americans. In Vietnam, for instance, an operator of a printing shop reported supporting his employees to the limits of his ability for six months after he was put out of business by government action. Americans probably would not expect the same responsibility from their employers. When Americans join an organization or a business, they do so as free agents and reserve the right to move out whenever their purposes are no longer served by being a member. Along with this right, however, goes their acceptance of the fortunes of the organization. If it fails, the individual is responsible for finding another position without support from other members of the organization. American unemployment insurance and other social welfare plans affect the logistics of this arrangement, but they do not change the basic expectations of either organizations or individuals.

The patron system prevalent in much of Latin America contrasts with American patterns of motivation by maintaining an intricate set of social relations between the individual and the patron. Patrons may be like godfathers to members of their estates and may extend, as a matter of obligation, personal services and considerations which would be unusual for American managers. As with the Vietnamese businessman, the obligations incurred by patrons are expected to transcend failure, poverty, or change of plans.

Ascriptive motivation introduces assumptions about the sources of action and purposes of behavior that differ from the view implied in the achievement motive. Individuals are perceived as belonging to social groups and as behaving according to the obligations, duties, and privileges inherent in their social and professional positions. The sources of motivation, then, are assumed to reside in the group or society. In the words of a Ghanaian government employee, "We do not concern ourselves with motivation, as Americans do. We know what our job is and we do it." American managers, as noted by this Ghanaian, must indeed contend with the personal intentions of individuals since Americans view achievement motivation as residing in those individuals. This difference in values impedes Americans abroad when they use the model of personal conflict to analyze difficulties in organizations. Such analyses are unlikely to make sense to members of ascriptive cultures, where conflict is more a matter of role confusion or an expression of long-standing antagonism between groups.

Measurable Achievement

In American culture, achievement is given a material meaning, which leads to an emphasis on technology and on publicity—making accomplishments measurable and visible. Acting on these assumptions, American technicians and advisors abroad define progress as technological change, more often than not reported in statistical data. Social progress comes to mean the number of schools erected rather than the quality of teacher training. This concern with visible achievement may lead Americans to lose sight of main issues. They may settle for a sensation, a personal triumph over a counterpart, or a specific visible accomplishment that can be reported as an achievement. One military advisor was described as becoming personally involved in the choice of headgear for a particular unit, which he finally succeeded in changing. This was his achievement and he was determined to have it before his tour of duty was over. Another frequent visible achievement in the military, the Peace Corps, and USAID is the building of latrines. This cannot be dismissed as lightly as the incident of the new headgear. The persistence of Americans all over the world in building latrines for people who refuse to use them suggests that their appeal as projects may be more their concrete visibility than their potential role in controlling disease.

Since achievement has to be visible and measurable, Americans become very sensitive to praise or blame—more so, perhaps, than any other people except the Japanese. They depend on feedback from associates to establish the visibility of their accomplishments. Both feedback and accomplishments are likely to be in short supply abroad. Achievements of any kind are more difficult in a different culture, and reactions of one's associates are likely to be both delayed and diffuse. American advisors abroad and foreign student advisors in the U.S. are often uncertain about the effects, if any, of their advising. Insofar as advisors are acting as catalysts to associates or clients by providing information, skills, and judgment, they may be deprived of visible, concrete achievements. In addition, foreign associates are likely to have an ascriptive orientation and therefore be relatively unconcerned with personal achievements of any kind. As noted in a previous section, Americans find this kind of situation very frustrating. They tend to shift their sights to another, future achievement or define the present situation as the fault of someone else.

Competition and Affiliation

Competition is the primary method among Americans for motivating members of groups. Americans, with their orientation toward individualism and achievement, respond well to this technique. But when a competitive approach is applied to members of another culture who do not hold the same values, the effort may be ineffective at best and may produce undesirable consequences. People for whom saving face is important or for whom dependency on others is desirable do not accept competition among members of the group with the same enthusiasm as Americans do. Thus, attempts to instill a competitive spirit in social, economic, or military activities in non-Western countries such as Laos and Vietnam were not very successful. In those countries, the intense attachment to family and village excludes an incentive to excel over others either as a member of a group or individually. An American advisor shows his bewilderment at the Lao's lack of competition in the following words:

> Watching them play a game—volleyball. To us, it's a game. I know when our teams compete, whether it's baseball or basketball—anything—we are serious, playing it because we like to win. With them, they aren't; they team up and have teams going, but they just don't give a hoot whether they win or not.

In Japan, groups compete seriously with one another, but individuals within groups experience the communal feeling that harnesses personal competition. This combination is sometimes confusing to Americans, who assume that the competitiveness of Japanese corporations with each other and in the international market is paralleled by open competition at the individual level. Their attempts to install American-style incentive plans and other personal motivation schemes for Japanese workers are unsuccessful because of this faulty assumption. The confusion is exacerbated by the Japanese use of *incentive* to refer to certain benefits given to employees. In contrast to the American use of this term, Japanese apply incentives to groups, not individuals. For instance, Japanese corporations commonly sponsor "incentive trips" to hot springs and other resort areas. Not only are the trips available to everyone in a work group, but attendance is practically required.

Non-Westerners, with their orientation toward ascription rather than achievement, value being a member of a family or of a group and usually exhibit a more strongly developed tendency toward affiliation. This is reflected in the intense commitment to family and community described earlier as part of the gemeinschaft orientation. Non-Westerners generally know, and know of, fewer people outside the family than do typical Americans. Both their direct interaction with others through travel, work, and social life and their indirect contact through the mass media are likely to be much more circumscribed than that of Americans. They are less self-conscious and less analytical of themselves as individuals than are Americans (see Bell 1965, 209-12). The world beyond the confines of their immediate region is often endowed with dangers that will harm the unwary who venture into it. An American advisor in Laos during the 1950s, who was training the Meo tribesmen for military service, reported that they were effective soldiers only within their own territory. Their knowledge of the outside world was meager and riddled with superstition, which made the soldiers fearful and ineffective in operations outside their own geographical area. But within their own domain, their willing acceptance of military discipline and complete dedication made them excellent trainees.

The characteristics of affiliation combine to make non-Westerners less committed to political entities, such as nations. This fact is often obscured by reports in the mass media of instances of intense nationalism on the part of individuals and groups in Third World countries. While nationalism is sometimes strong in non-Western countries, it tends to be weaker than the intense regional ties associated with affiliation. It is misleading to consider peoples such as the Lao and the Vietnamese to be self-conscious members of their respective nations in the sense that most Americans consider themselves to be citizens of the United States. In many non-Western countries, regional social bonds, often strengthened by ethnic bonds, place great demands on political leaders. They are compelled to coordinate sometimes inimical groups, such as tribes and clans, rather than center their energies on administering government bureaucracies as in Western countries.

To describe American society as gesellschaft suggests that achievement motivation is high and affiliation is relatively low. Americans display affiliation when they express their nostalgia for home-towns. But that does not indicate the presence of the kind of family, community, and status relationships, nor the acceptance of prescribed norms of behavior that are part of the warp and woof of ascriptive societies. It is instead a way of establishing an affiliation among people who have little in the way of "common origins and common expectations" (Mead 1965, 30). The value of affiliation may be on the rise as American individualism becomes subservient to organizations and the goals of groups and institutions.

The Implication of Achievement: The Individual

The dominant motive for the typical American is, as we have said, externalized achievement. Its impulse has been described as the key psychological factor in producing unparalleled economic abundance in the United States (McClelland 1961, 61, 105, 157; Potter 1954, 78-90). But hand in hand with the pursuit of achievement, Americans have been willing to exploit and control a physical environment that, until recently, has been perceived as unlimited. Although achievement and control are characteristic expressions of both individuals and collectivities, Americans typically accept the proposition that achievement is measured within the individual. The limit on success is not ascribed to resources, to the actions of others, to the agency of government, or to fate. For, as prescribed by the Protestant ethic, those who have the desire and work hard enough will have their labors rewarded with success—"Where there's a will, there's a way."

Furthermore, in this view the achievements of the individual are not gained at the expense of others. The vast land and opulent resources of the United States offer enough rewards—material wealth, prestige, popularity—for everyone who aspires and tries. Doctrines such as Marxism, which promulgate inevitable conflict among classes because the limited goods of the world are acquired by a few who exploit the masses, have rarely achieved great favor among Americans. Traditionally, Americans have seen failure as a lack of will and effort on the part of the individual. According to the Protestant ethic, successful accumulation of worldly wealth was a sign that the individual belonged to the select group that enjoyed the grace of God. The same idea is still present in a new version: a rich person cannot be completely bad—or else the person would not be rich.

This expansive view of achievement and of a world of economic abundance contrasts sharply with the perception of limited wealth prevalent throughout much of the rest of the world. This latter outlook is more than just a view appropriate to an economy of scarcity in which the individual's aspirations and potential achievements are necessarily limited. It is central to an ascriptive view of society, which tends to maintain the status quo in relationships among people. To explain the behavior of people in such societies, we turn to George Foster's idea of the image of the limited good as it appears in traditional peasant societies. (Peasant societies should not be equated with the non-Western world; the expression refers to agricultural areas where population is dense and land holdings limited.) The individual or family that acquires more than its share of a "good," particularly an economic good, is viewed with suspicion. The individual works to survive but not to amass wealth, which, like land, is perceived as inherent in nature.

> It can be divided up and passed around in various ways, but, within the framework of the villagers' traditional world, it does not grow. Time and tradition have determined the shares each family and individual hold; these shares are not static, since obviously they do shift. But the reason for the relative position of each villager is known at any given time, and any significant change calls for explanation (Foster 1965, 298).

Likewise, an individual who accepts a role of leadership will find his motives suspect, and

> he will be subject to the criticism of his neighbors. By seeking or even accepting an authority position, the ideal man ceases to be

ideal. A "good" man therefore usually shuns community responsibilities (other than of a ritual nature); by so doing he protects his
reputation (Foster, 303).

People in ascriptive societies do not compete for authority by seeking
leadership roles: they do not compete in material symbols such as
dress, housing, or food, nor do they act in any way that might make
the individual stand out from the rest of the members of the village.
For the sake of uniformity, people attempt to be inconspicuous in position and behavior.

But despite the stress on conformity in traditional peasant villages,
there is a place for individuality. Once people have fulfilled their obligation to family, community, and tradition, they may be allowed considerable freedom of personal expression. Both conformity and individuality can be found in non-Western societies where the individual
is recognized by ascriptive qualities. It is necessary, however, to as-
certain for each society those areas in which individuality or uniformity holds.

It follows from the above discussion that innovation or new techniques of working are also not perceived as related to wealth or, in
our terms, to achievement. Instead, achievement is a matter of fate, an
intervention by an outside agent that does not disrupt the relationships among the members of a community. One such agent is the lottery. By winning, the individual can improve his position without en-
dangering the community (see Foster, 308-9). People who have a "lottery
motivation," or a belief in an outside intervention in their behalf, are
difficult to convince of the virtues of hard work, effort, frugality, and
initiative. But even if this attitude does not exist, individuals may still
not accept the necessity of improving their position because it will
extend their obligations. Thus, a young Peruvian fisherman refused
aid to modernize his fishing technique because, he said, if he had more
money he would have more relatives to take care of (Foster 1962, 92).

An absence of achievement motivation is not necessarily connected
to the social and economic conditions of a peasant society. Apparently, a belief in fate or luck can be found in parts of the non-Western
world where density of population and limited land holdings are not a
problem. For instance, in the interior of Brazil, land holdings are not limited, population is sparse, and open land offering economic opportunities
exists to the west. Yet, the people are still motivated by luck, being more
concerned with buying tickets for the local game of chance than with
developing their resources or moving west. An explanation of the Brazilian attitude is not economic or entirely social, for in the same area
of their country, Brazilians are familiar with squatter's rights. Individu-

als and families take possession of land, work it, and eventually acquire a right to it. Even if Brazilians lack awareness of open land to the west, Brazilian custom provides precedents for possessing land. At least in the particular case of Brazil, indifference to personal achievement can be found where limited land holdings and density of population are not factors. Unlike Foster (1965, 308-10), who argues that "brakes on change are less psychological than social," this example suggests that absence of achievement motivation is, at least in part, a function of people's perception of fate, of themselves, and of the world. The growing popularity of state lotteries in the United States supports our earlier speculation that American society is transposing gemeinschaft features to larger segments of the population.

The Implication of Ascription: Total Power

In a society in which motivation rests on an ascriptive base rather than on achievement, status and inequality characterize the value system. People have their own fixed positions in a vertical, hierarchical tier. In some cases, as we have seen, ascriptive motivation is associated with an image of a world of restricted resources—in contrast to the American perception of a world of abundance. Some of the permissiveness and competitiveness of American society can no doubt be traced to the belief that there are enough material goods for everyone. David Potter (1954, 118) argues that most of the world, even Europe, assumes an economy of scarcity, so that the volume of wealth is assumed to be fixed. If there is not enough for everyone, if a generous volume of the goods of the society are restricted to only the select few, it is unlikely that the society will countenance perpetual (and probably internecine) competition for the economic and social spoils. It is to the advantage of the society to assign arbitrarily to each person a status which is transmitted by heredity and rigidly maintained by authority, where both the favored few and the unfavored masses maintain their respective statuses from generation to generation. Status-bound individuals often cultivate a sense of contentment and of dignity with their lot within its narrow sphere (Potter, 115). In some Eastern societies such as Japan, the value of harmony in social relations supports the social stratification of society.

The ascriptive way of life, flourishing in an economy of scarcity, most often develops a relatively rigid culture pattern in which authority rather than the individual becomes the center for motivation. In contrast, authority in American culture is seen as a social rather than as a motivational question, since the dominant pattern in American culture limits the role of authority to providing services, protecting the rights of the individual, inducing cooperation, and adjudicating differences. Certainly many variations on the dominant value exist in American society—the military, for example, or groups that seem to prefer strong, clear lines of authority. But these variations, which are deviant in American society, provide little help in understanding the display and acceptance of authority traditionally found in governments in many of the countries of Asia, the Middle East, and elsewhere. In these states, total power may be vested in the members of the government. The centralization of political and social power permeates the society, profoundly affecting the way of life of individuals by institutionalizing the values of status, loyalty, and conformity.

Delineating a few of the characteristics of a society organized according to what Karl Wittfogel (1957) calls "total power" should be helpful in putting into perspective American attitudes towards authority as they are contrasted with those of many non-Western people. Rather than picking a country with these characteristics and contrasting it with American patterns, we shall follow Wittfogel's analysis of total power in its political, social, and psychological characteristics. Wittfogel draws his materials from historical and contemporary examples and develops a theme regarding total power which, while not fitting any one society precisely, characterizes in a general way many societies around the world.

In societies with more or less absolutist governments, political power is not checked by nongovernmental forces as found in most Western countries. Historically, the power of the central governments in the West has been limited by constitutions, large individual landholdings, and political, cultural, and organizational subdivisions. In absolute governments, these checks are generally not present or not effective. Religious and military power are normally identified with the state and do not place a check on the government. There is no nongovernmental center of power. Intragovernmental balances such as those found in the American system also do not exist. Therefore, "...there develops what may be called a *cumulative tendency of unchecked power*" (Wittfogel, 106). The exercise of unchecked authority easily becomes arbitrary and results in intimidation, secrecy, unpredictability and—in the extreme—terror and brutality. The psychological climate thus created engenders mutual mistrust and suspicion among officials of the government. The key factor for officials is their relations to the authority figures. Promotions may relate to aptitude, but more often they depend on the loyalty and subservience of the individual. The prized quality for promotion is "total and ingenious servility" (Wittfogel, 364).

In an absolutist state, the central government makes official requests and imposes its authority through constables, tax collectors, and other kinds of government agents. The society is clearly demarcated into the ruled versus the rulers, with the people fearing involvement with the government and expressing little love for its representatives (Wittfogel, 156). There exist no serious competing interests to the government officials, who see the people tied to them by obligations. Government traditionally, as in Burma, for instance, is not concerned with problem solving or with improving society but with maintaining loyalty and status (Pye 1962, 78).

Parts of the society lie outside the control of the absolutist state. Government authority does not involve the assumption of responsibility for individuals which characterizes more decentralized governments. Where its authority and revenue are not jeopardized, the central government does not intrude. To varying degrees families and villages may enjoy autonomy to run their own affairs. In countries with a centralized government structure, the gemeinschaft values generate activity rooted in efforts to maintain status and govern social relations by personalized and traditional forms. The personal aloofness people may feel toward their government and toward fellow citizens with whom specific social relations have not been established may reach pathological proportions when perceived from an American point of view. For instance, assistance to the victim of an accident or a drowning may be withheld for fear the rescuer will be saddled with responsibility for the misfortune. The potential rescuer is involved in a unique web of gemeinschaft relations to which the victim is an outsider, if not a nonperson. If assistance were extended, the victim would probably become included within the social bonds of the rescuer, who might then be compelled to accept responsibility for or feel obligation toward the victim.

This very brief and simplified description of the nature of total power is not intended to describe any particular country at any particular point in time. (There are also contradictions: in democratic, urban America people may fail to come to the aid of others to avoid involvement or for fear of a lawsuit.) It nevertheless shows us some of the characteristics of states with highly centralized governmental structures and helps us understand certain aspects of the value systems that develop within them. There is little incentive for achievement or change. Significant relations are vertical; hence, the impetus for successful action or for change usually comes from above. There is little precedent for ideas, initiatives, or opinions to originate spontaneously with the people and move upward to the leaders.

When contrasted with American society, the nature of motivation may be quite different. Significantly, the clear acceptance of a personal bond between subordinate and superior in states under total power makes the authority figure a common source of motivation. Direct orders, explicit instructions, and demands for personal conformity may be much more acceptable, even desired, in the non-Western world than in the United States. Non-Westerners may perceive the American preference for persuasion as a weakness, and self-determination as egotism and a threat to others.

CHAPTER   FIVE

FORM OF
SOCIAL RELATIONS

Social Status

Although sociologists speak of class structure and status obligation in American society, most Americans see themselves as members of an egalitarian middle class. There are variations in parts of New England and in the Southeast, where the status and position occupied in the social structure carry influence; but, generally, in American society, social background, money, or power bestow perhaps fewer advantages than in any other major society. Lacking obligations to class and social position, Americans move easily from one group to another as they shift position or residence; consequently, their social life lacks both permanence and depth (C. Kluckhohn 1954a, 96). Styles of communication, social customs, and behavior are relatively smooth across classes. Personal relations among Americans are adapted to gaining emotional benefits from social interaction while preserving independence and avoiding obligations. In Germany, Great Britain, and Japan, for comparison, social status and inheritance enter into the ability of the individual to wield influence to a greater degree than with Americans.

The relative insensitivity to social status may interfere with American social judgment when moving in international circles. One of the authors recalls an evening in which an American invited a small group to her home in Washington, D.C., including two Germans because they were in a strange country and therefore might enjoy meeting each

89

other. One of the German guests, whose last name began with "von," came from the north while the second came from southern Germany. The styles of speech and of behavior—as well as their positions in Washington—were clear signs that the two Germans came from different strata of German society. During the evening, the exchanges between the two Germans were impeccable and tense, to say the least.

Another episode with American Peace Corps volunteers in Jamaica illustrates some of the psychological consequences of American insensitivity to social status. In the early seventies, Jamaica received a number of American Peace Corps volunteers each year to work in educational and community development programs. Many of the American volunteers saw in Jamaica an opportunity for the exercise of civil and human rights unimpeded by attitudes of racial prejudice. After a period of six months in country, many of them experienced a sharp turn in their attitudes as they began to realize that Jamaican society was highly stratified. Indeed, it became apparent to many volunteers that Jamaican civil servants valued the Americans for being willing to work and to communicate with members in all strata of society. Jamaican field workers and civil servants generally did not communicate or cooperate across class and status lines. The social anxiety created in some Americans was severe enough that the Peace Corps secured the services of a British psychiatrist to counsel American volunteers on a case-by-case basis. Yet, it seemed that volunteers visiting the psychiatrist left with exacerbated feelings of social turmoil, even though the competence and integrity of the psychiatrist were beyond dispute. When the situation was examined, it was found that in part the block was cultural. The psychiatrist typically explained Jamaican behavior according to social background using terms such as "upper-" or "lower-class behavior." The social class interpretation of human behavior cut against the grain of American social attitudes and particularly irritated the PCVs' strong feelings toward civil and human rights.

Equality

Running through American social relationships is the theme of equality. Each person is ascribed an irreducible value because of his or her humanness: "We're all human, after all." Interpersonal relations are typically horizontal, conducted between presumed equals. When a personal confrontation is required between two persons of different hierarchical levels, there is an implicit tendency to establish an atmosphere of equality. Thus, even within the clearly authoritarian structure of the military, a commanding officer may ask a subordinate a personal question or offer a cup of coffee before beginning a conversation.

Furthermore, the officer is expected not to call attention to his rank and authority or exercise his personal power over a subordinate. One mark of a good officer from the enlisted man's point of view is that he does not "pull rank" or "use his authority as a crutch." Outside the military, a parallel compliment is often made regarding people who are much richer or higher in position or status: "He's a regular guy—doesn't lord it over you." In short, the good officer and the respected higher-status person promote a feeling of equality, the preferred social mode among Americans.

Values associated with equality are not well accepted everywhere. Mead (1963) makes the following comment about Americans working abroad:

> Americans...find it very confusing to shift from high to low status as the situation demands and...respond by a continuous endeavor to stabilize relationships. Their uneasiness often leads to an assertive attempt either to establish a superficially egalitarian ethos—as in the ritual use of first names for everyone, which is most disorienting to persons of many other cultures—or else to attempt to establish hierarchies which are rigidly resistant to other considerations such as lineage and education (7-8).

It is clear that their cultural values predispose Americans to function most effectively on an interpersonal level of equality. They are often confused when confronted with persons of a different status—particularly when that status has been achieved through a legacy of special privileges. The ideal of equality makes it difficult for Americans to understand hierarchical patterns of organizations abroad; consequently, they tend to ignore political issues. For example, they usually do not consider the fact that the loyalty of members of an organization may be the primary principle that explains otherwise unintelligible actions and promotions. Noting the absence of an emphasis on both achievement and equality, Americans may fail to recognize the characteristics that determine who are the high-status opinion molders and decision makers.

> For instance, that impoverished aristocrats or ascetic priests, beggarly in dress and looks, can still command respect and allegiance, despite their lack of outward signs of visible achievement and "success," is a difficult concept for Americans to grasp. Some people, like the Japanese, present another enigma; for they practice a kind of faceless leadership in which string-pullers exert their authority behind conspicuous but powerless puppet or ceremonial figures in public office (Arensberg and Niehoff 1964, 135).

Another situation in which Americans may fail to recognize and respond appropriately to status difference occurs when they work with

Japanese business groups. The Japanese company is modeled on the Japanese household. The relationships among members of the company are precisely articulated along lines of the household. Americans, lacking both the terminology and the social psychology for understanding Japanese relations, perceive individuals first and their roles (and statuses) in the company second. This orientation perpetrates numerous social mishaps, as illustrated in the following episode.

> An American consultant returned to Tokyo after a long absence and decided to renew an old relationship with a manager in a Japanese firm, which we shall call Nihon. He phoned and talked with Mr. Suzuki, who invited him to visit his department any time. Several weeks later, the consultant took advantage of a Japanese custom and dropped by Nihon unannounced. He asked for Mr. Suzuki and some ten minutes later another man, Mr. Hara, came down to the reception room and greeted him. The American was glad to see Mr. Hara, whom he knew and liked. Mr. Hara was older, of higher rank, and in the same department as Mr. Suzuki The two had a pleasant conversation in the coffee shop, and toward the end, Mr. Hara explained that Mr. Suzuki was away for some days. Upon parting from Mr. Hara, the American thanked him for his courtesy and concluded by saying that it was really Mr. Hara he had wanted to see anyway because they shared interests and experience in the same regions of the world. Mr. Hara courteously and properly thanked the American for calling on Nihon. Some weeks later, the American invited both Mr. Hara and Mr. Suzuki and their wives to a reception. Both men expressed pleasure at the invitation, but Mr. Suzuki said that he did not know who would represent Nihon. Mr. Hara accepted. Just before the reception, Mr. Suzuki called to explain that the pressures of work would prevent his attendance, and furthermore, he was now working in another department of the company, but he said that Mr. Hara would be there. Mr. Hara attended the reception by himself but brought a card from Mr. Suzuki. The American remembered that years before, for another reception, two members of another Japanese company had been invited. The junior person had sent a gift a few hours before the reception while the senior manager attended with his wife.

This example illustrates the American difficulty in understanding networks in a Japanese company. The roles ascribed in those networks demand carefully calibrated behavior from the players and from the people who relate to them. Mr. Suzuki, being of lower rank than Mr. Hara, could not comfortably include himself in the relationship with the Americans on an equal basis with Mr. Hara. Americans tend to ignore the expectation of differential treatment, preferring instead to relate to individuals on the basis of personal liking and equality.

The American cultural value of equality is restricted in application. For instance, despite legislative efforts, equality has not generally been extended to African-Americans or members of some other racial and ethnic minorities. In these cases, cultural differences have been stigmatized by dominant groups, and different social norms have been developed to deal with them. Liberal- and conservative-minded people alike (including many blacks themselves) subscribe to

> a social etiquette that considers it impolite to discuss minority-group differences in public. This rule emerged over a period when such differences were regularly used as evidence of minority-group inferiority (Kochman 1981, 11).

The effect of this conspiracy of silence is to perpetuate the stigma attached to the different cultural patterns of some Americans. Without change in the basic acceptance of such differences, the social norm of inequality towards African-Americans and others is likely to persist.

Other restrictions in the application of equality exist in large-scale economic and political organizations with strong hierarchical and authoritarian emphases (Robin Williams 1961, 441). These may be related to the assumption that, although all persons are presumed to have equal rights and obligations, not everyone is presumed to be of equal talent and ability. The acceptance of unequal capability is tempered by the typical American belief that in any grouping there are some people with talent and leadership potential. Their emergence awaits the right opportunity. It is the equality of opportunity, then, that receives emphasis in American culture. Americans are usually individually interested in achievement and expect rewards commensurate with their accomplishments. Thus, historically, equality has not extended to achievements, success, or rewards (see Williams, 442). Under social and government pressure to compensate for racial and social injustices of the past, American individuals and organizations have at times modified their actions during the last twenty years to mask the distinction between equality of opportunity and reward. Nevertheless, as an ideal, the value of equality of opportunity remains pervasive in the culture.

When associating with persons either abroad or in the United States who do not share this value, Americans find it extremely difficult to understand how someone could comprehend the meaning of equality and still reject it. Yet persons accepting social hierarchies are likely to believe that equality in social relations spoils structured interactions among people, reducing the predictability of social responses. When social equality prevails, there is a tendency for everyone to be treated alike with little differentiation for personal and social characteristics. Many foreigners resent the sameness of perception and reaction exhibited by Americans, dislike the uncertainty of social relations introduced by American informality, and prefer a society which acknowledges social differences among persons.

The implicit dispute that many foreigners have with the American value of equality goes beyond surface culture and social manners. The contrasting view, well represented in the views of Max Scheler (1961), involves issues of philosophy and ideology. Scheler claims that equality offers a moral value only for that which everyone can do, even the least gifted. If all human beings are equal in moral values and talents, then the moral level of the least gifted is the criterion for the worth of all (Scheler, 139-41). Scheler finds this view objectionable and argues for what he calls *sacredness*—vitality and spirituality in cultural values (Scheler, 152). He scorns American commitment to such principles as utility as a subordination of ends to means. The views of Scheler lend themselves to a belief in absolute values more agreeable to aristocratic or privileged classes—a belief which most Americans find abrasive and dangerous. He has been called a fascist since his thinking can subsume ideas of cultural and racial superiority.

Even though Americans have frequently violated the assumptions of equality, their continued insistence upon it as an ideal demonstrates their inclination to perpetuate a value through a social norm which is part illusion and part reality. The illusion arises from the unrealized goal of equal opportunity for all. Each new generation must grapple with the ideal of equality and find ways to apply it in social and political life to the benefit of all Americans.

Obligation

While social activities occupy much of their time, Americans avoid personal commitments to others. They do not like to get involved. They accept and express gratitude for a social act such as an invitation or gift, but the recipient is under no obligation to reciprocate. There does exist the vague propriety of a return gesture, but it does not have the binding and formal quality of social obligations evident in other cultures. Americans usually prefer to pursue their social life under conditions that minimize incurring social obligations. The circumspection required to avoid social indebtedness is in direct contrast with conventions in most parts of the world. The American "thank you, I had a fine time" is a meager return for an evening's invitation. In European cultures, the guest is expected to bring flowers or candy, and in non-

Western societies, depending on the status differences involved, the obligation incurred by an invitation almost certainly demands some sort of reciprocity. One solution to social obligations, the Dutch treat, may seem crass to non-Americans who prefer the convention of individuals taking turns in being the host. It is probably accurate to say that in all of the world outside the United States, a relationship without obligation is simply not significant. In those societies, such as Japan, in which social relations are based on dependency and on a hierarchical social structure, the American custom of spontaneous, individually bound and duty-fee social relations is a social ornament rather than the fiber of the social system.

Cultural contrasts in patterns of relational obligation are readily illustrated by different customs of gift giving. In white, middle-class America, gifts are customarily given to commemorate a birthday, an anniversary, or a festival such as Christmas. Outside of these well-established occasions, circumspection is observed so that gift giving appears personally anonymous or offhand. The gift's significance is carefully limited to avoid a personal meaning that might be construed as offering a bribe, seeking special favors, or as requiring reciprocity. In the workplace, anonymity is commonly achieved by pooling donations from interested people for a gift to commemorate an event. In other cultures, the American convention of anonymity in giving gifts is often seen to deprecate the meaning of the act. If the gift does not inconvenience or deprive the donor, it has less meaning for the recipient. In parts of India, no expression for "thanks" exists; social conventions have not required its invention. A social act is seen as the fulfillment of an obligation or a duty and requires no verbal acknowledgement. If the action, as in offering a gift, is not the consequence of an obligation, thanks would still be inappropriate. To imply termination of social interchange by an overt expression of thanks places a finite value on the gift and cheapens its meaning.

Complex gift giving and receiving customs are simply the surface level of far deeper systems of obligation in some cultures. In Japan, for instance, the incurring of an obligation sets up a complex expectation of reciprocal repayments that might last for generations (Lebra 1974, 192-205). One loses face by refusing to recognize or accept an obligation or, once accepted, by failing to repay it. The repayment in turn obligates the original benefactor (or his children), and so on. This cultural mechanism is embedded in yet a deeper cultural pattern of maintaining the good will of others—an effort that "binds human beings in a dependent relationship" (Doi 1973, 34-35). Whereas digging below the surface of social relationships in American culture yields an inviolate individual, similar excavations in many non-Western cultures reveals a web of human relationships.

Two major variant patterns in obligation deserve mention. Among the American military, patterns of social relations are in many ways less anonymous and neutral than among typical middle-class Americans. As officers serve tours of duty throughout the world, they periodically encounter fellow officers with whom they have served before. Quite often strong friendships develop, usually including the entire family. Furthermore, there is a tendency in these relationships to specify expectations of social reciprocity that ordinarily are only vaguely felt by most other Americans. Although one social action does not necessarily require an explicit return gesture, there is the expectation that the association will be actively maintained. These informal social norms have probably developed under the influence of the social conventions of the formal military establishment, which is more ascriptive and gemeinschaft than dominant American culture.

Another major variant of the mainstream American pattern of social relationships is found among some racial and ethnic minority groups. Where a group finds itself beleaguered by negative attitudes toward its language, ethnicity, race, or even customs and traditions, its members are likely to fall back upon gemeinschaft ties of affiliation characteristic of societies living in political climates of total power. The social dynamic of affiliation provides protection for many African and Hispanic minority groups by providing their members with a sense of belonging and identity which can be used for political and social leverage. Affiliation in minority groups is expressed by a greater reciprocity in relationships than that found in mainstream white American culture. For instance, African-Americans in intercultural workshops will state, "You should do anything for a friend—give him all your money, if he needs it, or travel anywhere to get him out of trouble." The same kind of unequivocal statement about friendship will be heard from Arabs and people from other affiliative non-Western societies. These statements may be more expressive than declarative, but they do convey social sentiments rarely encountered among American whites.

Confrontation

When faced with a problem, Americans like to get to its source. This means facing the facts, meeting the problem head on, putting the cards on the table, and getting information "straight from the horse's mouth." Consistent with these tendencies, it is also desirable to face people directly—to confront them. Confrontation is not necessarily rancorous, but it does involve reporting one's feelings honestly, expecting reciprocal honesty, and dealing directly with the person involved in the problem. The strategy of confrontation seems to call for a temporary neutralization of social relations to allow the real facts of the case to emerge. A social moratorium is implicitly invoked in the name of frankness to permit objective reality to appear so that conflict can be averted while needs and purposes are expressed.

The social norm of confrontation is limited by two conditions. First, Americans accept the need to preserve surface cordiality, particularly when the problem is primarily social. Quarreling members of the same group can encounter each other at large meetings or parties and pass with only brief ritual exchanges. Under similar circumstances, Europeans, particularly the French and Germans, would more likely be provoked to create an incident. Second, a set of circumstances curtailing confrontation has emerged in political and social life. Where confrontation involves disclosure of weakness, Americans may attempt suppression, displacement, or denial, and fall back upon American ideology. Beginning in the 1950s, during the formative period of the civil rights movement, American social and political thought refined the idea of a pluralistic society in which varieties of ethnic groups contribute to a free and strong economy. Discussions critical of the social fiber of the society, particularly negative evaluations of minority groups or of minority political figures, are implicitly suppressed with epithets of "racism" and "prejudice." As a consequence, undercurrents of social, racial, and political feelings fester outside the domain of social and political debate. In recent years, the suppression of reality and the appeal to ideology has surfaced in trade negotiations with the Japanese as American political figures and business leaders have been reluctant to confront the structural "weaknesses" in the U.S. industrial system. Whether they are weaknesses or not is another question, but the ideology of the times prevents a confrontation on the issue.

A contrast to the American value of confrontation is supplied by the indirection of the Japanese in social matters. Frederick Hulse asserts, "Since so much of overt Japanese culture is purely arbitrary convention which must be accepted like the rule of passing to the right in driving, the importance of objective truth, which must be believed, is relatively minor" (1962, 304). Among the Japanese there even exist rules for what can and cannot be observed. "Guests do not observe their hosts until the latter are properly garbed, as many travelers in Japan have long pointed out" (Hulse, 304-05). The Japanese appreciate skill in social maneuvers and ridicule awkwardness which embarrasses friends.

Japanese social indirection is supported by several strategies that lack strong precedents in American direct communication. Takie Sugiyama Lebra (1976, 122-26) lists eight well-defined strategies that serve to protect "face" or avoid shame in interpersonal encounters. In *mediated communication,* a third person is asked to relay delicate information to the concerned party. Americans, of course, consider this technique unnecessarily cumbersome, if not hypocritical. An even more frustrating technique to Americans is the strategy of *refracted communication,* where statements intended for one person are made to a second person in the first person's presence. Alternatively, a Japanese person, a businessman for instance, may act as *delegate,* portraying himself as an emissary for another to surreptitiously state his own opinion, or he might allow *self-communication* such as notes or a diary to fall into the hands of the other concerned party. *Correspondence* can serve the same purpose of allowing uncomfortable communication to occur without the involved parties being physically present, and it may be preferred in business situations (or even personal ones) where rejection or other sensitive matters are the subject. In nearly all cases, Japanese indirect communication is characterized by understatement and *unobtrusive behavior,* both of which serve the purpose of an *anticipatory communication,* where the one is expected to empathize and accommodate to the unspoken needs of the other. Finally in the situations most likely to be encountered by Americans, *ritualism* may be used to maintain control of potentially embarrassing situations/ encounters where events are unpredictable, as they are when interacting with foreigners.

Many of the above Japanese strategies are common in other non-Western cultures. For instance, business in Thailand is often conducted through a third party, and in Truk one of the authors had a year-long argument with his school principal conducted entirely through the principal's brother. If there is face-to-face contact among parties in a mediated event, the strategy of ritual may be employed. Everyone in these situations acts as if nothing at all is amiss, even though they all know about the underlying negotiation or conflict. What is common to the strategies of indirect communication is their effectiveness in allowing both sides to accommodate each other or to withdraw without losing face. Although American culture incorporates some forms of indirectness as variants of the dominant cultural value of confrontation, it does not include the concept of face. Consequently, Americans easily underestimate the seriousness of indirect communication.

The American norm of confrontation consistently irritates human relations and endangers intercultural communication with foreign students and workers both abroad and at home. At the root of the American confrontational style is the concept that adversaries can compete against each other and at the same time cooperate under rules for interpersonal conflict. The language used by Americans in reference to communication carries the feeling of adversarial confrontation and depersonalization. Individuals conceive of themselves as subjects, but others in the role of intended receivers are social objects. Borrowing from the language of ballistics, social objects may be known as the "target audience." A direct and explicit message, such as a pointed question, is known as a "bullet question." Despite their occasional extreme admiration of American panache in face-to-face confrontations, foreigners often find this directness in communication harsh and destructive to the subtleties and indirection of interpersonal relations more common in other cultures.

Informality and Formality

The adversarial style encountered with confrontation is exhibited in the informality with which Americans tend to treat other people. For instance, Americans look directly into each other's eyes when talking, conveying informality, spontaneity, and equality in the exchange of glances. When eyes shift and avoid meeting those of the other, Americans sense connivance and infer deception. But the direct eye exchange can be forbidding in many societies where hierarchical relations exist among people and lowered eyes and sidelong glances express lower status or humility. The spontaneous informality indicated by direct eye contact sets a better stage for Americans' friendly, but adversarial, relations.

In conversation, American expressions of greeting are brief and often perfunctory, points in conversation are pressed directly and quickly, and forms in communication representing social relations are few and loose. Foreign students in the U.S. are frequently disoriented by these characteristics. Abroad, the directness and informality of Americans often seems brusque and may insult or confuse their foreign associates. The flowery language, complex methods of address, and ritualistic manners found in many other cultures reflect the social structure of the cultures. When Americans fail to use these forms, they violate the prescribed methods of structuring social interaction. Whereas the average American tends to consider formality, style, and protocol as somewhat pompous or arrogant, in other cultures these elements provide the context within which dependable expectations for the behavior of others is established. This function is particularly striking with the Japanese, who cannot communicate until they know the status of the other person. Not only does this information about status allow appropriate social forms to be observed, but it is also necessary for the use of the language, which requires specific linguistic forms to represent the different relationships between communicators.

American informality is coupled with the value of equality just discussed. Americans tend to address everyone in the same way. They use first names readily and early in a relationship, and they believe that treating everyone the same is ultimately respectful. If Americans develop a stronger than usual attachment to someone, they may experience difficulty in expressing it since exchanges from the beginning have been informal and friendly. Consequently, what at first may appear to be a personal way of treating others can ultimately become depersonalizing because it is extended to everyone alike. Few discriminations are made among people, each being kept at the same distance. Even enemies are likely to be treated with a controlled friendliness that may not look much different from behavior directed toward valued acquaintances.

The lack of discrimination in American interpersonal behavior can be extremely irritating to foreigners. Both Europeans and Asians comment with some distaste on the American habit of chatting casually with waitresses in restaurants or strangers in other public places. The surface equality which characterizes American social relations strikes at the heart of distinct role discriminations common to more ascriptive societies. At the same time, the casual style of Americans is often liked and even envied by people from societies in which personal relationships are more rigidly structured. This paradox is captured by the British playwright, Tom Stoppard, in the following excerpt from his play, *Dirty Linen and New-Found-Land*:

> BERNARD (the very traditional character, in response to ARTHUR, an enthusiast for things American): Americans are a very modern people, of course. They are a very open people too. They wear their hearts on their sleeves. They don't stand on ceremony. They take people as they are. They make no distinction about a man's background, his parentage, his education. They say what they mean and there is a vivid muscularity about the way they say it. They admire everything about them without reserve or pretence or scholarship. They are always the first to put their hands in their pockets. They press you to visit them in their own home the moment they meet you, and are irrepressible, good-humored, ambitious, and brimming with self-confidence in any company. Apart from all that I've got nothing against them (1976, 59-60).

Friendship

Although Americans have numerous relationships that are marked by friendliness and informality, they only rarely form the kinds of deep and lasting friendships in which friends become mutually dependent upon each other. Ideally, American friendship is based on spontaneity, mutual attraction, and warm personal feelings. People choose their friends. They also keep relations with friends separate from social or work obligations. It is important for the American to preserve personal initiative in pursuing friendships—in contrast to those societies where friendship patterns are inseparable from social obligations. In Japan, for instance, friendship apart from social obligations is virtually nonexistent except in special situations of temporary duration such as among classmates in college. The American qualities of choice, spontaneity, and personal warmth run strikingly counter to Japanese friendship patterns involving obligation, duty, and ritualized interaction.

A partial exception to this pattern of friendly but surface relations is met in the "best friend," who often turns out to be a friend made during high school or college days. Although the friendship may endure for decades or a lifetime, it is marked more by nostalgia and sentiment than by reciprocal dependence. Even best friends may subscribe to the lightheartedness of American patterns of friendship.

An American friend may refer to anyone from a passing acquaintance to a lifetime intimate. Friendship is formed and friends maintained in shared activities—doing things together. Thus, Americans have friendships which originate "around work, children, or political opinions—around charities, games, various occasions for sharing food and drink, etc." (Glenn 1966, 270). The various compartments of friendship are usually kept separate, so that a friendship that is centered around the office does not intrude into the relations with friends who participate in recreational activities. Even greater specialization may occur in leisure-time friendships, with certain people being, for instance, "bowling friends" and others being "skiing friends." Friendship tends to be generalized only to similar activities or events and to persons who have both social and personal commitments to each other. But these patterns of friendship among Americans—particularly the specialization of friends—do not imply a distrust of people. They signify more often the American reluctance to become deeply involved with other persons. In circumstances where a foreigner might turn to a friend for help, support, or solace, Americans tend to search for a professional, preferring not to inconvenience their friends. Nonetheless, Americans do sometimes call on their friends for what might almost be called "therapeutic" help.

The professionals sought out by Americans to help them overcome their feelings of depression or anomie are likely to counsel them to "get out and meet people" and "make new friends" (Bellah et al. 1985, 134-35). This utilitarian view of friendship may be compared to Dale Carnegie's advice on how to "win friends and influence people." Now, however, the profit to be gained from friends is not economic, but psychological. In a criticism that echoes the limitations of the action dynamic of gesellschaft in American society, Bellah et al. comment on this phenomenon:

> Are friends that one makes in order to improve one's health really friends enough to improve one's health? The popular language of therapy is so radically individualistic that it has difficulty imagining an alternative even when the inadequacy of "self-sufficiency" is recognized. Only occasionally do we find therapists who recognize, and then often only fitfully, that "community" is not a collection of self-seeking individuals, not a temporary remedy, like Parents without Partners, that can be abandoned as soon as a partner has been found, but a context within which personal identity is formed, a place where fluent self-awareness follows the currents of communal conversation and contributes to them (135).

In this statement, we sense the American loneliness of spirit and the emotional hunger for the security of intimate human relations.

In contrast, Russians, according to Glenn (1966, 270), expect to form deep bonds with their friends and to assume the "obligation of almost constant companionship, and the rejection of any reticence or secretiveness...." Whereas Americans tend to limit friendship to an area of common interest, the Russian "tends to embrace the whole person." French styles of friendship are in some ways like the Russian.

> They also tend to be organized in patterns of long duration, often with an expectation of family friendships extending over more than one generation. Where Americans are competitive even within the group of friends, for Frenchmen as for Russians, friendship excludes competitiveness; the coexistence of cooperation with competition, so natural to Americans, appears incomprehensible to French and Russian informants (Glenn, 271).

While American and Russian styles of friendship represent contrasting but consistent patterns, the French style poses contradictions stemming from simultaneous demands for privacy, independence, and long, close connections. When these divergent obligations cause a breakdown, they are reconciled through the French social norm of the *brouille:*

> Friendship is put in abeyance but not broken, the individuals concerned are not on speaking terms, but expect a reconciliation and stand ready to resume mutual help under some grave circumstances such as death in the family. Under similar circumstances, Americans would quietly drift apart, and Russians seek immediate resolution through a stormy scene (Glenn, 271).

These patterns of friendship reflect the willingness of both Russians and the French to accept obligations to others. This contrasts to Americans, who are generally reluctant to undertake deep obligations to their friends, preferring to keep the relationships more superficial.

Because cultural patterns of mutual obligation are usually found in ascriptive societies, the forms of relationships are more precisely defined in many such societies outside the West. Friends may be limited to specific classes of persons instead of to areas of activity. Most frequently excluded are members of the opposite sex. Arab men, for instance, do not generally include women among their friends. Their relationships to women are familial, marital, or sexual. Unlike the practice often found among Americans, friends in non-Western societies do not typically include parents, and friendships among persons of different status in society are avoided.

Finally, friends are not normally shared among non-Westerners as they habitually are among Americans. Friendship among non-Westerners is likely to be jealously guarded out of fear of losing or diluting it if other friends are brought into the relationship. As Foster (1965, 298) has suggested, for much of Latin America (and most of the rest of the world), true friendship is considered to be a scarce commodity. It is for this reason that so many foreigners are amazed when Americans announce, "I made a new friend this weekend."

Personalization and Depersonalization

Every culture provides methods for people to feel uniquely human— personalized—even if they are deviant members of the culture. Yet, what is personal for members of one society may not be for those of another. In each case, personalization conforms to cultural values, social norms, and the individual's concept of the self. Personal treatment in American life includes use of the first name; knowing biographical details such as hometown; and acknowledging specific acts, appearances, preferences, and choices of the individual. The behavior of salespersons and airline personnel typifies this kind of personalization. The pleasant smiles, brief expressions of interest, innocuous invasions of privacy, kidding, and swapping of personal anecdotes constitute a social norm of personalized behavior. The norm is loosely based on American cultural values of achievement, equality, and individualism. Activities are stressed, and individuals are more or less accepted as they present themselves.

The context for personalization differs from culture to culture. Americans consider things "personal" only if they relate to the individuals immediately involved, even when the expressions of interest are superficial. Indians, in contrast, are more inclined to become person-

ally involved while discussing a topic than while discussing a col-
league, the reverse of the American inclination. One group of Indians
undergoing training in an American university were observed to load
their words with emotion while discussing the problems of civil servants in the Indian government, but when the topic of conversation
veered toward the relationships among those in the group, comments
became unemotionally abstract and intellectual. Finally, one member
of the group eloquently proposed that they select some other topic that
would permit them to be personal and not allow the discussion to
degenerate into talking about each other "and all that." This comment
illustrates a view of personalism associated with opinions on issues
rather than with interpersonal relations. Americans are likely to encounter this approach to personalization in Europe, where initial "getting to know you" conversations are almost exclusively abstract. As one
European put it, "How can you really know someone if you don't know
how he thinks about important issues?"

Although Americans typically tend to see themselves as unique
individuals with private selves inaccessible to others, as a rule they see
others as representatives of depersonalized categories. The great divide in
American social relations is between the self and all others. Most Americans, therefore, are relatively impartial and objective in the conduct of
social relations—behavior that both equalizes and depersonalizes others.
In most of the non-Western parts of the world, the significant divide occurs
between one's own network such as family or work group and all other
social networks. This division personalizes most relationships and leads to
the paternal benevolence of the Japanese, the charismatic personal
leadership displayed by the Latin caudillo, and the nepotism endemic to
the non-Western world. In contrast, Americans value symmetrical working relationships, impartial leadership, and objectivity in hiring. Americans are likely to consider non-Western practices in these areas as
undesirable since they are personalized interactions in areas where
Americans are accustomed to depersonalized behavior.

The American form of personalization is, to some extent, symbolic.
Through personalization, individuals may depart temporarily from
conformity to the categories of American social relations, but individual
detachment cannot go too far. Americans typically yield to the unifor-
mities required by social life and work, becoming depersonalized while
preserving a symbolic appearance of personalization. The American
pattern is personalized in its surface emphasis on individual motivation,
preference, and choice, but at root it is depersonalized by the demands
of objectivity. In non-Western cultures, this pattern may be reversed.
An emphasis on conformity at the surface masks the deep personalization of gemeinschaft societies. Americans abroad may confuse this

surface conformity with depersonalization, creating confusion in social relations. In addition, Americans may expect trust and good will to accompany personalization, as it does in their society. They may be confused by the distrust and suspicion that frequently characterize relations among members of different groups in non-Western cultures.

The depersonalized behavior of Americans, along with the values of achievement and equality, nurture competition as a mode of social interaction. As we have seen, participants may perceive themselves as adversaries, each striving to achieve his or her own personal goals in relationships. This disposition is found in personal interactions among American men, where easy banter and joshing, freely given advice, quick repartee, and the "friendly suggestion" may all be subtle forms of competition. Individuals who have the last word are "one up" on their companions, at least until one of them tells a better joke or in some way gives a twist to the competition that elevates that person to the one-up position.

Although subtle competition in interpersonal relations may seem innocuous to Americans, such actions can assume the proportions of coercion to foreigners with more affiliative tendencies (see Wax and Thomas 1961). White Americans can comprehend this interpretation in terms of their own response to certain forms of African-American verbal behavior. Competitive verbal exchanges are more common among blacks than among whites (Kochman 1981). Verbal "play" such as *sounding* and *playing the dozens* (exchanging insults) and *woofing* (making verbal threats) is considered a kind of art form among some blacks. According to the white social norm, however, one makes threats only if one is prepared to carry them out. In commenting on the frequent misunderstandings that accompany this cultural difference, Kochman states:

> Whites need to learn that the more intense levels of black speech behavior are not per se intended to be provocative or threatening.... Blacks, for their part, need to learn what effect their speech behavior is likely to have on whites...(59).

Since both black and white American speech behavior is more intense than that of many other cultures, both groups need to heed Kochman's advice in dealing with foreigners.

Cooperation and "Fair Play"

Competition among Americans occurs within the context of cooperation, for competition requires a considerable amount of coordination among individuals and groups. The typical American ability to cooperate is one of the most important assets of advisors and managers abroad, where they may act as catalysts in inducing others to work together. One of the reasons Americans can do this—and they are well known for it—is that they do not commit themselves wholeheartedly to a group or organization. They pursue their own personal goals while cooperating with others who, likewise, pursue their own. They accept the goals of the group, but if their expectations are unfulfilled, they then feel free to leave and join another group. This separation between membership in a group and personal objectives allows the individuals to adjust their goals to those of other group members if it is necessary for carrying out joint action. To Americans, this compromise is practical, allowing them to achieve a benefit they could not attain on their own. Cooperation is given for the sake of action and it does not imply that the Americans are yielding their principles. They are in fact simply following one of the dominant values in American culture, that of *doing* (as discussed in chapter 4). Cooperating to get something done is more important than the personal relationships among the doers.

A sense of urgency and the importance of getting things done are often combined to gain the cooperation of those who dispute the principles or disagree with the objectives of the group. As discussed in chapter 4, a deadline or an appeal to future opportunities may be injected into group deliberations to overcome individual differences. Appeals may be made such as "Let's get the job done and then we can take care of these other problems." Each person is expected to make an individual accommodation to the joint action in a manner analogous to the "Dutch treat."

The American ability for cooperation and organization is not, as a rule, found in other cultures, even other Western cultures. The French, for instance, are less likely than Americans to embrace compromise easily; either no action at all is taken or each person has a turn at getting his or her own way—a parallel to taking turns as host. Latin Americans have a hard time adjusting their goals to those of the group or in making a practical adjustment to getting the job done since it represents a compromise of principles. Many Africans appear to share this reluctance.

The Americans' preference for the action dynamic of gesellschaft may work against their individualism in a social setting. The necessity for compromise in cooperative action may undermine other values, principles, or objectives. To insure that they adjust or compromise no more than necessary, Americans are likely to stress the means used to reach a group decision. In formal groups, for instance, they may be preoccupied with matters of agenda and procedure, which give some formal protection to the rights of the individual. Americans believe that "due process" establishes a frame for the use of persuasion to achieve compromises which are fair to each individual. In contrast, Latin Americans often regard appeals to the agenda or to group procedures as efforts to avoid the issue; they prefer to invoke concepts such as the dignity of man, honor, or other principled beliefs as a logic for settling differences. This abstract humanism of the Latin Americans contrasts with the instrumental technicism of Americans.

The American value of fairness, indicated by their concern with procedures, is not confined to formal groups. It has widespread ramifications, often appearing as the social norm of fair play. The essence of fair play is not so much that rules ought to be followed as it is "...the inclusion of the other person's weakness inside the rule..." (Mead 1965, 143). Rules should be applied with knowledge of the relative strength of the opponents, so that the stronger opponent does not use the rules to beat a weaker one. This American modification of the English notion of fair play is both an arbiter of personal relations among Americans and a motivating force. Americans will stand up for their fair share, but they will also be concerned that others are dealt with fairly. If they perceive themselves to be stronger, they tend not to initiate aggressive action since they do not believe in starting a fight. It is important for Americans to be able to say, "They started it," and then of course, "but we'll finish it."

Differences in how the weakness of another is treated fuels the mutual misunderstanding between Americans and members of other cultures. Americans cannot understand the deliberate and ruthless exploitation of a weak adversary by those with power and position in other cultures. On the other hand, to others the concept of fair play may seem foolish, hypocritical, and, in some languages, actually untranslatable (Mead, 143).

The Need to Be Liked

Americans usually react to others as achievers and participants in certain activities rather than as whole persons. As we have seen, they frequently establish interpersonal relationships with others who are instrumental in meeting their own needs—for companionship or for "mental health," for instance. It follows from this instrumental view that Americans are mainly concerned with the responses of others. They try to anticipate the effects of words and acts on others, envisioning the desired responses and gearing their actions accordingly. This emphasis on the other differs from the concern shown by some Asians that partners may say or do something which would lead to a loss of face for either person. The other person is seen as a whole entity, albeit perhaps a worthless one. To Americans, the other person is seen predominantly as a set of responses that are more or less satisfying. The characteristic way of seeing others largely as responses to themselves is reflected in the American emphasis on techniques of personal communication and in the great value they place on being liked.

Abroad, the American desire to be liked makes it difficult for them to implement projects that require an unpopular phase. In the words of an English anthropologist, signs of friendship or love are

> a necessity for the American. He is insatiable in his demands for them, for any occasion on which they are withheld raises the gnawing doubt that maybe one is not lovable—not a success (Gorer 1948, 133).

Americans want to believe that common people throughout the world will like them, and they tend to go to countries that fulfill this expectation. USAID projects and other foreign aid commitments are sometimes canceled in countries which seem "ungrateful," Peace Corps volunteers are pulled out of situations where they are "not wanted," and tourists are attracted to destinations where the people are "friendly." American ethnics or immigrants who express strong dislike of "the American way" are invited to go back to where they came from. Clearly, Americans base their esteem of others on being liked by them (Linebarger 1954, 384-85).

The glad handshake, the ready smile, the slap on the back, and other superficial signs of friendship are a part of American life. Whenever Americans are denied these expressions of friendship or popularity, they are confused, reacting as if one of the requirements for personal assurance has been denied. Social success is often a necessary part of achievement, and Americans tend to judge their personal and social success by popularity—almost literally by the number of people who like them. Being liked does not mean, however, that one needs to like others in return. To be liked or loved means simply that one is worthy of love, not that one is thereby obligated to the other person. Popularity and friendship are both matters of social success and not the conditions for establishing deep relationships.

Specialization of Roles

The perspective from which we have considered social relations in American culture has been that of the individual person. This point of view may be reversed as we look at the social roles cultures use to integrate the individual into society as a functioning member. Individuals assume patterns of expectations and behavior associated with certain roles according to their personal and social characteristics and the conditions under which they engage in a specific activity.

Middle-class Americans typically separate home roles from work roles. Behavior and attitudes associated with the family are left behind when one leaves for work, where the individual is expected to make a clear distinction between personal matters and the job. Work itself is separated into occupational roles. In American culture, specific functions and problems are dealt with by persons who specialize in dealing with them. The basic distinction in function is between line operations and staff or labor and management. Within this basic split, other specialized roles proliferate, so that the "job description" becomes a powerful and necessary means of establishing appropriate work behavior. As one might expect, role specialization is especially prevalent in highly bureaucratic organizations such as the military and government.

The separation of social and occupational roles in American society does not, as we have said, correspond to the patterns found in many other cultures. In more ascriptive societies such as those of Latin America and parts of Asia, the requirements of personal obligation extend into the workplace; managers are expected to know about the personal lives of their employees and to offer personal aid when necessary. While the distinction between leaders and followers may be strong in Latin American organizations, that between line and staff may be less clear. Any person in the organization may become a focus of power, setting up competing interests and diffusing authority. Authority may not be delegated because all functions are vested in the leader. These patterns correspond to the ascriptive orientation and to a view of the whole person that is resistant to specialization in work roles.

Americans may find it difficult to work abroad in situations where roles are not clearly defined and specialized. Channels of authority may not be clear, or they may encounter resistance to such ideas as the separation of planning from operations. To Americans, specialization equals efficiency, and so it is not surprising to hear Americans abroad complaining about the inefficiency of local organizations. But attempts to impose the specialized structures of American organizations on those in ascriptive cultures seldom succeed. Instead, advisors and managers abroad should be ready to adapt their ideas to local values, experiment with overlapping systems of organization, or develop some other form in which line positions gradually merge into staff positions.

The American tendency toward specialization of roles occurs in the social realm as well. Social roles tend to be linked to function rather than to position in society, as is the case in ascriptive cultures. This tendency is dramatically evident in the case of a sick person, whose role as patient has become so specialized in American culture that the person plays no useful part in society. If sick people remain on their feet, they are praised for not allowing their illness to interfere with their work. If they are secluded in their homes, friends and extended family members will probably pay a short visit with little purpose other than to express concern; then they will leave after dispensing advice to "get well fast" (so they can become functional again). When sent to a hospital, sick people become cases or patients. Their lives are regulated by the impersonal routines of the hospital, isolated from the active mainstream. They are deprived of a useful social role since their disease is defined as a physical breakdown demanding objective, and thus impersonal, treatment.

The lack of social roles for sick people in American society can be traced to the cultural understanding of illness. Although American psychologists recognize many social factors in disease, the typical American patient gives a sigh of relief when the doctor diagnoses a physical cause for his or her symptoms. Patients are assured that symptoms are real and physical, not imaginary, and there is the hope that a pill or shot will solve the problem. The common American view of illness as a purely physiological dysfunction is consistent with their definition of themselves as material beings driven by biological needs. These needs cannot be fulfilled socially, so American attitudes toward human nature and identity must incorporate the idea of radical individualism. In a loose application of Darwinism, it is the fittest individual who can command a place in society. Sick individuals are, by definition, not fit, and so they lose their functional roles.

Rooted in basic needs, American individualism is a departure from the much more common cultural assumption that the irreducible reality of human nature is social in origin. In socially oriented cultures, illness is defined more as a social condition, and sick persons occupy important social roles. An example of this contrast to American values is found among the mestizos of Aritama, a small mountain village in the northern region of Colombia.

Among the Colombian mestizos, the prevention and control of disease is essentially social. For most of the people of Aritama, the source of illness is the hostility of a "neighbor," who in fact can be a wife, sibling, relative, friend, or other person not so closely related. The people live under the unrelenting threat that they may become the object of a neighbor's envy and fall ill as a consequence. Although diseases are attributed to the "winds" and the "airs," their true cause is always believed to be in sorcery (G. Reichel-Dolmatoff and A. Reichel-Dolmatoff 1961, 309). In the anxiety-charged atmosphere pervading the entire village, it is not the disease but what it stands for, the neighbor's ill will, which is feared the most. When a person falls ill, the first question in everybody's mind is who caused the disease.

The healthy individual living in Aritama is considered an asocial person and dangerous. To openly admit that one is healthy is to challenge the social order. It is socially more acceptable to complain and exaggerate the importance of any boil, cough, or sneeze. To suffer is the best way in Aritama to demonstrate that one is a well-meaning and harmless member of the community (G. Reichel-Dolmatoff and A. Reichel-Dolmatoff, 313).

If healthy individuals are dangerous, then sick people should enjoy a valued social role, and such is the case in Aritama. Sick persons occupy privileged positions in the social order of the village. Being sick allows individuals to neglect obligations, to reconcile themselves with former enemies, and to receive favors without having to return them. They escape from social responsibilities by merely uttering the words "I am sick." The announcement is beyond dispute; doubting it would be an unforgivable insult to the complainer's self-esteem and dignity, even if no symptoms are apparent. The claim of illness places an individual in a special category, on another level of experience, action, and cognition.

> A sick individual is never impure or evil, but is almost "sacred," sacred because world-controlling forces are involved—forces which have made him an instrument and a victim in order to demonstrate their power (G. Reichel-Dolmatoff and A. Reichel-Dolmatoff, 312).

Though less drastic than Aritama, other societies also provide roles for illness that offer variations and shades of concern for the sick person as a social being. In parts of Italy, for instance, when people become ill, they may serve as a catalyst to bring together members of the family and friends. There may even be social activities associated with someone's illness and a sense of disappointment if the person recovers before the appropriate social activities occur. Diseases are often considered to have social, ethical, or magical meaning. An illness may be expiation for evil committed by an ancestor or a relative. In Japan, all physical disease is naturally and automatically diagnosed in the context of the social relations of the patient.

Social bases of disease are sometimes recognized in American society, but they are suppressed from consciousness, stripped of magical and social significance, and called "psychosomatic," or stress-related. The role for handicapped people in the United States has become more functional, although the shift seems to reflect more a sense of fair play than a change in attitudes toward disease. While the handicapped are supported in wider roles in society, the elderly are often still assigned to homes for the aged, where their roles are severely limited. Americans perceive aging as a progressive loss of function, and so it is not surprising that social roles based on functionality narrow with age.

The lack of a social role for the sufferer in American culture is linked to the values of individualism and control. Individuals in the culture are presumed to exercise some control over disease. In characteristic fashion, this control usually refers to actions such as exercising, dieting, and undergoing physical examinations that prevent the onset of illness. In some approaches to holistic health, people are assumed to have actually caused their diseases by maintaining unhealthy states of consciousness. Because in some way the individual is the implied agent of illness, actually succumbing to a disease is a failure of control, and the person is temporarily ostracized from functional roles in society.

PERCEPTION
OF THE WORLD

For Americans, human beings are unique, having a quality that is absent in all other forms of life: a soul. It follows that no other forms of life in the physical world possess souls, so they are conceived of as material and mechanistic. Western science and technology have elevated human beings to a separate plane from which they observe and manipulate reality, an idea captured in both language and thought.

In many cultures, human beings are just one form of life differing from others only in degree. Nature is alive and animistic. Animals and even inanimate objects have their own essence. In parts of the non-Western world no dividing line separates humans from plants, rocks, rivers, mountains, and valleys. Some Hindus and Buddhists believe life itself continues in endless cycles in which a soul can assume an infinite variation of forms. During one cycle the soul may inhabit the shape of a man or woman and in another take another form—that of an animal, perhaps, or an insect (Arensberg and Niehoff 1964, 127-28).

The American straightforward and practical interpretation of human nature stands in contrast to the vast and intricate architecture of Indian thought about the world and humanity. The tradition of India, extending more than three thousand years into the past, combines religion and philosophy into a deep longing for infinity and the unknown and a deep regard for universal being. Religion regulates the most minute details of everyday life (Nakamura 1964, 157). An obvious example is found in the Hindu, who refrains from raising cattle for food because the cow is sacred. Even the cultivation of plants has been known to stir up religious questions. Similar concessions to nature are unlikely for Americans, who see themselves as separate from animals and plants.

While Christianity is committed to the doctrine that human beings are evil by nature, most Americans are unlikely to give the concept much thought. They more commonly see humans as a mixture of good and evil or as creatures of environment and experience. A more representative American view is to stress the human ability to change: "Modern American religion inclines generally toward a remarkable perfectionism and optimism" (Robin Williams 1961, 338) reflected in the deep conviction that human nature is perfectible—people can change for the better. Furthermore, perfectibility can be approached through rational means as well as the more traditional avenues of religious faith. Perhaps no people in history have believed as firmly as Americans in the ability of education to improve the individual. The belief in human perfectibility and progress takes precedence over the doctrine of original sin which acts more as a reason to change than as an immutable condition—human beings can change and improve, and it is their duty to do so. The implied agent in American culture is transformed by experience into a rational manipulator and controller of the environment.

Human Relationship to Nature

The chief arena of American history has been nature rather than society, civilization, or other peoples (Boorstin 1958, 175). Discovery of the New World rekindled a traditional European belief that an earthly paradise lay somewhere to the west. Reports of the first explorers returning to Europe from the New World were embellished by promoters of colonization with descriptions of fabulous riches, a temperate climate, and garden-like natural beauty (Nash 1973, 25). But instead of a paradise, the early settlers encountered a "howling," "dismal," and "terrible" wilderness that stretched far beyond the European imagination of what "wild" was: an island, a bog, a heath, a peak, or a settlement surrounded by uninhabited land (Nash, 26).

The first need of the arriving colonists was an assured supply of food, and they used any method that would produce quick results, regardless of how it exhausted the land (Boorstin 1958, 260-61). Once survival was assured, the harshness of life encouraged a backwoods conservatism in farming. The pioneers developed a virulent enmity toward the wilderness, using military metaphors to discuss the coming of civilization.

> Countless diaries, addresses, and memorials of the frontier period
> represented wilderness as an "enemy" which had to be conquered,

subdued, and vanquished by a pioneer army....The image of man and wilderness locked in mortal combat was difficult to forget. Advocates of a giant dam on the Colorado River system spoke in the 1950s of that eternal problem of subduing the earth and of conquering the wilderness while a President urged us in his 1961 inaugural address to conquer the deserts (Nash, 27).

The early image of the dismal wilderness as an enemy was in part replaced during the nineteenth century by a romantic vision, created from a distance by the children and grandchildren of pioneers and by city dwellers (Nash, 43-44). But the separation between man and nature survived and remains securely in place to this day. The divide between humans and nature and the bias against the wilderness have long traditions in the Western world. The ancient Greek, Pythagoras, separated the human mind from the physical world and in so doing set the conditions for science and quantification to subsume physical phenomena and mysticism. In the East, both the Chinese and Japanese celebrate wilderness and preserve an image more integrated with nature. Human beings are just another form of the physical world, not in opposition to it.

The dominant assumption in the United States is that nature and the physical world should be controlled in the service of human beings (see F. Kluckhohn and Strodtbeck 1961). The Americans' formidable and sometimes reckless drive to control the physical world is perhaps unmatched as a dominant assumption in any other major society. It is best expressed by the engineer's approach to the world, which is based on technology and applied to social spheres as social engineering and human resource management. Americans have thrived in the well-controlled environment thus created. The natural laws assumed to underlie the physical world seem to be harnessed to the production of material welfare and hence are at the service of human beings.

Alternative assumptions regarding the relationship between humans and the world exist as variants in American society and are dominant in many non-Western cultures. One view prevalent in much of Asia stresses the unity among all forms of life and inanimate objects. This assumption of integration is expressed beautifully in traditional Japanese architecture. The form and lines of buildings and temples and the surrounding gardens appeal to the eye as a unity between the natural environment and the man-made structures. The observer easily passes from one environment to another without experiencing the discontinuity found in moving in and out of American structures, which are usually built to dominate their surroundings.

In contrast to the value of objective control, the relationship between human beings and the world is subtle when described by a member of a culture where integration is the dominant assumption. The

Japanese philosopher Nishida considers the world of historical actuality to consist of the subject and the environment (Tsunoda et al. 1958,
868). The environment (world) shapes and is, in turn, shaped by the
subject (human being). Nishida apparently considers that the world of
historical actuality is the result of a dialectical process between environment and subject. He describes Occidental culture, on the whole,
as moving from the environment to the subject. Movement of this kind
yields a "center of gravity" in the environment, meaning in our terms
that nature and the physical world become the focus of cultural and
historical interest. Oriental culture, in contrast, may be thought to move
from subject to environment. The subject itself is negated and becomes
environment—in our terms, a part of the natural world. This aspect of
Japanese culture represents a common thread in Oriental culture. The
essence of its spirit is to become one in things and events and to create
an identity between subject and world (Tsunoda et al., 869).

The Western and the American view of nature has led to objectivity
about the world and the development of science and technology. The
contrasting view has found expression in Asian arts and religion. Yet,
Oriental subjectivism does not prevent the kind of scientific and technological development known in the West, as demonstrated by Japan's
industrialization. Nishida identifies an additional quality in the Japanese
that has provided the impetus for this development: congeniality toward people and receptivity to foreign influences. In addition, as noted
in an earlier chapter, Japanese perception is concrete. This allows the
Japanese—unlike Indians, for instance—to move from universal principles to a particular event. The concreteness of the Japanese spirit,
according to Nishida, affects individuals emotionally and transforms
them "from being that which is formed to that which forms" (Tsunoda et
al., 872). While it is often assumed that separation from the natural
world and a desire to control nature necessarily underlie technological
progress, Nishida's analysis shows that these Western assumptions can
be supplanted by a more integrated concept of human beings and
nature, which, in conjunction with other cultural characteristics, can
also form the basis of technological development.

Not all peoples in the world share the assumptions that humans either
control or integrate with the natural world. There are those who take a
fatalistic attitude toward their environment, who feel overwhelmed by it.
The Colombian mestizo considers nature to be dangerous and animated
by the presence of spirits:

> Sun, moon and stars, wind and rain, heat and cold, light and
> shadow—all are believed to have occasionally harmful powers
> over body and mind. The cool air near the river or the reflected

heat from rocks or trails are thought to be dangerous, the same as the shadow of certain trees or the damp of the forest. Dangers are seen everywhere in nature and to try to understand them or to overcome them would be considered as foolishness (G. Reichel-Dolmatoff and A. Reichel-Dolmatoff 1961, 440).

Not all fatalistic attitudes toward nature are driven by animism. The yearly drowning of hundreds of people at the mouth of the Ganges River when it floods seems to indicate an acceptance of this phenomenon as a fact of life. This attitude of helplessness in the face of nature parallels similar attitudes toward the social and political orders. These beliefs, and those of the people living in poverty in many cultures of the world, may be described as an assumption that humans are subjugated by their environment (F. Kluckhohn and Strodtbeck 1961).

Materialism and Property

Guided by their emphasis on material things, Americans abroad almost invariably judge the local society by American standards of material welfare. Considerations of physical comfort and health are primary in this judgment and may lead Americans to promote physical improvements and health measures—for instance, latrines and vaccines—that demonstrate little immediate value. The intended benefactors see no evidence that these measures are successful in promoting health. American dedication to preventive health measures relies more on cultural assumptions than on demonstrated evidence of effectiveness, which often requires sophisticated observations and successive measurements over a period of time.

Associated with material comfort is the American genius for devising and employing machines to provide efficiency and convenience in daily life. The Americans' faith in, and love for, machines goes abroad with them. American advisors and technicians exhibit a strong tendency to perceive their tasks as requiring the use of machinery. The mechanical products of American factories have been shipped overseas in large numbers and placed in the hands of operators who may not have the skills or the spare parts to maintain them, and so the machines soon fall idle. Americans are usually correct in recognizing that machines can facilitate the tasks at hand, but they frequently overlook the fact that American machines and culturally based attitudes toward their operation and maintenance are both integral parts of American technology. The former cannot be successfully exported without an acceptance of the latter.

The American stress on material things is associated with a belief in the inviolacy of private property, a value commonly asserted to be at the root of the Constitution and the American conception of democracy. The popular assumption that private property is inviolate has frequently led to friction between Americans and the citizens or bureaucracies of other nations, with subsequent repercussions at the highest levels of government. U.S. relations with Latin American countries have often been strained over the issue of private property, and danger to property is usually reason enough for American intervention or threats to use force. The Panama riots of 1964 provide an example of this sort of action and reaction. According to newspaper reports, American forces withheld fire until private property was threatened by the rioters. Also, negotiations between the United States and Latin American countries often revolve around the charge that American emphasis on the protection of private property too often results in the loss of human rights for the Latin Americans (Northrop 1946, 42-48; 94-98). The governments of these countries have sometimes expropriated American property, or even that of their own nationals, without what Americans feel to be valid reasons or fair recompense.

Countering the threat of communism as a justification for intervention can also be seen as resting partially on the value of private property. Whether or not American property is threatened, Americans react negatively to the idea that free enterprise—the economic system based on the concept of private property—will be denied to anyone in the world. Americans regard free enterprise as an inalienable right that is worth fighting for, even if the threat is thousands of miles away. Consequently, reports from Vietnam, China, and Nicaragua of suppression of free enterprise help convince Americans to support efforts at containment. It is notable in this regard that rapprochement with China in the 1970s was accompanied by reports that some free enterprise was being reinstituted in that country. These reports always garner lavish coverage in the American press.

At the interpersonal level, many Americans also encounter difficulties in their dealings with non-Western persons who do not share with them a clear distinction between private and public property. American Peace Corps volunteers and expatriates in Micronesia are sometimes discomfited by the prevailing assumption that nearly all property is public—that is, capable of being shared. Personal goods such as clothing and flashlights commonly end up in the open possession of other people. Americans may be outraged by this flagrant "theft" while Micronesians simply consider it sharing. If asked to, they are quite happy to return the articles. On a larger scale, Americans may react quite negatively to bribery of government officials and other methods of directing public funds into private pockets. In many cultures, possession of such property is a right accompanying a person's position in society. Although the practice is frequently controversial within these societies, public service at a high level may justify appropriation of funds for personal use. The simple distinction between private and public property is blurred.

Americans consider it almost a right to be materially well off and physically comfortable. They expect swift and convenient transportation (preferably in a vehicle they can control), a variety of clean and healthful foods, and comfortable homes equipped with numerous labor-saving devices, certainly including central heating and hot water. The government is expected to ensure that food and drug products meet acceptable standards and that appropriate public health measures are observed by all people and agencies whose activities can affect the public's welfare. Associated with the values of physical comfort and health is the acceptance of cleanliness as being nearly identical with health, if not with "godliness."

Americans tend to project this complex of values, centered around comfort and material well-being, to other peoples. They assume that given the opportunity, everyone else desires to be just like Americans in this regard. Hence, they are disturbed by the sight of the rich churches of Latin America standing in the midst of poverty, the Buddhist meditating among the suffering, the masses of homeless people living on sidewalks outside expensive restaurants, and other examples of the rejection of American values throughout much of the world by people whose concepts of life are aesthetic, spiritual, or fatalistic. While some level of material comfort is certainly desired by most people of the world, the criteria for its distribution and attainment cannot be accurately judged by American values.

Progress

The intersection in American life of the values of material property with material well-being yields the powerful social norm of progress. On the surface, progress may be said to be universal. Throughout the world people wish for basic physical comfort, necessary material possessions, and good health and medical services that reduce the physiological harshness of birth, disease, physical abnormalities, and death. Both science and technology serve the surface value of progress, which has often been adopted as a political slogan. For instance, *progresso* appears as part of the inscription on the Brazilian flag. But beneath the surface and beyond the cant of its slogans, the core of the American concept of progress receives mixed responses in some places, is unknown in others, and may be rejected in still other non-Western parts of the world. In Iran and some other Islamic countries, the Western concept of progress has been perceived as a threat to traditional ways of life and has engendered violent reactions.

These adverse reactions to progress are aimed at the American view of rational man, separate from nature, relatively independent of the social order, and living in an objective world where the final arbiter of the good and desirable is economics. Based on those values, most Americans tend to believe that the basic problems of the world are economic and that technology offers solutions. The pervasiveness of this view in developmental projects throughout the world and the attendant neglect of political and social factors in favor of technology is, at least in part, to blame for the unsuccessful projects of recent times that strew the Third World like the archaeological ruins of ancient civilizations. Instead of progress, some see economic and social retrogression in both the Third World and in some Western countries, including the United States. The uncertain performance of technology in social and economic development invites a deeper analysis of progress.

Humanistic concepts, which were intertwined with the idea of progress, took hold during the Age of Enlightenment in the epoch when the American colonies threw off British rule and formed the United States of America. The leading thinkers of the period were rationalists and humanists who rejected the original Christian view of humans as inherently evil—being born, living, and dying in sin. In their eyes, humans were perfectible, and human history involved a continuous development from the low, primitive life of "savages" to higher civilization with the European way of life at the pinnacle. (The dissident Rousseau was a voice in the wilderness, deifying nature and exalting a cult of sophisticated primitivism.) Human beings were conceived to be the creators of their own destiny, using civilization as an instrument for perfecting humanity.

In this early period of national development, technology in the minds of many Americans was already dedicated to the creation of something better. The rocky New England soil, the wide rivers, the expanse of the land, and the height of the mountains defined the drama of nation building as conquest of the wilderness. There was a shortage of hands for the struggle, and to turn the battle more quickly in their favor, the settlers accepted technology as an instrument for improving their control of the natural world. Its use seemed compatible with the perfectibility of humanity and with progress as measured by rationalism.

In the nineteenth century, scientists in the fields of geology, biology, botany, and anthropology began to look more closely at human and natural history. Charles Darwin propounded his theory of biological evolution, which was soon translated into Social Darwinism. The concept of progress was inherent in Social Darwinism and was manifest in the idea of cultural evolution. Americans readily accepted these ideas and typically judged progress in sociopolitical terms, for example as democratic processes, individual rights, and personal improvement. These fundamental American values produced ethnocentric views and stubborn barriers to effective cross-cultural relations.

While not everyone accepts the cumulative growth of technology as the exclusive standard of progress, there is probably no significant view rejecting technology and science as a criterion of progress (see Kroeber 1948, 304). However, Americans are more committed to technical expressions of behavior than perhaps any other people. Beginning with the construction of the first assembly line in the eighteenth century, Americans have demonstrated a drive to simplify and standardize human performance by guiding and controlling it with technology in a way that we have termed *technicism*.

A contrast to technicism is found with the English "roundabouts," which are frequently used to control traffic where two or more roads intersect to form a circle. The roundabout demands that motorists make careful judgments about entering and leaving the circle and changing lanes within it. Although roundabouts have been used in the United States, they have never been as favorably accepted as in Britain. They have been transformed into traffic-circles studded with traffic lights or stop signs. The judgment which the motorist has to make in the English round-about is replaced in the traffic circle by simple responses to "stop" and "go" signals. The American motorist's performance is simplified. The same point can be made with the American development and use of training methods, job descriptions, methods of management, and with the use of word processors, the automatic shift in automobiles, and exercise machines. Although all of these are found in many countries, the development of technicism in American society is second to none.

In addition to technicism, the American idea of progress stresses facts, logical analysis, and practical results. This style categorizes experience as either subjective or objective, a notion which is central to scientific thought. Objective descriptions of experience reduce individual phenomena to typical cases of universal laws (see H. Frankfort and H. A. Frankfort 1946, 11). Subjective descriptions of experience, such as inspirations, dreams, and other products of altered states of consciousness, carry little weight in American culture. In contrast to cultures such as the Senoi, where dream interpretation is reported to be central to everyday life (K. Stewart 1969), or to some Native-American cultures in which the people accept the revelations attained during altered states of consciousness, most mainstream

Americans ignore such experiences or, at best, relegate them to the realm of "personal growth." Although praising subjective creativity, Americans persist with rational technicism, undistracted by the potential contradiction.

Another American criterion for measuring progress is the detachment of the individual from social customs and rituals that often occur in gemeinschaft societies to inculcate and maintain social control. The American idea of progress involves a decline in the traditional "obsession with the outstanding physiological events of human life" (Kroeber, 304). Each phase of life—infancy, childhood, adolescence, maturity, old age—is a time with characteristic qualities. In gemeinschaft societies, the individual is typically limited to positions in society occupied by the family. In addition, the transition from one stage of life to another is assisted or celebrated by community rites. For instance, puberty is the time for the formation and exercise of social controls. In some societies boys endure severe physical and psychological trials in the rites of passage to manhood. Marriage and death also receive a great amount of community attention in such societies. American culture provides a contrasting example in most respects. The conditions of one's birth are considered circumstantial and can be overcome by the self-reliant individual. Life transitions are given passing notice at best and are not seen as opportunities for exercising social control.

Americans consider success to result from individual effort, competence, and originality. Failure cannot be explained on the basis of physiological events such as fatigue, health, or mood cycles since these are the responsibility of the individual, who should take them into account in directing his or her performance. In contrast, the French find it more acceptable than Americans to plead fatigue, and the Japanese may dismiss commitments on the basis of illness. Brazilians, among others, seem more attentive than Americans to moods, and on occasion they find it useful to plot the mood cycles of people in positions of responsibility. Americans value competence and skill, which can be interpreted as technicism and which illustrates individualism. Americans define personal performance as a consequence of their ability and effort rather than as an outcome of life circumstance. Illness and other conditions in life may impair performance, but they do not control or contribute to it.

The extraordinary preference for individual and psychological explanations shown by Americans is part of their attitude toward progress. Because progress is seen as a composite of individual successful efforts, Americans may feel that progress is not possible in other terms, such as social development or political change. Their resistance to these more conceptual explanations of progress may generate difficulties in cooperation and communication with people who prefer them—the French and Japanese, among others.

Bound up with the idea of progress in American culture is a feeling of general optimism towards the future. Most Americans feel that through their efforts they can bring about a better future without compromising the welfare and progress of others. That there is enough for everyone is a valid belief for people living in a large country with an expanding economy and abundant resources. Foster's idea of the Image of the Limited Good, mentioned earlier in the context of achievement, again suggests a contrast to the American's expansive view of the world.

> By "Image of Limited Good," I mean that broad areas of peasant behavior are patterned in such fashion as to suggest that peasants view their social, economic and natural universe—their total environment—as one in which all of the desired things in life, such as land, wealth, health, friendship, love, manliness and honor, respect and status, power and influence, security and safety—*exist in finite quantity* and *are always in short supply,* as far as the peasant is concerned. Not only do these and other "good things" exist in finite and limited quantities, but in addition *there is no way directly within peasant power to increase* the available quantities. It is as if the obvious fact of land shortage in a densely populated area applied to all other desired things—not enough to go around. "Good," like land, is seen as inherent in nature—there to be divided and redivided if necessary, but not to be augmented (Foster 1965, 296).

Obviously, the exuberant optimism of Americans for future improvement is based on the opposite of the above view—an image of "unlimited good." With no restriction on the good available to all, individuals can progress, that is, acquire a larger quantity of the good for themselves without concern for depriving others of the same opportunity.

Progress and the Concept of Time

The American social norm of progress incorporates a number of assumptions, among them the basic one of *lineal time.* Progress is associated with the view that time is like a river flowing in one direction from its source to its mouth. The assumption of lineal time allows for a division into segments of past, present, and future. The temporal flow proceeds from the past, barely slows for the present, and rushes to the future. Americans find it important to cope with this flow ("keeping up with the times") and to look ahead ("keeping an eye on the future"), but the temporal orientation downstream should be qualified as "near future." (For businesspeople, six months, or perhaps one year, down river is a reasonable projection. More distant futures are usually considered impractical.)

The American notion of lineal time, particularly the hesitation to project to distant futures, finds parallels in psychology. It is possible to equate the present with perception and the past with memory, but no comparable mental faculty has been discovered that monitors the future. It is possible to make a case for the naturalness of both present and past orientations, but the future appears to be a cultural invention. Since the psychological experience of time is more like duration than flow, the perception of the present extends seamlessly into the past, and memory becomes a reconstruction of events lost to perception. The assumptions of lineal time and of the future, combined with the American value to project to the near future, are suited to a rational view of the world. One can distinguish various moments in time, note their sequence, and signal the relation between events of one moment to those of another, labeling preceding events "cause" and those following "effects." This causal view is often combined with one-dimensional descriptions of events, leading to the American predilection for explaining what happens in a single cause and effect sequence. ("Tom succeeded because he graduated with a high grade point average." Or "X was the best company to be awarded the contract. After all, X's profits had increased steadily over the past five years.") Although oversimplified, lineal time combined with Euclidean space strengthens the American belief in the individual's ability to master the environment—to "cause" progress.

Neither the concept of lineal time nor the idea of projecting the future is universal. Some people conceive of time as *cyclic*, associated with the recurrent changes of seasons. A close look at Hindu thought in India reveals that the concept of cycles extends far beyond the round of the seasons, or even the basic cycle of birth, life, and death, into an infinite and abstract universe of unending cycles (Boorstin 1983, 558).

The Chinese also perceive time as cyclic, but it does not usually reach the level of abstraction common in the West and India (Granet 1950, 86-113). The traditional Chinese concept of time is more in the nature of an expansion of the present into both the past and the future, with humans occupying the center of the stage. Rather than existing as an abstract quality, each cycle or period of time has definite limits that coincide with the beginning and end of a unified train of events. Futhermore, temporal relationships are practically indistinguishable from spatial relationships: an event (or an object) may be contiguous with the one before it or after it, but there is not necessarily a causal relationship between them. In effect, time does not provide the Chinese with a rational means of explanation and prediction as does the American concept. The Chinese demonstrate a much greater situation-centeredness and seek an explanation for a specific happening according to other factors occurring at the same time as the event in question. Certain events naturally go together. This view of time inclines the Chinese to integrate with the environment rather than master it and to adapt to a situation rather than change it. Mao, of course, attempted to alter these traditional attitudes, though how much success he had is open to question.

The assumption of lineal time replacing the cyclic notion of rotating seasons and the invention of the future, ironically, appear to have been generated together with the idea of history. The ancient Hebrews appear to have been the first to conceive of past events and of historical figures creating the events of the present. Once the Hebrews broke out of the link of cycles, they imagined a future state associated with their political subjugation. They came to believe that God would free them from bondage, making them into an independent nation in God's own time. The idea of a future was taken over by the Christians, who transformed God's time into man's time. The message that Christ might return to earth in the lifetime of the believer was a powerful incentive for receiving Christian baptism. The Christian Church consciously believed in lineal time and a future, and the modern world inherited these assumptions critical for the concept of progress.

The linking of history and the future set the stage for the notion of progress as continuous evolutionary development.

> In the sphere of human culture, which was man-made, there was continuous progress and transformation in the very organization of human life and society, as well as in the number and variety of human inventions and discoveries.... Culture history was progressive precisely because it was continuous and did not involve any radical breaks with the past. This meant also that time was an essential factor in the evolution of human culture and that time made for progress (Bidney 1953, 682-83).

With the scientific support of the theory of evolution, Americans see progress as ascending from the primitive past along a path in time toward a future in which the impediments of nature are dominated by individual human will and technology.

In India, perception of the past remained enmeshed in cyclic assumptions. Hindus did not develop a clear notion of past events linked in a great chain of history. To the north of India, the Chinese developed the concept of lineal time, but the cyclic assumption remained dominant. The Chinese view of history, even today, is sensitive to the present as well as the past. As events unfold, the Chinese may prudently rewrite the past to bring it in line with events of today. In both India and China, Western beliefs in progress and evolution acquire unusual forms from the perspective of American culture.

Quantification

Another fundamental aspect of the American view of progress is the importance of concreteness. But Americans do not require that they be able to touch, see, or in some other way personally encounter an object in order to establish concreteness, as the Japanese do. For Americans, the essential quality is measurability. They see the world as having dimensions that can be quantified. Apparently, every quality or experience can be at least partially quantified—if only as the first or last, least or most, biggest or smallest. Many otherwise unmeasurable phenomena may receive an arbitrarily assigned numerical value, such as ratings of individual preferences or other comparisons that simply translate subjective feeling into a number. Criteria that define success and failure are statistically measured, as are amounts of work, levels of ability, intelligence, and quality of performance. Even the number of minutes visitors spend with the president is routinely reported by the press.

The quantification of the world and experience is deeply ingrained in Americans, and it is only with difficulty that they can understand the reactions of others to this practice. To some foreigners the description of, say, the Washington Monument in terms of statistical information devitalizes the experience of seeing it. Americans are known to tourist guides in foreign countries for asking questions about size, cost, or age ("How big is it" or "How much did it cost") while visitors from other cultures (including Europeans) tend to ask questions about history or aesthetics. Sometimes the attempt to quantify can even be threatening, as if the numbers used in some way reproduce the phenomenon being measured and destroy its reality. The Kpelle of Liberia, for example, refrain from counting chickens or other domestic animals aloud to avoid some harm befalling them. The same practice has prevailed in other non-Western societies, including those described in the Old Testament "where it was not considered proper to count people aloud lest some die" (Gay and Cole 1967, 41).

The American use of statistics, such as the statement that an average family contains two and one-half children, assails the dignity of the individual for some foreigners. A similar reaction may be elicited by concepts such as the man-hour, which may include the efforts of one or several people expended over periods from minutes to many hours. Although such concepts as the man-hour are considered practical and efficient by Americans and form the basis of planning in many American organizations, their use is not necessarily considered commendable by others for whom only a qualitative feeling, an impression, has the character of concreteness which Americans can evidently find in numbers and charts.

Quantification of phenomena captures the essence of the American concept of progress. Insofar as they can express events in numbers, they can determine chains of causality with statistical reliability and fashion interventions in the flow of events with machinelike precision. When human behavior is also quantified, it becomes objective and can be treated like other controllable environmental forces. In areas that really count for Americans—economic gain and material comfort—the achievement of progress can be ascertained by measuring it.

Health and Disease

The American perception of the world is at the center of attempts to introduce health measures abroad. Improvement in public health is primarily achieved through programs of prevention in which success is measured by decreases (incidence of disease, injury, or infant mortality), and by increases (longevity). The evidence for the success or failure of programs of prevention is concealed in statistical rates of occurrences distributed in time and place. The cause and effect links for disease, many injuries, and for emotional disturbances are not readily perceptible for most people, including Americans, who tend to see the world in simple terms, especially in matters involving action. They regard the value of public health measures as self-evident, or at least as easily demonstrable. Thus, the average American finds it difficult to explain to non-Americans why they should make themselves sick or uncomfortable by submitting to vaccination when they are not sick at the moment, or why villagers should go to the trouble of using only clean water to prevent illness. The reasons for recommending both the vaccine and the clean water actually reside in an ability to anticipate consequences in the future. Essentially, preventive measures require individuals to anticipate a future event and connect it with present conditions and actions by means of a cause-and-effect relationship. This outlook requires an orientation to the future and faith in people's ability to control it through measures taken in the present. The optimistic belief that present action can change future events is an American view that is not always shared by persons who are oriented toward the past or present or who are fatalistic.

The attitudes people have toward health, the body, and the determinants of disease are important in establishing health measures. Western practices are firmly rooted in the concept of the body as a biological mechanism susceptible to invasion by external agents (germs, viruses), to unfavorable environmental conditions, and to dietary deficiencies which may cause disease and malnutrition. For Americans, disease and health are states of the biological organism, an entity separate from other aspects of the world. Many non-Western peoples have explanations for disease which are congruent with their different assumptions and values. In some of these cultures, disease is explained in ways that, in the American view, are irrational. An American in one African country reports that a sick child grinding his teeth is a sign of the evil eye while another writer says that in a Latin American republic, symptoms of malnutrition are often ascribed to "supernatural and other causes which bear little or no resemblance to Western medical explanations" (Erasmus 1959, 390). Villagers may continue to draw water from a contaminated pond because the resident water spirit would be vengefully jealous if another source of water was used. These and innumerable other practices may continue because the clear American distinction between humans and nature does not exist in many non-Western belief systems. Thus, there is little support for the Western materialistic explanation of disease.

In a subtle manner, the American idea of an independent person in control of the environment, together with an optimistic anticipation of the future, furnish the basis for public health measures. These techniques may be defended on the basis of social norms such as cleanliness, but most Americans employ them out of conformity to underlying values that lie outside their own understanding. Conscious or not, these assumptions go abroad with American advisors and volunteers and may be detrimental to the long-term success of public health projects. While the introduction of American or Western health practices may be effective in the short term, misjudging local values, mindsets, and social behavior patterns may result in abandonment of the project when the Americans depart.

Public health measures in the United States are buttressed by the specialized roles played by physicians (of different specialties), nurses, public officials, technicians, and scientists of all types. In many societies, these specialized roles may not be clearly distinguished, may not exist at all, or may go unfilled because too few people are trained to fill them. Health measures that are introduced will continue only if advisors adapt them to local social organizations, beliefs, and practices. In a potable water project in Laos, for instance, wells dug on village grounds fell into disrepair since no one in the village would naturally assume responsibility for maintaining them. Wells dug on the grounds of Buddhist monasteries were maintained and even improved although the need for the wells was no greater there than on the village grounds. The difference in result can be attributed to the organization of the monks in the Buddhist monastery, who had preexisting roles that included effectively maintaining shared facilities (Arensberg and Niehoff 1964, 112). Clearly, attention to social context is critical if innovative public health measures are to prevail.

PERCEPTION
OF THE SELF

Dimensions of the Self

The American self-concept is the integral assumption of the culture. Americans naturally assume that each person is not only a separate biological entity, but also a unique psychological being and a singular member of the social order. Deeply ingrained and seldom questioned, the dominant American self, in the form of individualism, pervades action and intrudes into each domain of activity.

Individualism can be identified by drawing a boundary around the person that separates the self from other people. Inside the boundary American selfhood has appeared in our analysis as the implied agent in perception, the individual source of action in activity, an independent individual in social relations, and a rational controller of the environment. The self is *subjective,* essentially outside awareness and inaccessible to outsiders.

Americans associate the self with words such as *me* and *my* (Deese 1965, 205), indicating the unexamined privacy of self-references. Its personal subjectivity sets the stage for one of the sharpest dichotomies of American culture—the distinction between self and others. Outside the boundary are others, whose behavior is attributed to their own subjectivity but who may also be seen as objective causes for our behavior (Houston 1985, 266-67). Social causation and ideology apply to others, but the self remains subjective.

The nature of their self-concept prevents Americans from fully comprehending that in other cultures people may not think that their own selves are much different from other selves. Many Indians, for instance, believe that all selves are manifestations of the same underlying consciousness: "In India the tendency is not to regard another's self as an independent subject of action opposed to one's self" (Nakamura 1964, 93). The difference between self and other is of the same order as the difference between other and other. But in American culture, the self subverts the perception that the difference between the self and other is the same as the difference between a first other and a second other. The perceived subjectivity of the self endows individuals with uniqueness of perception, placing priority on personal preferences, opinions, choices, and creativity. In contrast, the Japanese place emphasis on understanding and sharing general attitudes of others.

The radical subjectivism of the American self makes it incomparable with selves in other cultures until the concept is described at a more abstract level. The concept of self implies a faint and diffuse constellation of values and patterns of thinking which supply to the person a sense of continuity in time and the reflexive ability to introspect. As individuals move from event to event in their daily lives, they each have a subjective feeling of the same person, the *me*, participating in the events and reflecting upon them. The concept of the self answers the question of what it is that underlies the awareness of continuity.

Americans base their awareness of self on the assumption of doing. For instance, in one training workshop conducted by two German social scientists with a group of about twenty Americans and ten Europeans, the participants were asked to reach an agreement on the meaning of American individualism. Most of the predominantly American audience was satisfied with a definition of *independent* and *self-reliant* as "each one doing his own thing" (Emminghaus and Haupert 1989, 4). This view offers a vivid image of the subjective, private self that serves as the center coordinating activities. The American base for individualism contrasts with the German. In their thinking, Germans tend to stress history. Typically, they also know more about the social actualities of society such as language, traditions, and ideology than Americans. The German individual's attitudes toward political, social, economic, and humanistic issues become part of the person's identity. Americans generally do not assimilate such sentiments as part of the inner person. In the American self, there is a remarkable absence of community, tradition, and shared meaning which impinge upon perception and give shape to behavior (Cushman 1990, 600). The concept of self to Americans is singular; it is, in a sense, empty, something to be filled—or fulfilled. Self-realization or, in Maslow's terms, "self-actualization" is dependent upon doing. German identity, in contrast, is full and is dependent on becoming, knowing, and feeling. The American self may be portrayed as a quantum or unit of the culture, since intentions are not fulfilled except by achievements reflecting the individual rather than a member of the society. To be American is not part of the American self, but in Germany, the debate on identity has raged for two hundred years and continues unabated today.

On the other side of the globe from Germany, China offers a second instructive contrast to the American "empty" self. Among the Chinese, the self-concept has deep roots in the social stratum of the society. Identities of the people are inclined to form around the lineal family, including ancestors and future progeny. This implies that anything that has been done, is done, or will be done by members of the family is an action of the self. Continuity of the Chinese self thus spans generations and includes a wide range of events experienced by family members. In contrast, the American self-boundaries, at their greatest circumference, are likely to extend only as far as the nuclear family at any given moment in time. More typically, Americans do not identify with the actions of their own parents or their own children outside a given moment of shared experience. The American abstract view of time may even deprive the subjective and empty self of reflecting upon one's own behavior in the past as being "oneself." Continuity for Americans lies mainly in the immediate personal choices they make.

Another contrast is found with the complexity of Japanese selfhood (Lebra 1976, 156-68). The first member of a Japanese psychological duality is *honne*, an inarticulate and private sensibility of self. Honne is usually understood to be emotion, and in this form it is roughly comparable to the subjectivity of the American self. Honne is the source of feeling, sensitivity, and energy, but it is subject to the command of *tatemae*, which can be roughly described as the "social face" (Lebra, 136). The Japanese see themselves as inseparable from social face in the form of concrete networks of persons held together by obligations among members and forming a more extended social nexus (Nakamura 1964, 409-17). The Japanese self is usually described as an actualization of these social relations, and its continuity is based on the ongoing fulfillment of reciprocal obligations. The stress on human relations among members of a social nexus, rather than on single individuals, contrasts sharply with Americans, who participate in groups as individuals. Americans, generally, do not derive their identities from group interaction.

In many cultures individuals may subscribe to a perception of the self similar to that of Americans, but they do it in the context of the search for the meaning of existence, as in Buddhism, or as embodied in the concept of sacredness, as in Christianity. In social interaction, however, constraints of birth and circumstances prevail over the broader "self" concept. The social self may be rooted in an occupation, a family affiliation, an ethnic group, or a locale and thus be more narrowly conceived. The narrower the perception of the self, the more precisely delineated will be the type of contact individuals will have with others, including contact with people from other cultures (Mead 1963, 5). Their social interactions will seem to be set and unchanging, and their ability to be practical in choosing courses of action will seem limited. Americans tend to use the more narrowly defined roles as subsidiary definitions of self, while the major definition remains that of an individual human being of male or female gender. This wider perception of self allows Americans considerable freedom of choice in their actions in contrast to members of cultures where role is primary.

When confronted with people who do not locate the self within the individual, most Americans are bewildered. That the self can be centered in a role or in a grouping of some sort is to them a culturally preposterous idea. American foreign student advisors may display impatience with Chinese and other Asian students whose actions are guided by family considerations, especially when these students make career and life decisions that are detrimental to themselves but in compliance with the desires of others in their identity network. The advisors may be impelled to counsel them on the virtues of individuality—on watching out for themselves. To the Asian students, the family members **are** themselves. Similarly, Americans may be confused when their Japanese associates reject a practical and logical course of action because it might cause someone to lose face. Where this wider definition of self prevails, behaviors can best be understood as intentions to preserve affiliations in groups and identity networks and only secondarily to achieve personal goals.

When working abroad, Americans are often driven by the prominence of their individualism to clash with foreign associates whose identities are based on social meaning. For example, Bolivians will insist that their country has one of the most advanced systems of social welfare in the world, pointing as proof to the country's constitution, where social welfare provisions are clearly spelled out. Informed Americans may object to this claim, pointing out that Bolivian workers do not receive the benefits their constitution promises; therefore, according to American logic, Bolivia does not have a good welfare system. To Bolivians (and other Latin Americans), it is the abstraction that is important, but to Americans it is the individual benefits that matter. This difference in frame of reference is a recurrent issue between Americans and foreign associates.

Other abstract concepts of the self are even further removed from the individual self-reference of Americans, for example, when the self is completely submerged in or subservient to a state or to a cause dominated by a charismatic leader. Fanaticism and devotion to a cause or to a country (e.g., the Germans under Hitler or the Iranians under the

Ayatollah Khomeini) are little understood by Americans, who conceive of the state as an entity that exists to serve them. In the American view, the state assures individuals their freedom and rights, grants them security and protection, but respects their autonomy by not interfering unduly in their personal lives. That this view does not always correspond with reality does not lessen its importance in American politics or its significance as a basis for judging other systems.

Individualism and Individuality

The American concept of an individual self is rooted in a philosophical tradition represented by John Locke, a seventeenth-century English philosopher. Locke asserted that the biological individual is the basic unit of nature.[1] Social systems derive from the interactions of individuals who exist prior to the social order and who are acting in their self-interest (Bellah et al. 1985, 143). This view was influential in early American history, as was its application in economics by Adam Smith, who suggested that the "invisible hand" of self-interest coordinates free enterprise systems. But it was Benjamin Franklin who epitomized early American individualism in his writings and suggested that "God helps those who help themselves" (Bellah et al., 32-33).

The American stress on the individual as a concrete point of reference begins at a very early age. An episode from an American family demonstrates the encouragement of autonomy in children. It is early in the morning and the mother has placed her baby daughter, who is less than one year old, in her highchair and is preparing to give breakfast to the child. The mother selects two different kinds of baby cereal, each kind packaged in a box of distinctive color. The mother holds up a box in each hand before the child and encourages the small girl to select the one she wants. Before age one, the child has already learned to express her own preferences and make her own decisions, at least with regard to food.

In most societies such extreme forms of personal preference would not be cultivated, or tolerated. The child would be given what the mother considered best or what the mother thought social norms dictated. But American society implicitly accepts that children should be encouraged to make decisions for themselves, develop their own opinions, solve their own problems, have their own possessions, and, in general, learn to view the world from the point of view of the self.

---

[1] Although the concept of individualism can be traced to seventeenth-century English thought, the actual term was coined by Alexis de Tocqueville in his study, *Democracy in America*, first published in 1835.

The American is not expected to bow without question to the wishes of authority, be it vested in family, traditions, or some organization. Failure to develop self-reliance is seen as a threat to achieving material success. For instance, in a study of poor families in Appalachia, the researchers attributed the lack of economic development in that area to the fact that the families do not allow their children to challenge the authority of their parents in the way that most American families do. The children therefore grow up without the ability to change the economic situation in which they find themselves. The intense self-centeredness that most Americans learn in the home from the day they are born is manifest in the individualism that plays an important role in the American value system.

Individualism is the perception of the self as the cultural quantum in society. The self acts as the operational unit in action and as the locus of control for behavior. In the workplace, decisions are motivated largely by the pursuit of self-interest in career goals and other areas of personal achievement (Bellah et al., 27-39). American workers show relatively little loyalty to their organizations; their decision to stay or move on to another company is likely to be based on salary and advancement opportunities. American administrators and managers are mobile for the same reasons; and, in addition, self-interest may figure extensively into their supervisory decisions. For instance, incoming managers may routinely replace existing key employees with their own people and dismantle ongoing projects to make way for their own ventures. A common interpretation of these actions is that the managers wish to take personal credit for all activities under their jurisdiction.

American individualism may engender distrust when it is practiced abroad. For instance, in a Scandinavian study of joint ventures with Americans, several complaints were registered about the management style of the American managers. One Scandinavian observed that to understand American decision making in business, it was necessary to know the personal career plans of the decision makers since the Americans made decisions that furthered their own careers rather than the prosperity of the joint venture. A second Scandinavian compared the actions of an incoming American manager to a "new broom" who swept clean the projects of the predecessor. The new manager typically put his lawyers to work reviewing the contracts with Scandinavian companies, searching for legal loopholes which would allow termination of those least profitable for the American company. Absence of legal openings did not always deter the American from using legal technicism to arbitrarily terminate unprofitable contracts. On occasion, American companies threatened to sue the Scandinavian company. Unable to afford the costs of defending their interests in court against the larger American company, the Scandinavians buckled under to American intimidation. Both Scandinavians bemoaned the lack of "honor" that has characterized joint ventures with Americans since the 1970s.

In social relations, individualism asserts its influence as well—on morality, such as sexual and social behavior, or on ethics, such as prejudice or financial matters. In these areas, Americans may exhibit doubt about what is wrong and right. They are likely to resolve social and moral uncertainty by appealing to the subjective feelings of self attached to beliefs, motives, and values. The subjective side of individualism has been called *expressive,* and it has been identified with the pursuit of personal happiness and material comfort and with freedom of expression which has been released from outside constraints and conventions (Bellah et al., 27-39). The application of individualism to morality and ethics frequently yields only two conditions that distinguish right behavior from wrong; first, that all parties directly involved in the action consent (such as in sexual behavior), and, second, that no one else is harmed by the action. When these two conditions are met, Americans turn to personal criteria for further direction, which allows them a broad field of choice of action.

The personal naturalism of expressive individualism is represented in attitudes toward the fine arts. Americans resist canons of aesthetics that tell them what good painting or good literature is, preferring instead the position, "If you like it, it's good." The function of art is fulfilled by deriving pleasure from looking at the painting or reading the book, and it is not necessary to appeal to theories of aesthetics to classify objects as "art" or "not art." This attitude illustrates both individualism and the American rejection of sociological and philosophical principles, which are replaced with a simple psychological theory of preference, "I like it."

This untrammeled freedom of choice and autonomy of the self does not exist in a social vacuum. Social control and even a form of social coercion are found in the nebulous but imperative expectation that the individual will choose as everyone else wants him or her to. As Florence Kluckhohn has put it, the individual is "free to be like everyone else" (F. Kluckhohn and Strodtbeck 1961, 23). Since the individual in American society is a free agent, the pressures on the individual are informal but pervasive. The undifferentiated self lacks the resources to protect the individual from pressures to conform—from family, friends, the public, or associates in groups to which one belongs. The interface between the individual and the agents of conformity in the culture is like a frontier which affects all areas of the personality uniformly. Those agents, including government and the media, cross that frontier informally, almost surreptitiously, prepared to persuade or sell. If individuals choose to deviate from the norms expected of them, they run up against the American intolerance of "rate-busters" and "nonconformists." They fail to receive the fruits of approval, esteem, and popularity which are so important in American culture.

Americans abroad, valuing individualism, are sometimes surprised to meet people who display strong personalities, distinctive personal convictions, and idiosyncratic behavior. These people seem to be individualists in every sense of the word, and yet they live in cultures where authority (usually family) or tradition exercises considerable control over the person. This apparent contradiction points to a distinction between individualism and *individuality* (F. Kluckhohn and Strodtbeck, 23-24).

Individualism of Americans reflects a continuous frontier between the individual and the culture. In the interface between the person and the culture in some European cultures (English, for example), individuals are subject to the norms of their families, groups, and social class conventions but are allowed considerable room to cultivate personal expression as long as it does not interfere with social obligations to family and tradition. Individuality then implies the cultivation of differences but at the same time acceptance of obligations in narrow but well-defined spheres. With individualism, the self is the basic unit of the culture and the pressures from the society are ill defined but pervasive and uniform in all spheres of activity. The individualism of American culture does not prescribe specific obligations for the individual, but, at the same time, it affords much less freedom of self-expression.

Self-Reliance and Mythic Individualism

Of all the cultural norms associated with individualism, probably none is stronger than the idea of *self-reliance.* Americans talk fondly of "pulling themselves up by their bootstraps" to become "self-made men" (and women). Many of these ideas are based on myths of the Old West, where brave settlers carved out a new life without outside aid and lonely cowboys who shot straight imposed justice on equally lonely outlaws. This myth of the Old West has been tarnished by commentators such as Daniel Boorstin (1965), who has marshaled evidence to show it was casual, informal groups, readily formed and easily dissolved, that colonized the wilderness and stamped the American character from the beginning with its group consciousness. Still, the myth lives on, now in the form of the lonely detective or irate citizen who challenges the system imposes law and order personally. As with all myths, of course, it is more important that they be believed than that they be true. It should be noted that, like all myths, the mythic ideal occasionally appears in reality, producing heroes (the individual who bucks the system and wins; the inventor who creates a radical new and successful product in the garage).

Bellah et al. (1985, 144-47) have termed the social norm of self-reliance *mythic individualism:*

> Clearly, the meaning of one's life for most Americans is to become one's own person, almost to give birth to oneself. Much of this process...is negative. It involves breaking free from family, community, and inherited ideas (82).

> It is as if the myth says you can be a truly good person, worthy of admiration and love, only if you resist fully joining the group (145).

The mythic stories of cowboys and detectives carry within them the profound ambivalence about self-reliance that characterizes the reality of individualism.

> There we find the fear that society may overwhelm the individual and destroy any chance of autonomy unless he stands against it, but also recognition that it is only in relation to society that the individual can fulfill himself and that if the break with society is too radical, life has no meaning at all (144).

The fierce, utilitarian self-reliance originally advocated by Ralph Waldo Emerson has, to an extent, given way to more expressive forms. For many Americans, the search for autonomy, self-actualization, and personal growth has supplanted the mythic desire to save frontier towns single-handedly from outlaw bands. The social norm persists, however, as an avoidance of dependence. Since Americans can envisage few fates worse than dependence, they continue to stress self-reliance as a guard against desirable socialization becoming dreaded conformity.

Although rugged self-reliance lives on mainly in movies, Americans abroad are often quick to fall back on mythic individualism and fault the foreigner who shows no desire to be self-reliant. The meaning of this social norm is neither translatable into other languages nor is it self-evident in many other cultures. For example, in Latin American Spanish, *self-reliance* is translated as "independence" and carries the suggestion of political and social freedom as well as the implication of solitary action. The idea of the self as the source and sole limiting factor in action is missing. Indeed, the whole concept of self-reliance itself is not particularly congenial to Latin Americans, who have a strong attachment to their families and immediate groups. They do not deplore dependence as Americans do. Among the Chinese, dependence on others is desirable, for it strengthens the relationship among people and affirms a broad definition of self. Chinese parents, for instance, take pride in being dependent on their children and being supported by them. In Japan, to be self-reliant in the way it is meant by Americans is to be without an identity. In traditional Japan, the term *leaving home*, which is a normal event in an American's life, meant to enter the monastic life—to abandon all ties of ordinary existence (Bellah et al., 57). For the Japanese, dependence is a virtue. Americans working in Japan and elsewhere who automatically expect their clients or associates to value self-reliance or to be responsive to pleas on its behalf are swimming against the current of values in much of the non-Western world.

Self-Motivation

Unlike other societies, American culture does not attribute particular meaning to place of birth, family, or the other ascriptive considerations that can be used to define the self. The existence of the individual is a matter of chance. Self-definition is determined primarily by personal achievement. Individuals should set their own goals and then decide how to pursue them. Motivation, in the sense of long-range goals, as well as motivation for a specific and immediate task, should originate with the individual.

Because they dislike identification with groups and causes, Americans tend also to dislike others' motives being applied to them. They strongly resist motivation in the form of orders, injunctions, and threats emanating from authority. Probably it is this dislike that makes Americans suspicious and only grudgingly accepting of the military. While fighting and violence seem acceptable to most Americans, it is the overt authority of the military, based on enforced discipline and the prerogatives of rank that derive from status rather than achievement, that they find repugnant (Gorer 1948, 39). This is the case even though the American military characteristically deemphasizes the power and privileges of rank—in marked contrast to the military in most other countries.

The American concept of the self and self-motivation causes stress both in American institutions and in the general life-style prevalent in the United States. If coercion is disapproved of and authority rejected, how do Americans manage to coordinate their lives and activities? The answer is through *persuasion*. The desire to act according to the wishes of others is instilled in the individual by means of examples, incentives, and subtle hints of failure. It is perhaps the threat of failure that contributes the most to persuasion by providing an appeal to self-interest and the desire for achievement. Coercion, when necessary, is ideally applied informally so that the power of authority is masked. If possible, individuals are allowed to maintain the illusion that what they are compelled to do actually represents their own decisions made in their own self-interest. In the final analysis, it is not the conformity and the inevitability of authority that Americans dislike but the assault upon the self—the subjective and private core of the individual.

Although Americans tend to reject overt authority over people, they accept authority employed over things and processes. Control over natural resources, goods, services, and money is considered either natural or desirable (Gorer, 40-41). Organizations formed around this view of control ironically turn people into objective "resources." Individuals rightly feel that they and their associates are inherently replaceable, however much they may be valued. While seemingly contradictory to the value of individualism, this feeling apparently spurs the American on to greater achievement and avoidance of failure (Henry 1963, 29).

By defining people according to achievement, Americans can fragment their own personalities or those of other people. They do not have to accept others in their totality to be able to work with them; they may disapprove of the politics, hobbies, or personal life of associates and yet still work with them effectively. It is this trait of seeing others as fragmented, combined with the desire to achieve, that provides Americans with the motivation to cooperate. In contrast, people with ascriptive motivation tend to react to others as whole persons. Frequently, they cannot cooperate or work with a person of different religion, belief, or ethical code because they have rejected the other person totally. This tendency in other cultures to accept or reject another person as a whole is at the root of the observation that Americans abroad have to watch every act, for what they do away from work affects attitudes toward them in the workplace.

Another important consequence of the American tendency to view people in fragments is that actions, thoughts, and intents are evaluated separately. Legally, an American cannot be held liable for harboring undesirable thoughts. On the other hand, demonstration of desirable intentions is grounds for excusing an undesirable action. In parts of the non-Western world, however, there is no clear differentiation of this kind. Thus, indication of "wrong thoughts" may be grounds for censure even though undesirable actions may not have resulted from them. And actions, if wrong, are not easily pardoned; regardless of the intentions behind them, they are remembered. These values are found in the synthesis of action, thought, feeling, and intent of the Chinese. Some practical consequences of this integration are illustrated in a power struggle within the Chinese Communist party in 1954 (Ravenholt 1964, 175-84).

Two members of the central authority of Communist China, Kao
Kang and Jao Shushih, were ousted from power and deprived of all
titles and authority. The two men were accused of various "crimes."
The accusations against Kao Kang were that his crimes were "substantially those of violating basic tenets" (Ravenholt, 177). The charges
were substantiated by incidents that had occurred during the previous
twenty years, a period during which Kao Kang had exercised his
greatest power and influence. Essentially, Kao Kang was confronted
with his whole history with no effort made to isolate significant criminal
actions. The whole man was judged. The same strategy was employed
against Jao Shushih who was accused of defiant acts, crimes of attitude,
and crimes in the "sphere of thought." In his case, as in Kao Kang's,
there was little if any distinction made among actions, intentions, and
spheres of thought (Ravenholt, 175-84).

Resistance to Systems of Thought

Americans are pragmatists. They believe and act in ways that get things
done. If an idea works, they use it. That several ideas or values may
contradict one another does not bother most Americans. Nor does
inconsistency in living up to a value, which may be a goal relegated to
be achieved "in the near future." Coherent personal philosophies and
systematic ideologies are both rare in American culture. Values are
usually given specific applications and their contradictions are ignored
or rationalized. This social process has been called "situational speci-
fication of generalized values" (Robin Williams 1964).

> The implications of certain initially given values have been
> explored in a great variety of specific social contexts, resulting in
> numerous modifications and restrictions in application. Thus,
> "freedom" is now felt to be compatible with compulsory
> vaccination (and) compulsory school attendance... (27).

The burden of inequality placed upon African-Americans in the
United States has been the outstanding cultural contradiction in American history. In an attempt to make this situation compatible with the
assumption of equality, many whites simply denied that African-Americans were fully human. A more sophisticated rationalization, which
had elements of both politics and logic, was the "separate but equal"
doctrine, a justification that contributed to maintaining segregation for
many decades. At a more personal, emotional level, many whites often
acted as if blacks just did not exist. While their equal treatment in
American society is still an issue, it has probably been elevated to a

"goal for the near future" status—an improvement over earlier rationalizations.

A similar reluctance to generate an ideology or a philosophy exists at a more strictly political level in the United States. About as close as most Americans get to a political-economic philosophy is general support for the free enterprise system. Even then, Americans are likely to ignore or deny the implications of this system for Social Security, the GI Bill of Rights, minimum wage laws, and governmental assistance to agriculture and other industries. Each one of these issues and others with similar implications have to be fought out in their own terms. Minimum wage laws did not establish a precedent for a guaranteed annual income, and Social Security did not predispose acceptance of Medicare. These are somewhat general statements, but they do indicate one deeply rooted cultural value: Americans resist systems of thought that lose sight of the individual. Each of the above programs was justified in terms of its particular effect on individuals rather than as a general policy, and so every other similar program must repeat the process. Even when a program is instituted, it may continue to be evaluated in individual terms. Attempts by the Reagan administration to roll back portions of government welfare programs were supported by myriad anecdotes of individual "welfare cheaters," and counter-arguments were similarly buttressed by stories of the "truly needy."

The many elements of governmental responsibility and care for the individual are not usually unified into a system of ideology (Perry 1949). By clinging to the ideal of individual enterprise, Americans keep their self-identity intact. Their aversion to coherent systems of thought is again reflected in the traditional organization of political parties. The two major parties, Democrats and Republicans, are more aptly described as instrumentalities for securing political power than as representatives of ideologies. As Reston (1965) notes, the function of a political party in this country is not to preside over a philosophical debate but to control and direct the struggle for power.

Americans' distrust of systems of thought often leads them to underestimate the impact that a coherent, comprehensive ideology and philosophy such as communism can have on other peoples whose thinking does not revolve around the individual. For more ascriptive people, such a system provides an explanation of socioeconomic conditions, makes projections for the future, and, perhaps most important of all, provides a plan of action for the person as a member of a group or class rather than as an individual. Equally, Americans may overestimate the attractiveness of the self-oriented, pragmatic nonideology that Americans call the "democratic system" and others often call "Americanism."

Cultural Change

To live according to one's cultural patterns requires constant adaptation to different people and novel situations. As the individual matures and ages, even routine and familiar events acquire a different meaning. As a consequence, the guides to behavior that we have examined in the case of values, thinking, and norms are more like processes in flux than structures which convey instructions. Adaptation, adjustment, and change permeate the cultural atmosphere. According to this view, the well-known American disposition for the new is not exceptional. Indeed, it can be argued that either the German or the Japanese society has changed more than the American during the last generation; and specifically when compared with the Japanese, American industry has been resistant to innovation. What is distinct about the American attitude is that no other existing society has displayed equal or greater verve in institutionalizing cultural change into its thought. Whether as myth or as reality, change is woven into the fiber of the American ethos and interlocks with personal identity.

The American assimilation of change is largely based on the nature of the self. Although personality is fragmented, accommodating conflicting values and adjusting to the social and cultural diversity in people, the self provides a hub of identity, of integration, and of continuity for the individual. All messages, transitions, and activities which have impact upon the individual must make their way through the hub. But the self as the basic unit of the culture is subjective and unfulfilled, raising this question: what is the code used for passage through the hub? The answer is that all messages that reach the American self should be translated into the language of self-interest. Motivation is the key to American psychology, and the empty self acquires fulfillment in self-actualization. This dynamic quality of the American self, removed from any stable structure, makes the self receptive to what might be called the ideology of change if not change itself.

Americans' commitment to the individual self as the core of their cultural experience is to some extent based on mythic individualism. Myths and traditions of American history display more than their share of self-reliant Daniel Boones, but heroic individualism has always existed beside a slight sense of community and a strong disposition to cooperate. These dual themes impel Americans to seek social cooperation while preserving a self detached from the group. The tension that is generated by this dichotomy is resolved by the individual's perceiving others and the group as resources for pursuing self-interest. Nevertheless, the schism created by the contradiction of an individual self with a dependent self has, as one group of researchers found, produced a striking ambivalence in American culture.

> In our interviews…we found all the classic polarities of American
> individualism still operating: the deep desire for autonomy and
> self-reliance combined with an equally deep conviction that life
> has no meaning unless shared with others in the context of
> community; a commitment to the equal right to dignity of every
> individual combined with an effort to justify inequality of reward,
> which, when extreme, may deprive people of dignity; an insistence
> that life requires practical effectiveness and "realism" combined
> with the feeling that compromise is ethically fatal. The inner
> tensions of American individualism add up to a classic case of
> ambivalence (Bellah et al. 1985, 150-51).

The American self and social order convey an uncertainty of structure, reflecting more of "doing" in the outside world than projecting internal integration. The elusiveness of the self is increased by the American orientation to the future and the use of present choices as occasions for doing rather than being. The empty self encourages identification in process, explained as "growth" or "learning" and inducing openness in social relations. The attributes of an active self living in a mutable social order are an American-made prescription for change.

The centrality of change in U.S. culture raises at least three obstacles to an appraisal of it. The first obstacle is that change is ubiquitous in American perception; it is difficult to compare change to anything else. In visiting a new area of the country, visitors are usually provided with a description of how much things have changed. The visitors do not have to request this information since the American perception of objective reality and of the environment seems to depend on recognizing change primarily in the form of before-and-after comparison. Otherwise, Americans are relatively impervious to their environment. The impression of self as process makes novelty a significant value in American life, and every change, certainly in preference or taste, is accompanied by the clamor of immediate impact and meaning.

A second obstacle is that some changes occur in the context of private identity and deviant subcultures. All roads in the culture lead back to the self, which is irreducible but must remain private, vague, and ambiguous. An abstract and coherently defined self-concept would contradict the fragmentation of personality necessary to maintain an emphasis on achievement. These qualities of the self, existing detached from origins and uncommitted to any destiny, invite a search for meaning. The search is additionally fueled by the inherent polarities of individualism that are not clarified by tradition or education. Each generation of Americans is committed to the rediscovery of the self. To reinforce the uniqueness of the discovery, it becomes necessary to create social identities by means of a new youth culture. The development and exploration of the self takes place in cultural islands created outside the mainstream culture, to some extent hidden from view.

A third obstacle is the overlap of cultural change and stages of personal development. Personality does not remain stable over the human life span. Individuals change as they pass into adolescence, advance into maturity, and finally attain old age. Changes in culture that the youth of the 1960s (and other decades) claimed credit for may be attributable to the normal passage through a stage of *being* that seems to be a path traveled by all youth in this culture. These changes need to be separated from the genuine ones that alter the face of culture for future generations.

With these thoughts in mind, we can now turn to a brief examination of historical changes that are coalescing into a major shift in American culture. For generations the American mind was transfixed by the frontier and the conquest of the wilderness to the West. The arena of American history has been the battle with the wilderness and the Native-Americans. Western movies and novels have captured the epic struggle of the pioneer against these two antagonists and have helped create mythic individualism. Americans felt unique and distinct from the rest of the world, a feeling which prevailed during the nineteenth century but began to ebb in the twentieth as the United States attained the stature of a world power. "This declining sense of American uniqueness is the great trauma of the American mind in the last half-century" (Boorstin 1958, 121).

Since World War II, observers of the American scene have repeatedly commented on the expanding role of organization and the increasing depersonalization of American life. Americans are now apparently more willing to place themselves in the hands of the government or of an organization, accepting its policies and goals as their own, than were Americans of previous generations. More than thirty years ago, Clyde Kluckhohn noted that

> strictly personal values have receded in importance at the expense of more publicly standardized "group values," whether those of an organization, a community, social class, profession, a minority or an interest group (1958, 105).

More recently, Alasdair MacIntyre (1981) coined the term *bureaucratic individualism* to indicate Americans' new willingness to turn over public decisions to professional managers and agencies. This is an example of value redistribution in which the decision maker changes from the public to a professional group. The import of this change is that the influence of organizations and groups, which historically was mediated by informal pressures of individuals, is becoming more explicit among middle-class

Americans. The catch-all, "they say…," is increasingly identified as the voice of the government or some other large organization.

Along with the change in Americans' willingness to immerse themselves in groups, there have been parallel changes in the values of identity. Variations from the dominant value of individual freedom of choice have become more prominent. Traditionally, Americans perceived government as guaranteeing them certain rights rather than demanding obligations. Political institutions were kept to a minimum and drew their strength from the local scene. Throughout American history, and particularly since the 1930s, the position of the central government has strengthened. Similar centralization and increased organization have also occurred in business, labor, education, and recreation. The traditional American concept of complete freedom of choice has given way in many areas to selecting from among acceptable alternatives.

As a result of greater participation in organizations, self-interest and the willingness to compromise for achievement are increasing while unique personal expression is declining in importance. Boundaries of the self have become blurred with a loss of distinctiveness between the individual and others. In the context of American individualism, this change in self-concept has not led so much to a growth in general social consciousness as to an increased openness to special interest groups and causes. Perhaps as a reaction to the increased power of government and other organizations, individuals seem more willing to ally themselves with groups to promote particular interests.

The breakdown and blurring of boundaries is evident in innumerable other areas of American life, such as the change that has occurred in the traditional distinction between male and female roles. The differences in body image, dress, behavior, role expectations, and goals separating the two sexes are significantly reduced. This change is again one of a redistribution of values. Moving in the opposite direction, African-Americans have largely succeeded in widening the boundary of self to include an ethnic identification with blackness and certain aspects of African culture. Both these phenomena—one a blurring and deemphasis of boundaries and the other a redefinition and intensification—can be seen as yielding to perceived social and cultural necessities. The actions are politically and economically driven, although they may also, in the long run, serve the traditional American value of equality.

In the area of international affairs, the insularity of the twenties and thirties gave way to American receptivity to foreign influences after World War II. Foreign beliefs and practices, particularly if they appeared exotic and mystical, gained popularity. The struggle between communism and democracy replaced the struggle between the frontiersman and the wilderness. But even during the 1950s, when the idea of monolithic communism provided the binding factor in an otherwise disjointed foreign policy, emotions were unconsciously redirected toward the American South as a kind of social wilderness. It was on this familiar ground that matters of conscience and guilt for American culture were fought out around the issue of race. The external antagonists began to crumble. By the late 1960s, despite a growing war in Southeast Asia, the battle against communism was no longer able to provide direction and purpose to American national life. The antagonists of the culture were increasingly identified as inside the society.

In the late sixties and early seventies, an explosion of expressive individualism occurred. The gemeinschaft strains of American culture, muted until then by battles with nature and external antagonists, emerged in the form of religious revival and group consciousness raising. The inward-looking focus of that time represented a change in the American self-concept. It established a tension within the society and within the self that replaced the epic struggle between mankind and nature. For a time, self-examination brought values of love, identity, and power into prominence over the pursuit of success through change and achievement. The arena of American culture was no longer nature but society itself. The wilderness of American culture was absorbed into the self, producing vague and anxious feelings of unfulfillment.

Although the blush of new-found affiliation has faded, the experience of the last thirty years has continued to affect American values. Most individuals continue to pursue achievement, and they generally persist in maintaining the social norms of self-motivation and self-reliance. But an awareness of interdependence with others seems to have emerged in the culture. The American perception of self—individualism—now includes a more overt acknowledgement of how others are necessarily related to us.

> We find ourselves not independently of other people and institutions but through them. We never get to the bottom of ourselves on our own. We discover who we are face-to-face and side-by-side with others in work, love, and learning.... We are parts of a larger whole that we can neither forget nor imagine in our own image without paying a high price. If we are not to have a self that hangs in the void, slowly twisting in the wind, these are issues we cannot ignore (Bellah et al. 1985, 84).

The cross-cultural implications of this change in American perceptions of the self have already begun to unfold. The major effect on Americans working with foreigners is likely to be a sharpened awareness of alternative forms of social relations normally used. There is also evidence that Americans have become more interested in cultural differences and intercultural communication. In the academic world, the interdisciplinary development of cognitive science already displays openness to and assimilation of ideas and content from linguistics and culture. There is, as well, a greater demand from international business and international study programs for preparation to work abroad or within multicultural institutions. In the case of business, such training makes economic sense in the more competitive conditions Americans face in the world market. For international education, the desire for cultural education and communication training seems more clearly motivated by the new sense of an interdependent self. Americans are recognizing that they do have a culture and that learning about it enables them to relate more sensitively to the foreigners with whom they work and from whom they have much to learn.

INTERCULTURAL COMMUNICATION APPLICATIONS

The description of American cultural patterns in the preceding chapters has focused primarily on assumptions and values. These concepts are cognitive and, as a constellation of values representing dominant American cultural patterns, can be categorized as the *deep culture* that supports American behavior. Understanding deep culture is crucial to realizing the assumptions Americans bring to cross-cultural experience, but abstract cultural values offer only a raw template for actual behavior. The value of individualism, for instance, is hardly a discerning guide for how one should behave when caught in a situation of competing loyalties between the organization and one's own personal goals. The gap between the support of deep culture and the guidance of behavior is filled in part by *procedural culture*. The difference between deep and procedural culture is that of "knowing what" (or "about") versus "knowing how."

In decision making, for example, knowing how aims at a result. Its direction toward an objective separates it from deep culture and confines it to a context. Thus, procedural culture is a complex pattern with a goal orientation that combines surface behavior and deep culture in a specific context of application.

Although we are treating procedural culture only now in this last chapter, we have often touched on examples earlier in the book. The subject was unavoidable since procedural culture incessantly impinges upon the constellation of American assumptions and values. Perhaps more so than any other Western culture, American culture has developed decision making, negotiation, conflict resolution, management, communication, and other procedural systems. In this last chapter, we shall describe the dominant American style of interpersonal communication and examine how it fares in intercultural communication.

Emotion in Communication

We have been careful to include "emotion" in our definition of value, but in practice an abstract description of American culture can be presented that omits emotion altogether. The cognitive base of such a description provides an incomplete representation of the internal life of the individual. People experience fantasy and emotion, attend to bodily feelings, respond to percepts, and reconstruct memories. As Americans approach a moment of action, many of their thoughts, emotions, and fantasies must be carefully masked before they are expressed because they would be considered unseemly. Emotion and social feelings thus become undercurrents in American human affairs, seldom attended to and often disruptive.

Emotions influence behavior in nonsymbolic ways. In the dominant American cultural image of the mind, emotions appear in the dual form of feelings and desires. These two aspects of emotion are perceived to be different in important ways. The self, it is believed, cannot control desire and usually cannot control feelings. The self, nevertheless, is the agent for desire and the receiver of feelings. The implication is that the self cannot control emotion and is particularly hapless when functioning in the active modality of an agent (D'Andradei 1987, 117). Although interlinked with symbolic systems such as language, Americans consider emotions to be essentially outside the range of willful control, distrusted as guides for behavior, and essentially neglected in communication.

What Americans know about themselves and others, in the privacy of their thoughts, does not take clear form in surface behavior. Emotions are concealed in verbal expressions such as "I feel, " which is used to represent a commitment or opinion. Americans also abide by a strong convention to preserve surface cordiality in social interactions. Kind words and pleasant smiles are natural and expected; sharp opinions and critical positions in face-to-face encounters are avoided for fear of disrupting social conviviality. These behaviors suggest a mollification of emotions in the service of social interaction. The American emotional disposition is a friendly optimism, particularly among whites. African-Americans are more likely to believe that high levels of emotion can be controlled and thus are more comfortable with relatively intense emotional expression (Kochman 1981, 30-31).

In communication the American mentality is practical, favoring beliefs, resolutions, and intentions as the content of messages. These elements are controllable and consequently can be assimilated in communication. In fact, intentions can be loosely accepted as the psychological correlate of procedural culture. Emotions definitely take a secondary role to logical and factual strategies.

When we compare American emotional expression in communication with styles in other societies, we can conclude that emotion in American communication lies somewhere in midrange. Arabs and Latin Americans generally consider Americans to be cold, while the Japanese judge American communication to be emotional. At the same time, the Japanese consider American communication to be logical while their own cultural ways are based on emotion. Clearly, emotion has different meanings and presents various incomparable human states. It is in part this kind of intercultural confusion which makes the subject so important but also places it beyond the scope of our modest treatment of the role of emotions in American communication. We can, however, comment on one way in which the deep-culture value of equality guides Americans in their attempt to apprehend the dispositions of others.

Sympathy

The subjective and emotional aspect of the American self-concept is based on the perceived similarity and equality of everyone. This assumption yields a communication strategy typically employed by senders: in dealing with others, I can assume that what "I feel" will be identical to what the other person feels in the same situation. I can take my own feelings and project them to others as a way of understanding how someone else feels about the same situation. Americans typically believe that everyone is basically alike, and other people have the same basic needs that they have themselves. Since the important differences among people are believed to be individual, not cultural or social, Americans are sensitive to similarities in others rather than to differences. This American belief is similar to the perspective of the biblical Golden Rule, "Do unto others as you would have them do unto you" (M. Bennett 1979). The common American understanding of the Golden Rule is that the self is the point of reference for understanding how others might feel or wish to be treated. Understanding others by putting one's self in their positions describes the American concept of sympathy. The common American aphorism, "Imagine how you'd feel in their shoes," captures this feeling by implying that imagining one's self in different circumstances will yield to the different perspectives of others.

As a strategy in communication, sympathy is effective when people share common values. The difficulty appears when the "other" is significantly different from one's self, as is the case in cross-cultural situations. In seeking to communicate with people from other cultures, it is simply not enough to imagine how one's self as an American might feel in a given event. The feeling that results will lack correspondence with that of the other person because sympathy ignores human variations and cultural differences. The feeling of sympathy is bereft of the cultural influences that are brought to bear when interpreting the inner mental states of the other and is therefore inadequate to the task of understanding social relations. Empathy provides a better interface for cross-cultural communication.

Empathy

Empathy relies on the ability to temporarily set aside one's own perception of the world and assume an alternative perspective. Self-interest and purposes are held in check as one attempts to place oneself in the immediate situation and field (but not in the shoes) of another. Empathy assumes that the self is different from others; therefore, the shared qualities of subjective individualism upon which Americans build their interface of sympathy is not available. In empathic communication, the self and the other function as interlinked social objects since both are perceived to participate in social roles or as representative of groups. The subjective self in empathic communication is held in reserve (E. Stewart 1985).

Understanding empathy requires an analysis of social relations. In societies where empathy is a strong interface in communication, the social relations among people tend to be formal. India and Germany come to mind, but we shall use as an example Japanese *omoiyari* (empathy), which probably provides the best-known contrast to American sympathy.

Empathy for the Japanese is a social form for communicating and establishing interpersonal relations. Thus, the Japanese reflexively rely on anticipating how the other will respond. The empathic interface functions much better if people's actions are preprogrammed, explaining the value which the Japanese place on the right way of doing things.

First, the communicators establish a common perception. The Japanese prefer to sit alongside each other, exchanging side glances and looking jointly at something in front. Americans occupied with sympathy prefer to sit opposite each other, exchange eye glances, and establish communion on the basis of common experience or similarity of identity and origin. The highly structured social relations of Japanese culture lead each participant in a communication event to have specific expectations of how the other party will behave. The sincerity and genuineness of others' actions as well as deviations from expected forms are used to interpret the meaning and implications of communication. The empathic emotional interface depends on the perception of a shared event and an accepted common goal, and performances are evaluated against rather specific expectations of what people should do.

The high context of empathic events and situations transforms nonverbal communication into an essential channel. Its importance is illustrated by the response of a group of American and Japanese students to the question, "How can you tell if your wife or living partner is angry with you?" The Americans generally agreed that the anger would be expressed verbally with varying degrees of rancor. The first Japanese student to answer was quiet for a moment, and then he said that he also would know when his wife was angry. He would suspect it if a flower was askew in the entryway arrangement, but he would be sure of it if his teacup were only partially filled with lukewarm tea. The Americans said they would talk over the difficulty with their partners, while the Japanese said that they would make a special effort to be attentive to theirs, without actually bringing up the incidents. Similar subtleties exist in Japanese business negotiations, where difficult phases of a discussion may only be conducted through letter or by subordinates of the Japanese negotiators.

Unlike the Japanese, to the Americans empathy as an emotional interface is only a secondary variation. As we have said, their culture predisposes them to use sympathy, not empathy. In the intercultural situation, however, it is clear that empathy may be the better alternative.

The American Style of Communication

In describing the American style of communication, we shall define communication in the broad sense of the interaction among people which facilitates cooperation in work or sharing in daily activities. This meaning of communication implies that it covers almost all sectors of behavior. We begin our description of the American style with a few comments about the four functions of communication—expressive, persuasive, referential, and phatic—in a cultural contrast frame of reference.

Expressive communication can be illustrated by an event in a fashionable street in Moscow on a cold Sunday afternoon. Some seventy-five to one hundred people had gathered to listen to a middle-aged man recite a poem he had composed to convey his feelings about life in the Soviet Union, his attitudes toward political leaders, and his thoughts on the subject of the politics of *perestroika*. When he finished, another man took his place, and later a third, each reciting or reading his own poems and giving vent to his own thoughts and emotions.

The audience did not respond with praise or with questions. The message was conveyed by the metaphors of language, the cadence of sound, awareness of the situation, and sensitivity to the event, but not by a dialogue with the audience. Communication was one-way. The image and identity of the poet was more important than the response of the audience.

This event in Moscow is illustrative of the Russian tradition of the artist as the guide to the meaning of life, not the scientist or the philosopher. For example, when a Soviet official was asked for suggestions of books which would inform foreigners about the Soviet Union, he answered with the names of writers of short stories and novels, including Dostoyevsky. No mention was made of social scientists, historians, or philosophers.

Although expressiveness exists in American communication, only with some ethnic groups does this form of communication attain significance equivalent to that attributed to Soviet communication. The dominant American communication function is *persuasion*. The American at heart is a salesperson, committed to convincing others of his or her own point of view. In keeping with the American distrust of emotion, efforts to persuade usually depend on technical information and logical reasoning. "Get your facts right, control your feelings, and give it to them straight" reflect the American approach. This function of communication, called *referential*, supports persuasion in American culture. Second in importance, the referential function is the base for the technical and logical cast of American communication. It also places a heavy burden on the structure of language, requiring that the words used in communication be precise and technical, unlike the words of Soviet poets reciting on the street in language saturated with metaphors and allusions. American communication relies on language which conveys information abstractly apart from the contingencies of situations and events. It reaches for objectivity, unlike Japanese, which is based on the social logic of interpersonal relations.

There remains a last function of communication—*phatic*, the purpose of which is social processing. It includes small talk, rituals of communication, and other practices aimed at maintaining or developing human relations. The Japanese are masters at phatic communication, but Americans rank its importance low. It is based on nonverbal communication and empathy, both cultivated far more in Japan than in the United States.

The functions of communication—expressive, persuasive, referential, phatic—and their supporting structures of language, content, form, and channel provide us with a base for describing the American style of communication. It follows that the American style should display qualities that are specific to American cultural patterns adapted to the pattern of communicative functions. Drawing on this discussion and those in earlier chapters, we can summarize American communication style as problem-oriented, direct, explicit, personal, and informal.

PROBLEM-ORIENTED

As we discussed in chapter 4, Americans tend to see events as problems to be solved, based on their concepts of an underlying rational order in the world and of themselves as individual agents of action. Americans often try to organize information into statements of "wrongness" so courses of action can be recommended that will rectify the situation. For instance, American political campaigns are judged effective if the candidates can put their opponents on the defensive by labeling them as supporting a wrong policy or having something wrong with their characters. Candidates can then speak about how their own character and policies will redress the problems that have been created by politicians of their opponents' ilk. In interpersonal relations, discussion may center around needs—problems in the form of personal deficits—that should be fulfilled (solved). Similarly, a problem is often simply assumed without being stated. Thus, many American interchanges are of the form, "I'm thinking of going to graduate school" or "I'm considering going on a diet," to which the response is a solution to the implied problem—"Let me suggest some good schools" or "I know a terrific weight-loss program you should try."

Americans commonly assume that problems and solutions are basic ingredients of reality. For the Japanese, however, statements of problems often serve as conversational tools to change the subject away from an embarrassing topic. When a Japanese associate brings up a problem to an American, the American tends to immediately search for a solution and may miss the point entirely. For Arabs, problems are severe twists of fate that cannot be solved. As noted earlier, attempts to push Arabs into accepting that there is a problem may well be met with mystifying resistance. For the Trukese, the closest synonym to *problem* is "confusion," a condition that is best addressed by stopping whatever one is doing and waiting. Any attempt to solve a problem is likely to be interpreted by the Trukese as contributing to the confusion. Europeans tend to interpret Americans' pragmatic bent as a failure to conceptualize. According to most Europeans, solutions should be attempted only after the problem is thoroughly understood. Americans are far more likely to engage in trial-and-error solutions, actions which earn them the label of "impetuous," both in foreign relations and interpersonal encounters.

Direct

Americans, valuing pragmatic action, are quick to come to the point in conversations. They generally eschew long greeting and leave-taking rituals, preferring to exchange only minimal pleasantries before stating, "The reason I wanted to talk with you is…." If a greeting ritual goes on too long by American standards, the recipient of the visit is likely to say, "What's on your mind?" or some other prod to "get down to business." This tendency continues throughout conversations. Americans are impatient with digressions and rich contextualizations. If the subject seems to waver or if too much detail is provided, one of the conversationalists is likely to intrude with, "Let me see if I understand your main point here." This style of conversation is known as *linear*, where speakers are expected to come to the point by moving in a straight line of logical thought through the subject to an explicitly stated conclusion. American students who do not follow the rules of direct style in writing receive comments on their papers such as, "seems vague" or "point not clearly stated." Similar directness is encouraged in face-to-face interaction with nonverbal indications of impatience during digressions or, as noted above, outright interruptions. As may be the case with many aspects of American communication style, an exaggerated form of directness is reinforced by television. The short, direct statement—often a confrontation—is the *sine qua non* of television news "sound bites," and television talk-show hosts are quick to panic when their guests begin to digress from the one point they have been invited to make.

In contrast to the American style of directness, many cultures encourage a style that is more *contextual*. The elaborate greeting rituals of Asian, Arab, and Latin American cultures provide a social context for eventual discussion of the topic at hand. Inquiries about family members, health, and other general matters are likely to exceed American dictates of politeness by far. Yet to members of many other cultures, such questions are necessary for making the social judgments that dictate, for example, the choice of language or the extent of familiarity that can be assumed in the conversation.

The contextual style does not require that material be presented in a linear form. Speakers need mainly to establish the context in which a conclusion can be reached, but the materials need not be presented in any particular order. In addition, conclusions are often not stated explicitly; it is up to the listener to divine the conclusion implied by the context. Particularly in some African communication styles, excursions into related subjects are normative, and listeners are expected to embellish the theme rather than to prod for the main point or the problem. In the words of one African student, "I know I have been understood when the other person makes statements that express the same idea as mine."

Asian contextual styles are more likely to use the subtlety of nuance and silence. As discussed in chapter 5, the direct confrontation common to American style is ill-advised in societies where face is of primary concern, since frequently the indirectness of statements masks feelings that, if stated, might cause embarrassment to both speaker and listener. This concern was captured by a Japanese communication student in her article, "Sixteen Ways to Avoid Saying 'No' in Japanese" (Ueda 1975). Americans who believe that "deep down" everyone appreciates honest directness will continue to exact a heavy toll of tolerance from their more indirect foreign associates.

Explicit

The American reliance on digital representation discussed in chapter 3 forms the basis of explicit communication style. Digital representation is associated with language—verbal symbols representing concepts—rather than with the nonverbal signals—gestures, facial expressions—that are closer to analogs of perceptual states. Americans assume that language is primary while nonverbal behavior accents and modifies the meaning of words. Substance in American conversation is based more on what is stated than on what is not. Indeed, great stress is placed on developing the skill to say exactly what you mean. In the American legal system, the verbal code is supreme, relying for meaning on contracts and other documents with high specificity and low contingent content. As a general conclusion, American communication is more or less independent of the context in which it takes place. In contrast, Japanese communication is highly contextualized. Condon (1984, 45-46) notes this difference in saying that American culture has low reliance on context and high trust in words as compared to Japanese culture's high reliance on context and low trust in words. Cultures such as Japanese have been called *high-context*, while those such as American are *low-context* (Hall 1976, 79-90).

In high-context cultures, issues would be expected to have lower clarity and specificity and their meaning to be contingent on context. This expectation is consistent with the greater Japanese reliance on unwritten contracts based on mutual trust. In Japan, nonverbal behavior is more highly valued as a means of sincere communication than is language. Japanese leaders are not required to have highly developed rhetorical skills and may even be distrusted for too much verbal facility. This contrasts with the American preference for leaders with highly developed verbal skills, and it points to another implication of the high- and low-context distinction. Cultures differ in their social norms regarding whether the speaker or the listener is more responsible for the meaning created in a communication exchange.

In low-context American culture, the responsibility for meaning falls mainly to the speakers, whose job it is to formulate ideas into clear language. The more lucid speakers are, the more highly they are regarded as communicators. In high-context Asian, African, and Native-American cultures, the listener is more responsible for deriving meaning from the nonverbal and relational cues surrounding an often ambiguous verbal message. An eloquent speaker may be judged as patronizing—acting as if the listeners are incapable of fulfilling their responsibility. Although Americans place the major responsibility for clarity on the speaker, the value of equality leads them to assign part of the responsibility for understanding a message to the receiver. If a misunderstanding occurs, Americans typically assume that the wrong words were used, the sender garbled the message, or the receiver was not listening. The explanation is usually technical and requires the sender to review how the message was transmitted, and the receiver to ask questions. Reciprocal questions and comments are a matter of course when sender and receiver are associates, but sensitivity to instrumental equality in communication prevails even where there are marked status differences between communicators. Thus, students are encouraged to ask questions of professors. Where status is markedly different, as with a corporate or military officer addressing subordinates in a formal meeting, the high-ranking sender may ask for questions or may phrase the message as answers to questions anticipated by receivers. In all cases, the sender shares responsibility with receivers for successful transmission of the message, regardless of difference in status or authority.

The American pattern of responsibility for meaning contrasts with others. In German society, social distance among people is greater and more clearly defined than in American. German communicators do not cultivate the same equality as Americans. German students do not ask questions of professors; such behavior would be perceived as challenges to the professors' authority and knowledge. Responsibility for understanding the message therefore resides in the receiver and is not shared with the sender. Conversations among Germans lack the back-and-forth pattern found among Americans since Germans do not acknowledge or reciprocate comments from senders to the same degree.

Personal

American emphasis on the individual self finds its purest expression in the personal communication style. As discussed in chapters 5 and 7, Americans tend to rely on their personal experience for knowledge of the world, and their communication patterns are weighted in that direction. Upon first meeting, Americans typically sift through a number of topics until they find an experience they have in common. After brief exchanges on that topic, they begin the search again until all obvious subjects such as sports, vacation spots, work, marriage and children, etc. have been exhausted. If there is sufficient overlap of experience, the conversationalists may judge that they "have a lot in common," and additional conversation will ensue, generally on more intimate commonalities of experience. Conversely, "having nothing in common" is a sure indication that the relationship will not be pursued. Opinions, theories, and even education (unless it was at the same school) do not figure significantly into this acquaintance ritual, although they may be broached later in a relationship. The basis of relationship for Americans is commonality of action and experience, not commonality of thinking. And since most American relationships are relatively superficial (by gemeinschaft standards), actions and personal experience become the predominant topics of nearly all American conversation. In combination with direct and explicit styles, this personal communication style leads Americans to be extremely free in revealing much about themselves in virtually any situation where conversation occurs.

The American ease of self-revelation is shared by people of few, if any, other cultures. As an extreme contrast, research comparing Japanese and American reports of comfort with self-revelation indicates that Americans are far more comfortable disclosing aspects of themselves than are Japanese (Barnlund 1989). The research compared "willingness to disclose" on a scale that listed possible topics of discussion, including interests and tastes (such as food preferences), opinions, work or studies, financial status, personality, and physical attributes (such as feelings of sexual adequacy). Possible conversational partners included mother, father, same-sex friend, opposite-sex friend, stranger, and untrusted person. Americans and Japanese agreed on the ranking in terms of comfort with both topics and target persons (the order in which they are listed above). But Americans reported themselves more willing to disclose about every topic to every person, including the most threatening case (discussing sexual adequacy with an untrusted person) than were the Japanese, except about food and their mothers.

A consideration of American communication with Europeans reveals a somewhat less stark contrast in personal style but one that is troublesome nevertheless. Europeans are surprised when Americans open conversations with reports of activities and experiences. For Europeans, acquaintance is more typically made through discussion of intellectual issues—politics, religion, or philosophical topics. Disclosure of experiences and other personal matters comes later in the relationship, assuming that interest has been established on the intellectual level first. Although this difference in style is more one of timing than of substance, it is enough to cause many Europeans to judge Americans as shallow. Conversely, Americans tend to judge the initial European reticence about personal experience as arrogant.

INFORMAL

Closely related to the style of personal disclosure is the American commitment to informality in nearly all communication situations. As discussed in chapter 5, American individualism is closely coupled with the notion of equality. Ideally, each person is equal by virtue of his or her individuality; therefore, no person is inherently better than any other. This idealized egalitarianism is expressed in American communication style by a willingness to converse freely about activities and experiences across a wide range of social class and circumstance. Americans chat casually with waitresses in restaurants or strangers in other public places. While they are willing to engage in formal communication in some situations and sometimes demand it of their leaders, Americans are also likely to deride people who are excessively formal and look for opportunities to puncture the facade they present. People who insist on being treated formally are judged by Americans to be stuffy, and no higher compliment can be paid to an important person than the statement, "He's just a regular guy—real down to earth." Americans tend to address everyone in the same way. They use first names readily and early in a relationship, and they believe that treating everyone the same is ultimately respectful. As we have mentioned earlier, if Americans develop a stronger than normal attachment to someone, they may experience difficulty in expressing it since exchanges from the beginning have been informal and friendly. The consequence is that what at first may appear to be a personal way of treating others ultimately becomes depersonalizing because it is extended to everyone alike. Few discriminations are made among people, each being kept at the same distance. Even "enemies" are likely to be treated with a controlled friendliness that may not look much different from behavior directed towards valued acquaintances.

The degree of informality found in American communication patterns is uncommon in other cultures. In most Latin American and European societies, for instance, there are levels of formality attached to status difference. In Asian cultures, formal communication may be demanded by greater age as well as by higher status. In Japan, formality is also extended to strangers with whom a relationship is demanded. This formality is no joking matter, since a failure to follow appropriate form may suggest to others a severe flaw in character.

This discussion of the American style of communication suggests some of its strengths and weaknesses for intercultural communication.

Using a problem-oriented approach, we shall now examine obstacles to intercultural communication and how they come into play in American interactions.

Implications of American Ethnocentrism

Many of the difficulties with intercultural communication can be traced to the obstacles created by *ethnocentrism*, which means, literally, "centrality of culture." When one's own culture is considered central to all reality, the values, assumptions, and behavioral norms of that culture may be elevated to the position of absolute truth. There are several implications of this definition. First, ethnocentric beliefs about one's own culture shape a social sense of identity which is narrow and defensive. Second, ethnocentrism normally involves the perception of members of other cultures in terms of stereotypes. Third, the dynamic of ethnocentrism is such that comparative judgments are made between one's own culture and other cultures under the assumption that one's own is normal and natural. As a consequence, ethnocentric judgments usually involve invidious comparisons that ennoble one's own culture while degrading those of others. With these costs, ethnocentrism establishes identity and belonging in the context of culture.

Ethnocentrism produces significant effects on cross-cultural interaction and international affairs. The patterns of other cultures may be ignored in deference to the naturalness of the reference culture. Or the other cultures may simply be treated as deviations from reality or normality rather than as variations. In either case, the effects of ethnocentrism can be seen in the way Americans perceive themselves and in their perception of others. First, we shall look at the inward face of ethnocentrism and briefly suggest some of the factors in American ethnocentrism that affect cross-cultural interactions.

The image of the ugly American prevalent in the 1960s has become increasingly rare. Although an occasional traveler still behaves as if the world owes him or her tribute as an American, overt displays have yielded to more subtle expressions of ethnocentrism. Statements such as "Deep down, everyone in the world is really just the same" and the advice to fellow Americans, "Just be yourself," betray the peculiarly American mix of individualism and egalitarianism that pervades American cultural self-perception. While these values and their attendant behavior may function well within American culture, their application, as we have seen, is not universal. Yet Americans are inclined to act on the false assumption that all people consider themselves autonomous individuals, that all people desire maximum material gain, or that all people value social mobility.

Americans commonly assume that circumstances such as oppressive governments or restrictive social norms have frustrated people's "natural" desire to value those things that Americans also value. When this assumption is used in intercultural communication, the result is likely to be misunderstanding. For example, a recent United States president on a trip to Central America called for governments in the area to "get off people's backs" so they could do what they really wanted to do—engage in individual entrepreneurship. Since many Central Americans do not share the American value of individual entrepreneurship, the statement was interpreted as another attempt by North Americans to impose their way of life on others. In another case, an American businessman responsible for hosting some Japanese visitors to his U.S. company was asked about what problems he thought might occur during the visit. "Nothing," he was reported as saying, "except that they won't want to go home after they have a taste of the social freedom we have in this country." The American's lack of acknowledgement that the Japanese visitors may find their own ways preferable will almost certainly be interpreted by the Japanese as disrespect, and communication will suffer in subtle but definite ways.

Ethnocentric self-perception tends to vary from culture to culture. The Japanese, for instance, generally assume that they are different from people of all other cultures. Superficially, this stance may seem to be less ethnocentric than the American view, but it is not. The Japanese commonly assume that because they are so different, foreigners can never really understand them, nor can foreigners really be understood. European ethnocentric self-perceptions are more likely to be based on yet another premise: cultures are "evolving" toward more civilized states, and the pinnacle of civilization is assumed (mostly by Europeans) to be in Europe.

An American form of the premise of cultural evolution can be found in the notion of "developing nations," where the goal of development is American technicism. As we have seen in previous examples, advisors may be drawn by this idea to help people (whom they frequently misunderstand) develop towards a goal that is also misunderstood and perhaps, if understood fully, would be spurned. Cultural, political, economic, and religious "missionaries" are particularly inclined to accept cultural evolution. Even if adept at intercultural communication, they may nevertheless use those skills to further their own ethnocentrism by helping other cultures to be like them. The point is not that there is anything wrong with cultural, social, and economic change but that the assumptions about how these changes should take shape are too easily derived from the values of foreigners.

The outward-looking face of ethnocentrism directs the perception of others and the interpretation of events in simple terms, conforming to familiar cultural experience. Judgments are parochial and lack a base for making objective interpretations. Insofar as people are restricted to the categories of only their reference culture, they may fail to perceive the meaning of specific events in other cultures. Indeed, they may fail to perceive the events at all. For example, American tourists sometimes return from Tokyo or other large foreign cities and report that "It's just like New York" (or some other large American city). These Americans have perceived as figure only the large buildings, heaving traffic, and fast-food outlets that do, indeed, exist in most large cities of the world. The unique conditions that make these cities different from one another remain hidden from the travelers' views by the constraints of their own culture-bound perceptions. It is not just Americans who suffer from parochial perception. Japanese tourists in the U.S. are more attuned to recognizing differences than similarities, but their perception still tends to depend on already existing categories of meaning. Thus, it is common for the Japanese to report extensively on the wide-open spaces of America—which are made important in Japan by their absence—and which don't exist in most of the large American cities they visit any more than they do in Tokyo.

An ethnocentric perception of others has no single name but is based on "units" which are called *stereotypes*. This form of social perception is not an aberration of cross-cultural contact; it is the individual's natural defense in confronting cultural difference (M. Bennett 1986). An ethnocentric vision composed of stereotypes simplifies the social perception of others by means of a rigid belief that all members of a culture or group share the same characteristics, and thus, challenges to ethnocentric assumptions are avoided. It is not surprising that simple contact between ethnocentric members of two cultures is likely to exacerbate existing stereotypes and perhaps generate new ones. Unless intercultural communicators are aware of these processes, face-to-face interaction is not likely to improve awareness of and tolerance for cultural differences. Stereotypes can be attached to any assumed indicator of group membership, such as race, religion, ethnicity, age, or gender as well as national culture.

Stereotypes fail to distinguish among members of broad categories. For instance, many Americans do not differentiate among Gulf State Arabs (in particular, Saudi Arabians), other Middle Eastern Arabic speakers (e.g., Syrians), and Iranians. To lump these different cultures into a single broad category of "Arabs" is both inaccurate and a source of great frustration to people of those cultures. Similarly, the category "Asian" or "Oriental" clouds important cultural differences among Japanese, Koreans, and Chinese. Although Americans now commonly differentiate Southeast Asians from Asians in general, even this category ignores crucial differences among Vietnamese, Cambodians, and Laotians. This kind of restricted or parochial perception can have dramatic practical consequences. One case occurred in the Portland, Oregon Rose Parade, where a float was entered honoring Sapporo, Japan, Portland's sister city. Dignitaries flown from Japan were quite upset when they observed that some of the young women waving from the float were Chinese, not Japanese. The parade director, when questioned on the point, responded with a statement of stereotypic perception: "Japanese...Chinese—close enough." More troubling, many Saudi Arabian students were subjected to verbal (and sometimes physical) abuse during the Iranian hostage crisis. Aside from the questionable justification for abusing anyone because of nationality or culture, this confusion of Arabs and Iranians, who have quite different histories and cultures, again indicates the practical consequences of inadequately developed categories for cross-cultural perception.

We should not leave the topic of parochial perception without mentioning one of the chief sources of irritation to foreigners in communicating with Americans. Foreign visitors to the U.S. universally report that Americans ask them stupid questions. Typical of these questions is (to Africans) "Do you have lions around your house?" Europeans are surprised when Americans ask them if they have ice cream or cars in their countries, and nearly everyone is irritated by geographical questions that place their countries on the wrong continent. While these questions may occasionally be expressions of negative stereotypes, more often they are well-motivated attempts by Americans to express interest or friendliness toward the foreigner. Of course the questions betray ignorance about other countries, but beyond that, they display parochial perception. Operating with broad categories that fail to differentiate critical differences among peoples and societies, Americans may have to select from a small array of elements to formulate their questions. For instance, the mental category for Africa may include only the elements "blacks live there" and "lions live there." Thus, the only question or comment that can occur is one that links an African black person with lions.

The realities of ethnocentrism and of limited information obstruct the development of objective assessment of cultural differences. Our examples thus far have been drawn from the area of stereotypes which typically involve beliefs, concepts, and images. Many of these stereotypes derive their content from simplistic word-of-mouth sources and from woefully incomplete information on television and in cartoons and comic books. While these cultural distortions are troublesome for communication, the content of the stereotypes is based on deep culture and is thereby accessible to description and analysis and is responsive to education.

Furthermore, deep-culture ethnocentrism among Americans is not so different from that in other cultures. The true challenge for intercultural communication appears when we consider procedural culture. In the next section, we examine some of the issues involving ethnocentrism in the American style of communication. The novelty of this section is that we associate obstacles to understanding with procedural rather than with deep culture.

Procedural Ethnocentrism in Communication

The ethnocentric impression that one's communication style is natural and normal predisposes Americans to evaluate other styles negatively. Such evaluation is likely to elicit a defensive reaction, forming a *mutual negative evaluation* that stems from blindness toward differences between procedural cultures. For instance, Americans may evaluate Japanese indirect communication style as "ambiguous," while American directness may be received by Japanese as "immature." When communicators engage in mutual negative evaluation, the recriminatory interaction may be enough to block communication. If the communicators then attempt to overcome the difficulty through ethnocentric procedures, the communication event may deteriorate even further. The American, sensing Japanese reluctance to confront a problem, becomes even more personal and aggressive. The Japanese, reacting to an embarrassing social indiscretion, becomes even more formal and indirect. With each turn of this *regressive spiral*, negative evaluations are intensified; "ambiguity" may spiral to "evasion," "deviousness," "deception," and finally to "dishonesty." On the other side of the culture curtain, "immature" may spiral to "impolite," "brash," "impertinent," and finally to "offensive." In this pattern of mutual compensation, the actions of each person intensify the reactions of the other (Wilmot 1987). Recognizing regressive spirals and predicting their effects are major concerns in the procedural domain of intercultural communication.

Negative evaluations and spirals are not limited merely to American-Japanese interactions. The following situations illustrate regressive spirals common to Americans communicating with people of a variety of other cultures.

> An American student listens with growing impatience to a Nigerian student, who is responding to a simple question about his religion with several long stories about his childhood. Finally, the American breaks in and makes her own point clearly and logically. The American evaluates the Nigerian negatively as being stupid or devious (for talking "in circles"). The Nigerian evaluates the

American as being childish or unsophisticated (for being unable to understand subtlety). The American urges the Nigerian to state his point more clearly, and in response the Nigerian intensifies his efforts to provide more context.

The American states that there is a problem that needs solving (by direct action of a participant). An Arab counterpart denies there is any problem at all, stating that the situation is ill-fated. The American evaluates the Arab as lazy and unperceptive while the Arab sees the American as unperceptive (of the larger context) and egotistic (in thinking he can change things). The American seeks to convince the Arab of the severity of the problem, prompting the Arab to emphasize even more the inevitability of the situation.

To avoid appearing "status conscious," the American manager requests that a Thai employee address him by his first name. The employee agrees but continues to use the manager's formal title in conversations. The American evaluates this action as unduly subservient and unfriendly. The Thai evaluates the American as naive and disrespectful (of the special place held by the employee in the organization's hierarchy). The American insists on pursuing casual friendliness, engendering even more formality in the employee's behavior.

An American trainer presents a proposal to her British counterpart. The Briton states that it is the most ridiculous hogwash she has ever seen. The American responds by saying that her feelings are hurt (by the attacking tone of her counterpart). The British woman enlarges on her original statement by pointing out the specific shortcomings of the proposal. The American says she must have been mistaken about considering the woman her friend, and the Briton becomes silent.

The main factor in these and endless other examples of intercultural communication spirals is a lack of awareness of specific cultural differences in communication style. In the first case of the Nigerian, both people are unaware of the American preference for a direct and explicit style in contrast to the more contextual African style. Both these communicators are likely to leave the situation less inclined to ask or answer questions of each other again. The Arab example illustrates a typical tendency for people to "educate" each other. Unfortunately, the education is not about cultural difference but is instead an unconscious attempt to convert the other to the "best" way of interpreting a situation. As in the Nigerian example, all participants are likely to leave with their negative stereotypes of the others as "obtuse" confirmed. In the Thai case, there might be an ironic conclusion: the Thai may eventually acquiesce in calling the supervisor by his first name, but rather than the action being one of American egalitarianism, it will be a confirmation of the higher-status person's right to demand compliance. The misunderstanding will go underground.

The British situation illustrates a particularly troublesome clash of American personal and European intellectual styles, and it deserves closer attention. Europeans tend to use a low-context approach to intellectual confrontation—they state their points explicitly and without the ambivalence considered polite by Americans in intellectual matters. In personal matters of feeling and relationship, however, Europeans use a more high-context style, relying on suggestion and nonverbal nuance. One is far more likely to hear a European say "I think…" than "I feel…". Americans, on the other hand, treat a relationship in a low-context manner. They verbalize emotions far more often, including direct expressions of how they feel about the person with whom they are communicating. But Americans are more likely to handle intellectual confrontation in a high-context manner. They tend to indicate disagreement nonverbally with tone of voice or facial expression, for example, "Well (pause), that idea certainly has **some** merit." Americans commonly stereotype Europeans as being adamant in intellectual matters, while Europeans stereotype Americans as lacking strong convictions (or as being ignorant). On the other side of the coin, Americans often think Europeans are unnecessarily coy about interpersonal relationships, while Europeans see Americans as lacking subtlety in personal affairs.

Certainly not all negative evaluation is inappropriate. People in most cultures are critical of aspects of their own society. While it is possible that a long-term visitor will achieve enough understanding of the host culture to be knowledgeably critical, such ability is long in coming, rarely insightful, and nearly always unappreciated by hostcountry nationals. To avoid complicating the already difficult task of intercultural communication, participants in a cross-cultural situation need to consider first the possibility that a negative evaluation might be based on an unrecognized cultural difference rather than the result of astute cross-cultural analysis. Each person needs to be aware that he or she is evaluating the other, often on similarly ethnocentric grounds, and seek to suspend these kinds of evaluations until the potential spiraling effects of the action have been considered. Suspension of judgment is particularly difficult for professionals, since much of their credibility and self-esteem may lie in being able to exercise quick, accurate evaluation. Professionals operating cross-culturally might usefully define their primary goal as communication rather than evaluation. It would then become apparent that swift evaluation is likely to be ethnocentric and detrimental to effective intercultural communication.

Americans can overcome the tendency to stereotype and generate negative evaluations by approaching every cross-cultural situation as a kind of experiment. They should assume that some kind of cultural difference exists but that the nature of the difference is unclear. Using available generalizations about the other culture, they can formulate a hypothesis and then test it for accuracy. Lacking a generalization about the other culture, the hypothesis can be based on possible contrasts to a typical American pattern in the situation. The hypothesis should be tested by acting tentatively as if it were accurate and by watching carefully to see what happens, as illustrated in the following example:

> An American student in a homestay in Germany is sitting down to her first dinner with her host family. (The family speaks English.) She avoids the initial pitfall in a cross-cultural encounter—intolerable ambiguity—by treating the occasion as a chance to learn and not as a "command performance" at which she might fail. Nor does she fall back on her American behavior patterns, which might involve somewhat nervous chatter about what happened during the day and how she felt about it (importance of personal experience). By allowing the family to initiate the conversation, the student may be able to ascertain the pattern of topics that are appropriate for dinner conversation. But what if they wait for her? One hypothesis she might consider is that Germans typically do not engage in conversation during a meal. Thinking over what she knows about Europeans in general, she decides that this is not likely (although it is typical in some other cultures). Because she has not received a very complete predeparture orientation, the student is unaware of the generalization that Germans prefer to discuss intellectual or political issues over meals (and at other times as well). But the student does remember her mother telling her never to discuss politics and religion at the dinner table. Perhaps the German pattern is a contrast to this American social norm? She tentatively broaches the topic of the political problems of American forces stationed on German soil, ready to back off from the topic if it seems uncomfortable. However, the family engages this subject heartily, the student is relieved, and the homestay is off to a good start.[1]

Generating and using cultural generalizations effectively while avoiding stereotyping is one of the most demanding skills of intercultural communication. Cultural self-awareness is necessary, as is some knowledge of predominant patterns in the target culture and their variations (e.g., generational, gender, ethnic group). Although this knowledge is usually

---

[1] This example represents dozens of reports by exchange students interviewed by the authors. Unfortunately, most students did not discover the procedure described until well after the first dinner.

limited, it can still be used to hypothesize likely areas of contrast and possible communication problems. As more knowledge of relevant cultural differences is acquired, generalizations can become more specific, hypotheses more particular, and communication difficulties more predictable. However, if Americans (and others) seek sure answers that will eliminate all ambiguity from communication, the result is likely to be stereotyping.

Empathy and Action

We have looked at the obstacles to intercultural communication in the procedural domain of American culture. We turn lastly to action. Americans often conceptualize performance in a context of confrontation, which may attain the proportions of conflict or, at least, competition among adversaries. In the cross-cultural situation, the confrontational approach is seldom desirable. Americans do better to establish an interface of empathy with coworkers. While sympathy builds on similarity among people, empathy begins with difference and builds the interface on common goals and context. To employ empathy, Americans should gain a clear view of their mission and attempt to integrate their efforts within the existing organizational or social context in which they are working.

There exists empirical evidence from the Peace Corps that Americans perform better in countries such as Korea, where cultural differences are immediately confronted, than in countries like Jamaica, where English is spoken and most observations convey the impression of a contemporary developing society. Taking stock of such informal experience, we surmise that the perception of cultural differences might naturally impel Americans toward empathy, not sympathy. Unfortunately, however, awareness of cultural differences is not enough to guide Americans toward empathic performance. The American impatience for action often gets in the way. The temptation to get something done may become so strong that Americans abandon their advisory or supervisory roles and attempt to do the job themselves. This reaction reflects both their preference for "doing" as a form of activity and the emphasis they place on the self as the responsible party. Americans strive for a quick-impact project, attempting to complete something before the end of their tour abroad. They fail to integrate their work adequately into the social structure and neglect the cultural customs and traditions needed for success. These roadblocks toward empathy can best be illustrated by a few examples where American values intervened to work against the mission at hand.

The American assumption of doing sometimes blocks efforts to advise, train, or teach others. For instance, on an American mission in Laos, American military personnel were advising Laotians on training, but the American advisors frequently resorted to giving the training themselves rather than fulfilling their mission of teaching Laotian trainers. A similar event took place in the Philippines, where Peace Corps volunteers had the mission of training teachers. According to verbal reports from the volunteers, the Filipino teachers resented being observed by the volunteers, and when the volunteers taught the classes, the Filipino teachers left the classroom. Finally, the volunteers themselves took over the classes, although after three or four months they realized that their approach, based on American values of efficiency and time-consciousness, was a hindrance to cooperation and to the accomplishment of their goals. The volunteers also mentioned that "when a problem came up, it was the Americans who immediately decided what to do about it." The Filipinos made no effort to do anything about a problem they had, outside of mentioning it. The Americans added that they felt they took action primarily "because of the great difficulties involved in the Filipinos doing anything about it."

The third example concerns a Peace Corps project in Micronesia, where a group of volunteers was being trained for assignment elsewhere. With three months to go before training was completed, the group wanted to complete some kind of "model" public works project to show what they could do. Despite repeated (but subtle) statements from island leaders that a new school building was wanted, the trainees insisted that an obviously needed water supply system take priority since plastic pipe and other materials were already available. When local men were reluctant to carry one-hundred-pound bags of cement up the mountainside to build catchment tanks, the trainees carried them up themselves. Overriding local insistence that only a few pipes be run into village centers, the trainees laid pipes into individual houses. Glowing with the success of the project, most of the new volunteers left the island to go to their permanent assignments.

The two volunteers who remained on the island received an education in cross-cultural innovation as they observed the following events: (1) small children routinely urinated in the catchment tanks so no one would drink the water; (2) village women persisted in carrying laundry to streams on the mountainside, where they had always exchanged information and gossip; (3) during droughts village chiefs were unable to control the overuse of water by some people in individual houses; (4) fights between youths of different villages resulted in nighttime machete raids on the plastic pipes in each other's villages. Within one year the system was inoperable, and a new school-building project was begun.

The situation in Micronesia represents an inept intervention of the American values of doing and of producing a concrete product. It also illustrates a failure of communication in a situation where the Americans received ample "messages" about the needs of the islanders. If empathy had been used, the trainees would have been more attentive to the relatively subtle protestations of the host nationals. Such sensitivity could have been encouraged with training that linked technical and language preparation with intercultural communication. An emphasis during training, and in the field as well, on procedural culture would have contributed to a better performance on the part of the trainees.

On the other hand, it can be argued that complete empathy on the part of change agents is ineffective since it would probably block the undertaking of projects that are not already recognized as necessary. One approach to this dilemma is that of using empathy to integrate a new technique into an already-existing cultural pattern. The following example from India shows how a new technique in agriculture was introduced despite cultural barriers.[2]

An agricultural project introducing the new practice of green-manuring had failed to take hold in the village of Ikari. When the villagers showed no interest in plowing under the *san* hemp for fertilizer, the project advisory team, composed of Americans and Indians, went to the village and soon learned that the functioning village leader was not the man who held title but his uncle, an older man and the head of a family known for its scholarly tradition and respected for its devout religious life. Recognizing that the basis of leadership was different from what they had expected, the advisors were able to approach the real rather than the nominal source of influence.

When they finally sat down with the uncle, Shri Sanehi, to discuss the use of green manure, they did not broach the main point immediately. When the subject was brought up, Shri Sanehi agreed that green-manuring would be effective. He added, however, that according to the precepts of his culture, fulfilling the average needs of the family was enough and one should not be greedy and anxious for more economic production. One of the Indian advisors, understanding Shri Sanehi's perspective, argued that most people in villages nowadays were not able to meet the above-mentioned obligations to the family, the self, and religious mendicants. Thus, it was even more important today to produce more, and green-manuring was one of the tried methods for better production. There was no harm in doing so.

---

[2] The source used for this case is Albert Meyer and Associates, *Pilot Project India. The Story of Rural Development at Etawah, Uttar Pradesh* (Berkeley: University of California Press, 1959) 207-10.

These words reflect the Indian definition of the self, the relationship of the individual to others, and intimations of how the individual should conduct his life. In each instance, the concepts are different from those of Americans. But the apt endeavor of the advisor to attach the cause of green-manuring to the Brahmin's beliefs was not immediately successful. Shri Sanehi replied, "I consider that for human beings, righteous conduct is vastly more important than all the wealth of the world," hinting that green-manuring would be an impious act. Indeed, plowing under the san hemp leaf and stalk before they are ripe, he said, is an act of violence— and nonviolence is the greatest virtue. This remark makes sense only from the point of view that nature and plants have an essence similar to humans, a nonmaterialistic definition of the world. The advisor's answer to the Brahmin deserves to be related in full quotation.

> The [advisor] first argued that even if a plant had a soul, it was immortal and, therefore, plowing it under would be no sin; he quoted the *Bhagavad-Gita* extensively, but in this he was no match for the Brahmin and his village followers. However, he continued in humility to explain that the farmer's profession was sacred, but in its pursuance many violent acts had to be committed—insects and worms were killed in the process of plowing, green grasses and weeds were rooted out for the benefit of the planted crop, and the draft animals were forced to work. Yet, the farmer did many sacred acts. He fed his family and cattle, supported the temples and priests, teachers and mendicants, and performed many other acts of hospitality and charity. Without the violent acts necessary to grow his crop he could do none of these acts. His sins of violence were outweighed by his acts of charity. Moreover, the land was getting poorer each year because of improper manuring. If the green-manuring were done, more of the righteous acts would be possible.

This case illustrates several empathetic adjustments by the team of American and Indian advisors to place their case in the relevant cultural context. Modifications were needed in terms of definition of the self, perception of the world, and basis for motivation. Interpersonal relations were conducted with meekness, humility, and indirection (the advisors did not always talk directly to the Brahmin but often wondered aloud about a subject, allowing the Brahmin himself to connect it with the purpose of the meeting). The Indians in this example do not look to the future but to the traditions; they do not favor "doing" for its own sake, but incline toward "being"; they do not value progress. The arguments which Americans might be tempted to use under these circumstances— progress, a better life, material benefits, and a greater yield—were generally avoided by the advisors.

What is important in this case study—and absent in the previous ones—is the consciousness and control of cultural differences and the use of empathy and the comprehensiveness of the understanding of both deep and procedural culture. With this conscious understanding, the change agents were able to communicate in an appropriate style, their message congruent with the perception and understanding of the Brahmin.

The two advisors were also able to use to their advantage two important cultural bridges. First, they were aware that culture is more like a river composed of many channels, currents, and ripples than it is a monolithic structure which precisely controls the behavior of the cultural being. Cultures are composed of variations and provide guidance, not control. It is incumbent on the American sojourner to become sensitive to cultural variations, keeping in mind that a variation in reference culture may be very similar to a variation in the host country cultures. Thus, patterns of culture which are variations of dominant cultural patterns may well be discovered which provide a cultural bridge between two distinctly different dominant variations. Although the content of the arguments in the case study are Indian and refer to the *Bhagavad-Gita*, the pattern of communication and the feelings expressed resemble the metaphors which can be heard in southern churches in the United States, delivered by speakers steeped in rich oral traditions. Precedents can be found in variations of American culture for the thought and feelings of the Brahmin, even though the dominant American cultural pattern is far removed from the traditions represented in the case study.

The second bridge the agents used was the creation of a *third culture* composed of deep and procedural elements from both cultures—American and Indian. Change agents in international development carry out their work in the milieu of a third culture which is "created, shared, and learned by men of different societies who are in the process of relating their societies, or sections thereof, to each other (Useem, Useem, and Donoghue 1963, 169-79). In our example, both the Indian and American advisors were convinced of the practical benefits of green-manuring for Ikari. Both realized, however, that an American approach would fail or, if accepted by the force of pressure, would not "take" in the village and endure after they left. Thus, the advisors were able to skillfully weave together Western notions of progress and material benefit with the Indian sense of obligation to family, self, and religious mendicants to achieve a mutual goal.

Certain themes are characteristic of the third culture. It is assumed that the relationship between the members of the two societies, as well as the two societies themselves, should be coordinate. Often they are not, but the ideal is still present and the failure to realize it creates areas of conflict between advisors and counterparts. Programs sponsored in the third culture are considered to be rational, secular, and future-oriented. Expected to show concrete results, they are construed as a beginning and are expected to grow and perhaps diffuse throughout the society. Hence, they are conceived of as expansive and open-ended (Useem, Useem and Donoghue 171-72). The American advisors respected their Indian counterparts' knowledge of and sensitivity to their own culture, letting them take the lead in negotiations. Yet, the program itself was rational and open-ended, designed to serve as a model for future expansion to other villages.

Conclusion

Americans frequently have difficulties in communicating and cooperating with their foreign counterparts. The original obstacles to cross-cultural understanding may be conceptualized as differences in cultural assumptions and values. The Americans' values and assumptions prevent them from objectively perceiving and understanding the underpinnings of the behavior of their counterparts. Their performance overseas would be enhanced if they understood both their own culture and that of their counterparts.

Although a cultural pattern is an integrated whole, it may be analyzed into patterns of thinking and the four components we have examined in this book: form of activity and motivation, form of relation to others, perception of the world, and perception of self. This cultural base deeply influences how Americans interact with and perceive those who are culturally different. The typical American emotional interface of sympathy projects the cultural qualities that hinder their performance in cross-cultural situations. Cultivating empathy or even striving to function from a position of an appropriate third culture would accommodate both the American and host cultures in reaching common goals.

The exploration of American culture presented here from a cross-cultural perspective is intended to encourage Americans involved in intercultural interaction to achieve the following objectives:

> 1. *Establish conceptual cross-cultural bridges.* The terms used to describe American culture should serve as bridges to other cultures. Although some of the cultural concepts which have been discussed in this book cannot be literally translated into other cultures, all cultures will contain patterns of thinking, assumptions, values, and norms of behavior which can be classified somewhere within the scheme provided.

2. *Foster an attitude of cultural relevance.* Since a culture provides a complete system of meaning for conducting life, each culture possesses integrity and, generally speaking, is neither inferior nor superior to any other culture. But in a structured situation and for a specific purpose, one cultural system may in fact work better than another.

   A cultural characteristic represents only one of a number of possible assumptions, values, or norms of behavior. Alternative characteristics will be found in the same culture, options that can be found in other cultures, but the emphasis on particular characteristics will differ from culture to culture. Thus, the American way will quite likely not be the most desirable and certainly not the normal or natural way in non-American cultural contexts.

3. *Work toward self-understanding.* An awareness of American culture along with examples of contrasting cultures contributes to the individual's understanding of her- or himself as a cultural being. This understanding assists in preparing for the hardships of culture shock and the frustrations common to working abroad or dealing with foreign nationals at home. Obtaining objectivity in appraising oneself as well as one's counterparts and an ability to separate cultural from idiosyncratic factors in oneself and others is important to effectiveness in foreign cultures.

4. *Identify facilitating and interfering factors.* Individuals should be better able to identify those specific American predispositions that usually help them work with foreign counterparts, as well as those that are usually a handicap.

5. *Develop cultural judgment.* The effect of this book in the service of intercultural communication and cross-cultural performance should be to improve judgment, which guides behavior. Experience in education and training over the last twenty years indicates an increase in awareness of deep culture, in sensitivity to cultural differences, and in improved employment of proce-dural culture in intercultural communication. These gains have contributed to the adaptation and

performance of Americans overseas. In the perspective of these improvements, our purpose in writing this second edition is to inform judgment and to assist readers in becoming intercultural communicators who are capable of making the necessary observations about themselves and their counterparts. It is not our purpose to change American culture or dissuade Americans from taking pride in their ways of being in the world. We are convinced that any success we may have achieved relies on judgment, good will, and cross-cultural commitment. It is necessary to maintain a curious and open mind, to question and inquire, and to test our analyses and suggestions. The readers' cross-cultural understanding should enable them to adapt their American modes of operation to a form appropriate to the local situation. Thus, they should be able to develop guides for personal behavior, recasting desirable goals overseas and at home into realistic activities by becoming truly masters of the art of the possible. With informed judgment, it is possible to abandon the idea that cultural differences are impediments to communication and cooperation and instead accept the challenge that cultural differences are resources that can be used for the mutual benefit of members of the societies involved in cross-cultural cooperation.

BIBLIOGRAPHY

Arensberg, Conrad M., and Arthur H. Niehoff. *Introducing Social Change.* Chicago, IL: Aldine Publishing Company, 1964.

Arnheim, Rudolf. *Visual Thinking.* Berkeley, CA: University of California Press, 1969.

Barna, LaRay. "The Stress Factor in Intercultural Relations." In *Handbook of Intercultural Training, Volume II: Issues in Training Methodology,* edited by Dan Landis and Richard Brislin. New York: Pergamon Press Inc.,1983.

Barnlund, Dean C. *Public and Private Self in Japan and the United States.* Yarmouth, ME: Intercultural Press, 1989.

Bell, Daniel. "The Disjunction of Culture and Social Structure: Some Notes on the Meaning of Social Reality." *Daedalus* 94, no. 1 (Winter 1965): 208-22.

Bellah, Robert, and Richard Madsen, William Sullivan, Ann Swindler, and Stephen Tipton. *Habits of the Heart: Individualism and Commitment in American Life.* Berkeley, CA: University of California Press, 1985.

Bem, Daryl J. *Beliefs, Attitudes, and Human Affairs.* Belmont, CA: Brooks/Cole Publishing Company, 1970.

Bennett, J. "Transition Shock: Putting Culture Shock in Perspective." *International and Intercultural Communication Annual* 4 (1977): 45-52.

Bennett, Milton J. "Overcoming the Golden Rule: Sympathy and Empathy." In *Communication Yearbook 3, edited by D. Nimmo. Philadelphia: International Communication, 1979.*

_____. "Towards Ethnorelativism: A Developmental Model of Intercultural Sensitivity."In *Cross Cultural Orientation: New Conceptualizations and Applications,* edited by R. Michael Page. Lanham, MD: University Press of America, 1986.

Berger, P. J., and T. Luckman. *The Social Construction of Reality.* Garden City, NY: Doubleday, 1967.

Berlin, B., and P. Kay. *Basic Color Terms.* Berkeley, CA: University of California Press, 1969.

Bidney, David. "The Concept of Value in Modern Anthropology." In *Anthropology Today,* edited by A. L. Kroeber. Chicago: University of Chicago Press, 1953.

Boorstin, Daniel J. *The Americans: The Colonial Experience* vol. 1. New York: Random House, 1958.

_____. *The Americans: The National Experience* vol. 2. New York: Random House, 1965.

_____. *The Discoverers.* New York: Vintage Books, 1983.

Brislin, Richard W. *Cross-cultural Encounters.* New York: Pergamon Press, 1981.

Brogan, Denis W. *America in the Modern World.* New Brunswick, NJ: Rutgers University Press, 1960.

Bross, Irwin D. *Design for Decision.* New York: Macmillan Publishing Company, 1953.

Brown, Richard D. *Modernization: The Transformation of American Life, 1600-1865.* New York: Hill and Wang, 1976.

Brown, Roger. "Language and Categories." Appendix to Bruner, J. S., J. J. Goodnow, and G. A. Austin. *A Study of Thinking,.* New York: John Wiley and Sons, 1956.

_____. *Words and Things.* Glencoe, IL: Free Press, 1958.

Bruner, J. S., J. J. Goodnow, and G. A. Austin. *A Study of Thinking.* New York: John Wiley and Sons, 1956.

Chang, Tungsun. "A Chinese Philosopher's Theory of Knowledge." *ETC* 9, no. 3 (1952): 203-26.

Christian, Chester C., Jr. "Language and Culture." In *Language and Communication,* edited by Helmut Esau. Columbia, SC: Hornbeam Press, 1980, 230-55.

Cleveland, Harlan, Gerard J. Mangone, and John C. Adams. *The Overseas Americans*. New York: McGraw-Hill, 1960.

Cohen, Morris R. *American Thought: A Critical Sketch*. New York: Collier Books, 1954.

Cohen, Rosalie A. "Conceptual Styles, Cultural Conflict, and Nonverbal Tests of Intelligence." In *American Anthropologist 5*, Vol. 71 (October 1969): 828-56.

Cole, Michael, and Sylvia Scribner. *Culture and Thought: A Psychological Introduction*. New York: John Wiley and Sons, 1974.

Condon, John C. *With Respect to the Japanese: A Guide for Americans*. Yarmouth, ME: Intercultural Press, 1984.

Condon, John C., and Fathi Yousef. *An Introduction to Intercultural Communication*. Indianapolis: Bobbs-Merrill, 1975.

Cushman, Phillip. "Why the Self Is Empty." *American Psychologist 45*, 1990.

D'Andradei, Roy. "A Folk Model of the Mind." In *Cultural Models in Language and Thought*, edited by Dorothy Holland and Naomi Quinn. Cambridge: Cambridge University Press, 1987, 112-48.

Deese, James. *The Structure of Associations in Language and Thought*. Baltimore: The Johns Hopkins University Press, 1965.

Diaz-Guerrero, R. *Psychology of the Mexican: Culture and Personality*. Austin: University of Texas Press, 1976.

Doi, Takeo, *The Anatomy of Dependence*. Tokyo: Kodansha International, 1973.

DuBois, Cora. "The Dominant Value Profile of American Culture." In *American Anthropologist 6*, Vol. 57, Part 1 (December 1955): 1232-39.

Emminghaus, Wolf B., and Bernhard Haupert. "What's Cultural in Intercultural Training?" Manuscript, University of Fribourg, Department of Social Work, Fribourg, Switzerland, 1989.

Erasmus, Charles J. "An Anthropologist Looks at Technical Assistance." In *Readings in Anthropology, Volume II: Readings in Cultural Anthropology*, edited by Morton H. Fried. New York: Thomas Y. Crowell, 1959.

_____. *Man Takes Control*. Minneapolis: University of Minnesota Press, 1961.

Erikson, Erik H. *Childhood and Society*, 2d ed. New York: W.W. Norton, 1963.

Finke, Ronald A. "Theories Relating Mental Imagery to Perception." In *Psychological Bulletin* 98 (1985): 236-59.

Fisher, Glen. *Public Diplomacy and the Behavioral Sciences.* Bloomington: Indiana University Press, 1972.

Foster, George M. *Traditional Cultures and the Impact of Technological Change.* New York: Harper and Row, 1962.

_____. "Peasant Society and the Image of Limited Good." In *American Anthropologist* 67, no. 2 (April 1965): 293-315.

Frankfort, Henri, and H. A. Frankfort. "Myth and Reality." In *The Intellectual Adventure of Ancient Man,* edited by H. Frankfort, H. A. Frankfort, John A. Wilson, Thorklid Jacobsen, and William A. Irwin. Chicago: The University of Chicago Press, 1946.

Fried, Morton H., ed. *Readings in Anthropology, Vol. II: Readings in Cultural Anthropology.* New York: Thomas Y. Crowell, 1959.

Gay, John, and Michael Cole. *The New Mathematics in an Old Culture.* New York: Holt, Reinhardt and Winston, 1967.

Geldard, Frank A. *The Human Senses.* New York: John Wiley and Sons, 1953.

Glenn, Edmund S. "Semantic Difficulties in Intercultural Communication." In *ETC.* 11, no. 3 (1954): 163-80.

_____. "The Use of Epistemological Models in the Analysis of Cultures." In *Proceedings of the VI International Congress of the Anthropological Sciences.* Paris: Musée de l'Homme, 1963.

_____. *Mind, Culture and Politics,* mimeographed, 1966.

_____. "The University and the Revolution: New Left or New Right?" In *The University and Revolution,* edited by G. R. Weaver and J. H. Weaver. New York: Prentice-Hall, 1969.

_____. *Man and Mankind: Conflict and Communication between Cultures.* Norwood, NJ: Ablex Publishing Corporation, 1981.

Goodenough, Ward H. *Cooperation in Change.* New York: Russell Sage Foundation, 1963.

Gorer, Geoffrey. *The American People: A Study in National Character.* New York: W. W. Norton, 1948.

Granet, Marcel. *La Pensée Chinoise.* Paris: Editions Albin Michel, 1950.

Gregory, R. L. *The Intelligent Eye.* New York: McGraw-Hill, 1970.

Hall, Edward T. *The Silent Language.* New York: Doubleday, 1964.

Hall, Edward T. *Beyond Culture.* New York: Anchor/Doubleday, 1976.

Hall, Edward T., and William F. Whyte. "Intercultural Communication: A Guide to Men of Action." In *Human Organization* 1, Vol. 19 (Spring 1960): 5-12.

Helson, Harry. *Adaptation-Level Theory*. New York: Harper & Row, 1964.

Henry, Jules. *Culture Against Men*. New York: Random House, 1963.

Hoopes, David. "Intercultural Communication Concepts and the Psychology of Intercultural Experience." In *Multicultural Education: A Cross-cultural Training Approach*, edited by Margaret D. Pusch. Yarmouth, ME: Intercultural Press, 1979.

Houston, John. *Motivation*. New York: Macmillan Publishing Company, 1985.

Hsu, Francis L. K. *Americans and Chinese: Two Ways of Life*. New York: Schuman, 1953.

Hulse, Frederick S. "Convention and Reality in Japanese Culture." In *Japanese Character and Culture*, edited by Bernard S. Silberman. Tucson: University of Arizona Press, 1962.

Jacobson, Nolan P. *Buddhism: The Religion of Analysis*. London: George Allen & Unwin, 1966.

Janowitz, Morris. *Sociology and the Military Establishment*. New York: Russell Sage Foundation, 1959.

Jayatilleke, K. N. *Early Buddhist Theory of Knowledge*. London: George Allen & Unwin, 1963.

Jones, J., and J. W. Pfeiffer, eds. *The 1977 Annual Handbook for Group Facilitators*. La Jolla, CA: University Associates, 1977.

Kaplan, Abraham. "American Ethics and Public Policy." In *Daedalus* 2, Vol. 87 (Spring 1958): 48-77.

Kay, Paul, and Willett Kempton. "What Is the Sapir-Whorf Hypothesis?" *American Anthropologist* 86, no. 1 (1984): 65-79.

Kerlinger, Fred N. "Decision-Making in Japan." In *Social Forces* 30 (1951).

_____. "A Critique of Three Studies of Japanese Personality." In *Japanese Character and Culture*, edited by Bernard S. Silberman. Tucson: University of Arizona Press, 1962.

Kluckhohn, Clyde. "American Culture—A General Description." In *Human Factors in Military Operations*, edited by Richard H. Williams. Technical Memorandum ORO-T-259, Operations Research Office. Chevy Chase, MD: Johns Hopkins University, 1954a.

_____. "Some Aspects of American National Character." In *Human Factors in Military Operations*, edited by Richard H. Williams. Technical Memorandum ORO-T-259, Operations Research Office. Chevy Chase, MD: Johns Hopkins University, 1954b.

_____. "The Evolution of Contemporary American Values." In *Daedalus* 87, no. 2 (Spring 1958): 78-109.

Kluckhohn, Clyde, and Florence R. Kluckhohn. "American Culture: Generalized Orientations and Class Patterns." In *Conflicts of Power in Modern Culture: Seventh Symposium*, edited by Lymon Bryson. New York: Harper and Bros., 1947.

Kluckhohn, Clyde, et al. "Value and Value-Orientations in the Theory of Action." In *Toward a General Theory of Action*, edited by Talcott Parsons and Edward J. Shils. Cambridge, MA: Harvard University Press, 1951.

Kluckhohn, Florence R. "Some Reflections on the Nature of Cultural Integration and Change." In *Sociological Theory, Values, and Sociocultural Change: Essays in Honor of P. A. Sorokin*, edited by E. A. Tiryakian. New York: Free Press, 1963.

Kluckhohn, Florence R., and Fred L. Strodtbeck. *Variations in Value Orientation*. New York: Row, Peterson, 1961.

Kochman, Thomas. *Black and White Styles in Conflict*. Chicago: University of Chicago Press, 1981.

Kohls, Robert. *Survival Kit for Overseas Living*. Yarmouth, ME: Intercultural Press, 1979.

Kroeber, Alfred L. *Anthropology*. New York: Harcourt, Brace and Company, 1948.

Kunkel, John H. "Values and Behavior in Economic Development." In *Economic Development and Cultural Change* 3, Vol. 13 (April 1965): 257-77.

La Barre, Weston. "Some Observations on Character Structure in the Orient: The Japanese." In *Japanese Character and Culture*, edited by Bernard S. Silberman. Tucson: University of Arizona Press, 1962.

Leach, Edmund. "Anthropological Aspects of Language: Animal Categories and Verbal Abuse." In *New Directions in the Study of Language*, edited by Eric H. Lenneberg. Cambridge, MA: MIT Press, 1964.

Lebra, Takie Sugiyama. "Reciprocity and the Asymmetric Principle: An Analytic Reappraisal of the Japanese Concept of *On*." In *Japanese Culture and Behavior*, edited by T. Lebra and W. Lebra. Honolulu: University of Hawaii Press, 1974.

_____. *Japanese Patterns of Behavior*. Honolulu: University of Hawaii Press, 1976.

Linebarger, Paul M. A. "Problems in the Utilizations of Troops in Foreign Areas." In *Human Factors in Military Operations*, edited by Richard H. Williams. Technical Memorandum ORO-T-259, Operations Research Office. Chevy Chase, MD: Johns Hopkins University, 1954.

Lundstedt, Sven. "The Interpersonal Dimension in International Technical Assistance: Statement of a Problem." *Mental Hygiene* 3, Vol. 45 (July 1961): 324-82.

MacIntyre, Alasdair. *After Virtue*. South Bend, IN: University of Notre Dame Press, 1981.

Marr, David. *Vision*. San Francisco: W. H. Freeman, 1982.

Martindale, Don. *The Nature and Types of Sociological Theory*. Boston: Houghton Mifflin, 1960.

Maslow, Abraham H. *Toward a Psychology of Being*. Princeton, NJ: D. Van Nostrand, 1968.

Mayer, Albert and associates. *Pilot Project India: The Story of Rural Development at Etawah, Uttar Pradesh*. Berkeley: University of California Press, 1959.

McClelland, David C. The Achieving Society. Princeton NJ: D. Van Nostrand, 1961.

McConnell, James V. *Understanding Human Behavior*, 5th ed. New York: Holt, Rinehart and Winston, 1986.

McNeill, William H. *The Pursuit of Power*. Chicago: University of Chicago Press, 1982.

Mead, Margaret. *Sex and Temperament in Three Primitive Societies*. New York: William Morrow and Company, 1963.

_____. *And Keep Your Powder Dry*. New York: William Morrow and Company, 1965.

Mouer, Ross, and Yoshio Sugimoto. *Images of Japanese Society: A Study in the Structure of Social Reality*. London: KPL, 1986.

Nakamura, Hajime. *Ways of Thinking of Eastern Peoples: India-China-Tibet-Japan*. Honolulu: East-West Center Press, 1964.

Nash, Roderick. *Wilderness and the American Mind,* rev. ed. New Haven, CT: Yale University Press, 1973.

Needham, Rodney. *Primordial Characters*. Charlottesville: University Press of Virginia, 1978.

Niehoff, Arthur H. "Theravada Buddhism: A Vehicle for Technical Change." In *Human Organization* 2, Vol. 23 (Summer 1964): 108-12.

Northrop, F. S. C. *The Meeting of East and West, An Inquiry Concerning World Understanding*. New York: Macmillan Publishing Co., 1946.

Oberg, K. "Culture Shock: The Problem of Adjustment to New Cultural Environments." In *Practical Anthropology* 7 (1960):177-82.

Ornstein, Robert, and Richard Thompson. *The Amazing Brain*. Boston: Houghton Mifflin Company, 1984.

Ouchi, William. *Theory Z*. New York: Avon Books, 1981.

Pascale, Richard, and Anthony Athos. *The Art of Japanese Management.* New York: The Free Press, 1981.

Perry, Ralph B. *Characteristically American.* New York: Alfred A. Knopf, 1949.

Platt, John R. "The Two Faces of Perception." In *Changing Perspectives on Man,* edited by Ben Rathblatt. Chicago: University of Chicago Press,1968.

Potter, David M. *People of Plenty: Economic Abundance and the American Character.* Chicago: University of Chicago Press, 1954.

Pye, Lucian W. *Politics, Personality and Nation Building: Burma's Search for Identity.* New Haven: Yale University Press, 1962.

Rathblatt, Ben. Changing Perspectives on Man. Chicago: University of Chicago Press, 1968.

Ravenholt, Albert. "Feud among the Red Mandarins." In *American Universities Field Staff Reports Service, East Asia Series* 2, Vol. XI (1964): 175-84.

Reddy, Michael J. "The Conduit Metaphor—A Case of Frame Conflict in Our Language about Language." In *Metaphor and Thought,* edited by Andrew Ortony. Cambridge: Cambridge University Press, 1979, 284-324.

Reichel-Dolmatoff, Geraldo, and Alicia Reichel-Dolmatoff. *The People of Aritama: The Cultural Personality of a Colombian Mestizo Village.* Chicago: University of Chicago Press, 1961.

Reston, James. "Washington: Tweedledum and Tweedledee." In New York Times, November 7, 1965.

Richardson, Alan. *Mental Imagery.* New York: Springer Publishing Company, 1969.

Rogers, Carl H. "Toward a Modern Approach to Values." In *Journal of Abnormal and Social Psychology* 2, Vol. 68 (1964): 160-67.

Rogers, Everett. *Diffusion of Innovations,* 3d ed. New York: The Free Press, 1983.

Rosch, Eleanor. "Universals and Cultural Specifics in Categorization." In *Cross-cultural Perspectives on Learning,* edited by Richard Brislin, Stephen Bochner, and Walter J. Lonner. New York: John Wiley and Sons, 1975.

Rosenfeld, Lawrence, and Jean Civikly. *With Words Unspoken: The Nonverbal Experience.* New York: Holt, Rinehart & Winston, 1976.

Ryle, Gilbert. *The Concept of Mind.* New York: Barnes & Noble, 1949.

Scheler, Max. *Ressentiment.* Glencoe, IL: Free Press, 1961.

Seyle, H. *The Stress of Life.* New York: McGraw-Hill, 1956.

Shils, Edward. "Primordial, Personal, Sacred and Civil Ties." In *British Journal of Sociology* 8, no. 2 (1957):130-45.

Singer, Marshall. "Culture: A Perceptual Approach." In *Intercultural Communication: A Reader,* edited by L. Samovar and R. Porter. Belmont, CA: Wadsworth Publishing Company, 1985.

Smyth, Herbert W. *Aeschylus.* Cambridge: Harvard University Press, 1956.

Snell, Bruno. *The Discovery of the Mind.* Oxford: Basil Blackwell, 1953.

Stanley, Manfred. "Dignity Versus Survival? Reflections on the Moral Philosophy of Social Order." In *Structure, Consciousness, and History,* edited by Richard H. Brown and Stanford M. Lyman. Cambridge: Cambridge University Press, 1978, 197-234.

Stcherbatsky, F. Th. *Buddhist Logic* vol. I. New York, Dover Publications, 1962.

Steinberg, Rafael. "Olympics Only One Star Turn." Washington Post, June 7, 1964.

Stewart, Edward. "Culture and Decision Making." In *Communication, Culture, and Organizational Processes,* edited by William B. Gudykunst, Lea P. Stewart, and Stella Ting-Toomey. Beverly Hills, CA: Sage Publications, 1985, 177-211.

Stewart, Kilton. "Dream Theory in Malaya." In *Altered States of Consciousness,* edited by Charles T. Tart. New York: John Wiley and Sons, 1969.

Stoppard, Tom. *Dirty Linen and New-Found-Land.* London: Faber and Faber, 1976.

Stouffer, Samuel A., et al. *The American Soldier.* Princeton, NJ: Princeton University Press, 1949.

Tönnies, Ferdinand. *Community and Society.* East Lansing: Michigan State University Press, 1957. Originally published in German in 1887.

Tsunoda, Ryusaku, et al. *Sources of Japanese Tradition.* New York: Columbia University Press, 1958.

Ueda, Keiko. "Sixteen Ways to Avoid Saying 'No' in Japan." In *Proceedings of International Christian University Conference,* 1975.

Useem, John and Ruth, and John Donoghue. "Men in the Middle of the Third Culture: The Roles of American and Non-Western People in Cross Cultural Administration." *Human Organization* 3, Vol. 2 (Fall 1963): 169-79.

Wallace, Anthony F. C. *Culture and Personality.* New York: Random House, 1961.

Watzlawick, P., J. Beavin, and D. Jackson. *Pragmatics of Human Communication*. New York: W.W. Norton & Company, 1967.

Wax, Rosalie H. and Robert K. Thomas. "American Indians and White People." In *Phylon* 4, Vol. 22 (Winter 1961): 305-17.

Whorf, B. L. *Language, Thought and Reality: Selected Writings of B. L. Whorf*. Edited by J. B. Carroll. New York: John Wiley and Sons, 1956.

Williams, Richard H. *Human Factors in Military Operations*. Technical Memorandum ORO-T-259, Operations Research Office. Chevy Chase, MD: Johns Hopkins University, 1954.

Williams, Robin M. Jr. *American Society: A Sociological Interpretation*. New York: Alfred A. Knopf, 1961.

_____. "American Society in Transition: Trends and Emerging Developments in Social and Cultural Systems." In *Our Changing Rural Society: Perspectives and Trends*, edited by James H. Copp. Ames: Iowa State University Press, 1964.

_____. *American Society*, 3d ed. New York: Alfred A. Knopf, 1970.

Wilmot, William W. *Dyadic Communication*. New York: Random House, 1987.

Wittfogel, Karl A. *Oriental Despotism: A Comparative Study of Total Power*. New Haven, CT: Yale University Press, 1957.

Woodard, James W. "The Role of Fictions in Cultural Organization." In *Transactions of the New York Academy of Sciences* 8, Series II, Vol. 6 (June 1944): 311-44.

INDEX

U

USAID, 108

V

Values, definition of, 12-15. *See also* Specific values
Verbal dynamics, 55-56

W

Whorf, Benjamin, 46
Whorf hypothesis, 46-50
Wilderness in the New World, 114-15
Williams, Robin M. Jr., xiii
Wittfogel, Karl, 85
Work and play, 71-72
Work ethic, 72